ROUTLEDGE LIBRARY EDITIONS: WW2

Volume 28

ROMMEL'S LAST VICTORY

ROMMEL'S LAST VICTORY
The Battle of Kasserine Pass

MARTIN BLUMENSON

LONDON AND NEW YORK

First published in Great Britain in 1968 by George Allen & Unwin Ltd

This edition first published in 2022
by Routledge
2 Park Square, Milton Park, Abingdon, Oxon OX14 4RN

and by Routledge
605 Third Avenue, New York, NY 10158

Routledge is an imprint of the Taylor & Francis Group, an informa business

© 1966 Martin Blumenson

All rights reserved. No part of this book may be reprinted or reproduced or utilised in any form or by any electronic, mechanical, or other means, now known or hereafter invented, including photocopying and recording, or in any information storage or retrieval system, without permission in writing from the publishers.

Trademark notice: Product or corporate names may be trademarks or registered trademarks, and are used only for identification and explanation without intent to infringe.

British Library Cataloguing in Publication Data
A catalogue record for this book is available from the British Library

ISBN: 978-1-03-201217-9 (Set)
ISBN: 978-1-00-319367-8 (Set) (ebk)
ISBN: 978-1-03-207972-1 (Volume 28) (hbk)
ISBN: 978-1-03-207978-3 (Volume 28) (pbk)
ISBN: 978-1-00-321232-4 (Volume 28) (ebk)

DOI: 10.4324/9781003212324

Publisher's Note
The publisher has gone to great lengths to ensure the quality of this reprint but points out that some imperfections in the original copies may be apparent.

Disclaimer
The publisher has made every effort to trace copyright holders and would welcome correspondence from those they have been unable to trace.

ROMMEL'S LAST VICTORY

The Battle of Kasserine Pass

MARTIN BLUMENSON

London

GEORGE ALLEN & UNWIN LTD

RUSKIN HOUSE · MUSEUM STREET

FIRST PUBLISHED IN GREAT BRITAIN IN 1968
SECOND IMPRESSION 1969

This book is copyright under the Berne Convention. Apart from any fair dealing for the purposes of private study, research, criticism or review, as permitted under the Copyright Act, 1956, no portion may be reproduced by any process without written permission. Enquiries should be addressed to the Publishers.

© *Martin Blumenson, 1966*
SBN 04 940024 X

A ma chère et belle Mitou, Hélène Aldebert

Contents

Part I	The Setting	1
Part II	Faid	71
Part III	Sidi bou Zid	113
Part IV	Sbeitla	173
Part V	Kasserine	213
Part VI	The Aftermath	301
	Note	323
	Chart: The Allied Command	327
	A Brief Chronology	329
	Index	333

Illustrations

		facing page
1.	A light American M-3 tank, captured by the Germans The plain of Sbeitla	22
2.	General Dwight D. Eisenhower and General Henri Giraud	23
3.	General Sir Harold R. L. Alexander	54
4.	Field Marshal Erwin Rommel	55
5.	Generaloberst Juergen von Arnim	86
6.	Lt. General Sir Kenneth A. N. Anderson	87
7.	General Louis-Marie Koeltz	118
8.	Djebel Lessouda Djebel Ksaira	119
9.	Major General Lloyd R. Fredendall Major General Orlando Ward	150
10.	Sbeitla	151
11.	An American antitank gun crew	182
12.	Kasserine Pass, the Allied View	183
13.	The village of Kasserine	between pages 294 and 295
14.	Kasserine Pass, the German View	
15.	Major General Ernest N. Harmon	

ILLUSTRATIONS

Maps

North Africa	10
Tunisia	75
Faid	106
Sbeitla	182
Kasserine	229

Part I

THE SETTING

1

"PSYCHOLOGICALLY," a master once wrote, "it is particularly unfortunate when the very first battle of a war ends . . . [in] a disastrous defeat, especially when it has been preceded by . . . grandiose predictions. It makes it very difficult ever again to restore the men's confidence."

The psychologist was Field Marshal Erwin Rommel, one of the astute German generals of World War II. What he said applied to the Americans.

There had been "grandiose predictions" of swift victory — the result of the landings in North Africa. The troops coming ashore gained an easy triumph because they met halfhearted opposition from French soldiers caught in an agonizing dilemma between duty and desire, but in their exultation they overlooked the reason for their quick success. Certainly, the Americans thought, along with their people back home, we have but to appear and the enemy will be terrified and fall before us.

And suddenly there was "a disastrous defeat" — inflicted by the master himself. The blow sent the Americans reeling back in Tunisia, more than fifty miles across the parched plain of Sbeitla between the mountain passes of Faid and Kasserine.

The news of Kasserine went halfway around the world and struck the United States with the blast of a tornado, scattering illusions and leaving in its wake the devastation of a numbing consternation and the shock of disbelief.

To the American people, the event was incredible. It shook the foundations of their faith, extinguished the glowing excitement that anticipated quick victory, and, worst of all, raised doubt that the righteous necessarily triumphed.

How could the forces of evil win over the youth of America? How was it possible for the oppressors of Europe, the soldiers of tyranny and darkness, to destroy the crusaders of freedom and liberty?

Like the inexplicable reverses suffered by earlier Crusaders in North Africa at the hands of the Sultan's paladins, Kasserine made no sense. The confused picture of havoc at Kasserine flashed across the American consciousness like a nightmare.

The start seemed trifling in February, 1943, when "German tanks, infantry and artillery," Drew Middleton reported in the *New York Times*, "brushed aside a small French force defending Faid pass . . . with great gallantry." The pass had strategic significance, but the German gains were slight, nothing more than an effort to secure the flank of Rommel's army in the Mareth Line by keeping the Allied army in Tunisia off balance.

There seemed little to fear as a calm descended over the battlefield.

The quiet lasted two weeks.

Then came the eruption, "sledgehammer blows," the papers reported, driving the Americans back, compelling them to abandon their airfields, to burn their supplies, to flee for their lives.

Officials in Washington tried to be reassuring: the setback, they announced, was only a local retreat.

But soon thereafter, headlines admitted that Rommel had taken three more towns, had subjected the Americans to a five-day mauling, and had driven across Tunisia to come close to Algeria.

Speaking at his weekly press conference in Washington, Secretary of War Henry L. Stimson was candid. He admitted "substantial casualties, both in personnel and equipment." He called the situation "a sharp reverse." He termed the development "a serious local setback" that should be neither minimized nor exaggerated.

But he also said, curiously enough, that Kasserine was "a not unexpected development."

Had the Americans, then, expected the defeat? To some observers, Mr. Stimson's statement sounded like an apology for a mistake that was recognized while the error was being made.

The "local setback," editorialized the *New York Times*, could hardly obscure the fact that the Germans had scored a victory of considerable importance to their whole military and political strategy. Despite a forced retreat across fifteen hundred miles of the desert in Libya, Rommel had somehow found the strength and the energy to turn and leap against the Americans. His success delayed the course of the entire war. The Germans would now be able to consolidate their hold on Tunisia. They would have more time to prepare their defenses along the European periphery and crush guerrilla fighters in France and the Balkans. The Allies would have to postpone their invasion of northwest Europe. The conquered nations would have to wait longer for their deliverance.

"How," asked the *Times*, "could these setbacks arise [three months] after the brilliant execution of the [North African] landing?"

How indeed?

Had political squabbles over fictitious issues deflected attention from military tasks? Could the Axis be defeated only by an overwhelming superiority of men and materiel in North Africa? Were the American troops too inexperienced for the Axis veterans? Were "our boys" too soft to stand up to the thugs? Or was there something else?

The questions appeared to be answered a week later as the Secretary of War held his usual press conference: " 'Clear-Cut Repulse' in Tunisia Dealt to Foe, Stimson Asserts." Rommel was withdrawing. The Americans had met the challenge at Kasserine and, according to Mr. Stimson, "came back with a vigor which the Germans were unable to withstand."

In short, the bad guys had knocked down the good guys. And then, as in the movies, the good guys got up off the ground and thrashed the bullies.

The American dream remained intact. The facile, phony script explained everything.

Yet the bad moment stayed too, never quite forgotten, rather pushed aside, replaced by better images of strength and purpose, courage and valor, know-how and confidence. Quiet toughness rather than bluster.

The outcome was more than a bad memory, more than an uncomfortable sensation. The crushing defeat swept aside the illusions of a time of innocence. Complacency at home and on the battlefield vanished. Kasserine, Mr. Stimson declared, "serves to remind us that there is no easy road to victory and that we must expect some setbacks and considerable casualties. We will not have an easy nor a quick victory."

The war would continue for more than two more years. As the Secretary said, there would be additional setbacks and casualties. But Kasserine had shocked Americans at home and overseas into an awareness of the grim and brutal facts of war.

They learned some unpleasant but valuable lessons — and quickly. They discovered the terrible ignorance bred of inexperience, the high cost of poor equipment, the tragic effect of sterile bickering among themselves and their allies, and the need of a special kind of man for leadership in battle.

In a country strange and mysterious to most Americans, where the squalor of life made the civilization of a Roman province two thousand years earlier seem resplendent, where Arabs in rags rode half-starved camels and donkeys across a barren and eroded land, where a field full of marble fragments, tumbled about a solitary arch or portal still standing, marked an ancient forum — in that part of the world where Numidians, Berbers, Carthaginians, Romans, Vandals, Byzantines, Arabs, and Turks had fought and plundered, American soldiers learned the trade of war at the hands of a master craftsman, who showed them, by the disaster he wrought, the extent of their mismanagement and inefficiency.

What happened, and why?

2

It would have been difficult to find a more captivating villain — handsome, buoyant, talented, a husband and father who adored his wife and young son.

He led the English not so merry a chase, kept a good part of North Africa in turmoil, and threatened for two years to smash one of the pillars of British empire and power, the Middle East. Yet his opponents admired Rommel.

No Nazi, he was a professional soldier uninterested in politics until much later in the war, too late as it turned out. Yet his implication in the plot to assassinate Adolf Hitler — he was an uncomfortable conspirator — and his forced suicide would make him even more attractive to his adversaries.

He compelled respect because he regarded the exercise of arms as an honorable métier, without blind hatred or vulgar disrespect for the enemy; because he scrupulously followed the rules of conduct laid down in an earlier age — and perhaps outmoded in the twentieth century — for officers and gentlemen; because he inspired his men and was considerate of them, leading them personally on the field of battle where the action was critical and the danger real; and because he worked hard at his profession and was good at it.

A pity, some said grudgingly in the Allied camp, that he was on the other side.

Some of his colleagues who regarded the officer corps as a monopoly of the Prussian aristocracy denigrated his accomplishments because he was only a middle-class Württemberger.

Yet Hitler, who was only an Austrian, recognized Rommel's proficiency and fostered his career. He made Rommel a colonel in 1939, a major general a year later, a field marshal in 1942, and decorated him with the senior grade of the Knight's Cross, the highest German military award.

A leading exponent of the blitzkrieg theory, Rommel executed it with remarkable results. In employing that hard-hitting combination of rapidly moving weapons — the tank, the airplane, and motorized infantry — he showed his genius in his power of imagination to create surprise, to produce the unexpected. He upset his enemy by mobility and speed, motivated by an audacity that was shrewdly calculated rather than reckless or hotheaded.

Originally an infantryman, he took command of an armored division in February, 1940, during the so-called phony war, and a few months later he was in the forefront of the breakthrough that brought Germany heady victory and France dismal defeat.

At the beginning of the following year Rommel was in North Africa. There he commanded a relatively small German force called the Afrika Korps that Hitler had sent to help his friend, Benito Mussolini.

Mussolini had entered World War II late. He waited until Germany had mortally wounded France before delivering the stab in the back. Then, while Hitler initiated the Battle of Britain to bring the English to their knees, Mussolini waged what he termed a parallel war, embarking on what was to be a glorious adventure in Africa: the restoration of the old Roman Empire. From the Italian territory of Libya he decided to march to the Nile and conquer Egypt.

His army in Libya of 250,000 men had few mechanized vehicles and only obsolete weapons — light and underpowered tanks and trucks, artillery pieces dating from World War I, old-fashioned antitank and antiaircraft guns, outdated rifles and machine guns — but had succeeded against primitive African tribesmen. Against the handful of British troops in Africa and the Middle East, the triumphs continued, and the

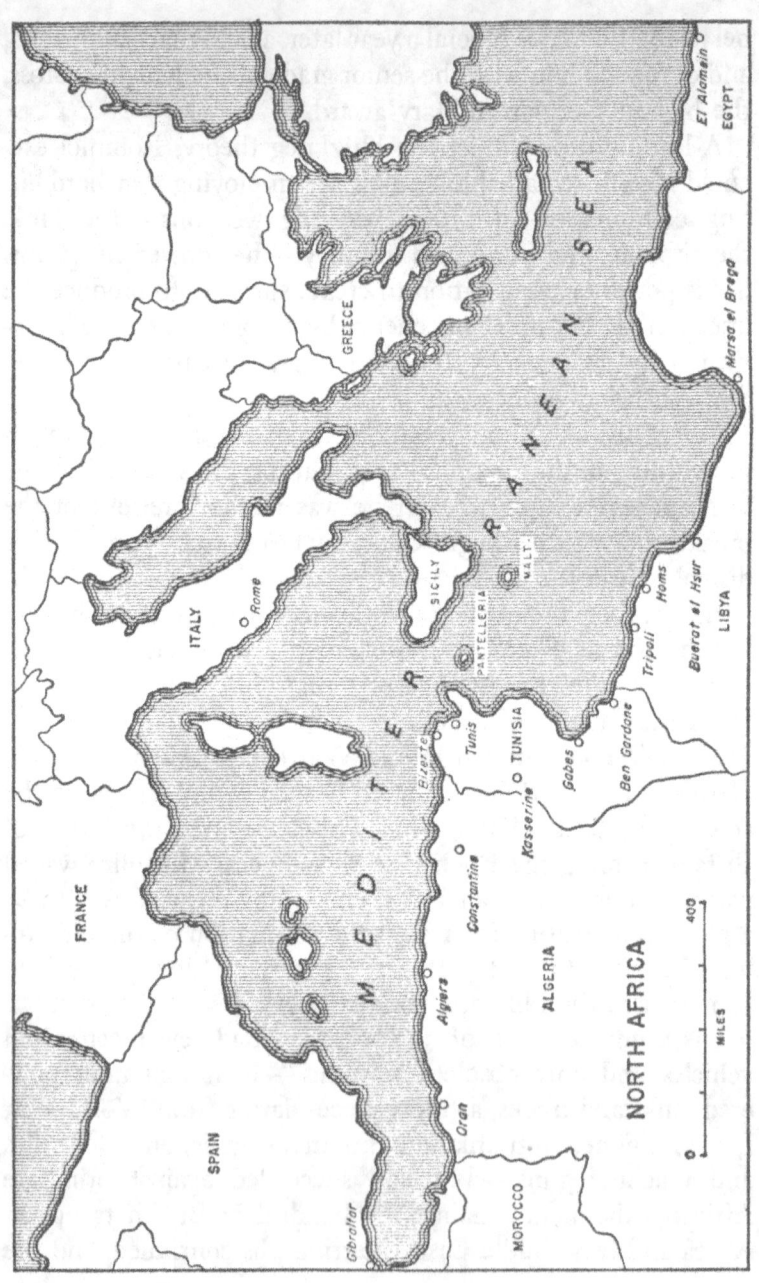

Italians moved into Egypt. There they had to stop and await additional supplies — gasoline, ammunition, rations, clothing, and the other items needed by units in the field.

They waited in vain. Not only was Italy ill-prepared to furnish the economic requirements of modern warfare, but Mussolini was letting his ambition dictate to his good sense. Instead of sending supplies to Egypt, he invaded Greece. Instead of overrunning Greece quickly, he saw his units bog down.

The British, who had meanwhile hurriedly assembled a modern, mechanized army in Egypt — with tanks, airplanes, long-range artillery, and motorized infantry — attacked the Italians in Africa, virtually destroyed them, and drove them out of Egypt.

Mussolini called for help, and Hitler came to the rescue. He dispatched an air force to southern Italy — to protect Axis convoys in the Mediterranean. And he sent Rommel and the Afrika Korps to Libya — to spearhead the ground operations. Acknowledging Mussolini's paramount interest in that area, he placed Rommel under Italian control.

Though Rommel was supposed to maintain an aggressive defense, he launched an offensive in April, 1941, and swept across Libya to the Egyptian border. "I took the risk against all orders and instructions," he later said, "because the opportunity seemed favorable." It was a characteristic statement.

Beyond the border he was unable to go, for he too needed supplies. He too waited in vain. General shortages, the requirements of the Russian front, poor lines of communication, British air attacks against Mediterranean shipping, and disinterest and incompetence in Rome deprived him of the essentials.

Though he was promoted to command a larger force — Panzer Group Afrika, consisting of the Afrika Korps and several mobile Italian divisions — the increased prestige failed to give him the material means to resist a British attack in December, 1941. Preferring to lose part of Libya instead of part of his army, he withdrew from the Egyptian frontier.

Hitler again came to the rescue. To prevent British planes based in Egypt and Malta from destroying Italian ships carrying supplies to Africa, he sent additional air units to Sicily and southern Italy, plus an energetic air force commander, Field Marshal Albert Kesselring.

The senior German officer in the Mediterranean theater, with headquarters at Frascati, near Rome, Kesselring had will and drive, a capacity for organization, a talent for diplomacy, and a thorough knowledge of technical military matters. He was responsible to Hitler for the proper employment of all the German forces in Italy and North Africa; yet for operations, he too, like Rommel, was subordinate to Comando Supremo, the Italian Armed Forces High Command.

Mussolini exercised supreme command in North Africa through Comando Supremo, which issued operational instructions and sent copies of them to Kesselring for his information. Since he had direct communications with Rommel and Mussolini, as well as with Hitler, he was a key figure. In 1942, after Rommel became a field marshal, he too would enjoy the privilege accorded to all officers of his rank of direct contact with the Fuehrer. Thus, by virtue of their direct access to both Hitler and Mussolini, the German commanders could bypass Comando Supremo. Yet the amenities of coalition warfare imposed certain courtesies. The Germans tried always to act in a respectful manner toward their allies. The Italians felt patronized and were usually uncomfortable.

"Thanks to the initiative of Field-Marshal Kesselring," Rommel later wrote, German planes attained superiority over the Mediterranean. As they beat off British aircraft that attacked Axis shipping, Rommel received an increasing flow of men and materiel. With sufficient supplies to launch an offensive, with his Panzer Group Afrika expanded and upgraded to the status of an army — now called Panzerarmee Afrika and consisting of all the German and Italian combat units at the front — he attacked late in May, 1942. He swept eastward across Libya and into Egypt.

A month later, having made his deepest penetration into Egypt, he was at El Alamein, sixty miles short of Alexandria and the Nile. Though complete success, an end to the British power, had come within immediate reach, he had to stop. He had again outrun his supplies.

While apathy reigned in Rome, the peril in which the British found themselves moved them to extreme exertions. They transported considerable amounts of men and war materiel to Egypt.

As Rommel continued to await the arrival of additional resources, the British harassed him, selecting Italian sectors as targets for local and limited attacks that brought many units close to exhaustion and disintegration.

No inherent fault could be attributed to the individual Italian soldier. The blame lay instead on the entire state and military system, which had failed to provide good weapons, modern equipment, proper training, adequate commanders, and moral incentive. In contrast with the well-trained, well-equipped, and well-disciplined German troops, the Italian units were, for the most part, second rate.

Carefully husbanding his strength and building up his reserves, Rommel launched a final effort in August to reach the Nile. After a week he had to go over on the defensive. Hope of overrunning El Alamein, of reaching Suez, and of occupying Egypt vanished. Gone too was Hitler's grand illusion of a march through the Middle East to a meeting with German forces in the Caucasus, the greatest projected pincer movement in history.

With bitterness — and with some exaggeration — Rommel ascribed his failure to a single cause: "our sources of supply had dried up — thanks to the idleness and muddle of the supply authorities on the mainland [of Italy]."

Now mutual resentment and suspicion arose between Germans and Italians, and muttered accusations began to be heard: that the Italians were incompetent, unreliable, unwilling or unable to pull their fair share of the weight; that the Germans played favorites, letting the Italians take the brunt of the fighting and a disproportionate share of the losses.

At this point Rommel left Africa. His health had begun to give out. After a year and a half of front-line responsibility and command, he was tired. Plagued with fainting spells, stomach and intestinal troubles, and circulatory difficulties, he was also discouraged. He saw no permanent solution to the problem of sustaining and nourishing his army. As long as Hitler was preoccupied with the Russian campaign, as long as Mussolini and his bungling henchmen directed the African campaign, the flow of supplies, he believed, would be less than satisfactory. Without gasoline, ammunition, and rations, armies could not function. For the first time, Rommel expressed doubt of Germany's eventual victory. Medical authorities suggested that he take a vacation in Germany to restore his health, and he agreed.

He flew first to Rome, where he talked with officers of Comando Supremo. They promised more supplies for Africa.

He spoke also with Mussolini, saying frankly that if the Axis nations were unable to furnish additional support, they ought to pull out of Africa altogether.

Evading the issue, Mussolini said nice things about Rommel's ability as a tactical commander. The inference was clear: Rommel should avoid strategic and political questions, which were outside his sphere of responsibility and competence.

Several days later Rommel reported to Hitler.

After complimenting him on his success, the Fuehrer talked about the supplies scheduled for Africa. He also mentioned some newly developed weapons that would certainly bring victory — the enormous Tiger tanks and the multiple rocket projectors or Nebelwerfer tubes ejecting what Americans would later call screaming-meemies.

Far from reassured, Rommel traveled to a mountain resort near Vienna to rest and clear up his liver condition and erratic blood pressure.

* * * *

The British Middle East forces, which defended Egypt, had two big jobs — guarding the Suez Canal and destroying the Axis military power in Africa. Twice the British had pushed into Libya, and both times the requirements of other theaters — the Balkans in 1941 and the Far East early in 1942 — robbed them of the strength to exploit their initial successes or even to retain the territory they had gained.

In August, 1942, shortly before Rommel launched his final attack, a new commander arrived from England to take charge of the Middle East forces, General Sir Harold R. L. Alexander. Sartorially splendid, quietly self-assured, suave sometimes to the point of nonchalance, with charm, personal courage, a high measure of intelligence, and a magnificent war record, he was an outstanding soldier.

Chosen to command the British Eighth Army under Alexander, Lieutenant General W. H. D. Gott, flew from the desert front to Cairo. As his plane was landing, enemy aircraft attacked the airfield. While he was helping to remove wounded occupants from his plane, he was killed.

He was replaced immediately by Lieutenant General Sir Bernard L. Montgomery, a wiry, caustic, and somewhat personally eccentric officer. Montgomery studied the art of war with an ascetic intensity that reached the edge of fanaticism, and he extorted by means of a querulous magnetism a fierce loyalty from his subordinates. He had still to make his reputation, and was not yet, as a high-ranking American officer said after the war, the nuisance he later became.

Alexander and Montgomery had stopped Rommel's final effort at El Alamein, and they waited almost two months to launch their own offensive. By this time, they had several American air force units that were knocking out Axis tankers carrying fuel to Africa; and three hundred brand-new Sherman tanks, sent from the United States around the Cape of Good Hope to give the British for the first time weapons that were the equal in armor, armament, and performance to the best German panzers in the desert.

When the British attacked at El Alamein on October 23, 1942, they broke through the Italian and German defenses, gained a major triumph, and inflicted a decisive, perhaps mortal, defeat.

In Austria, Rommel received a telephone call from the Chief of the German Armed Forces High Command on the afternoon of the 24th, the second day of the attack. He learned that the officer who had replaced him at the head of Panzerarmee Afrika was missing in action. Was Rommel sufficiently recovered from his illness, he was asked, to be able to return to Africa and reassume command if his presence was needed?

Yes, Rommel replied, he was feeling much better. He could cut short his leave.

That evening his telephone rang again. This time it was Hitler. Was Rommel able to start for Africa immediately if necessary?

Yes, of course.

Shortly after midnight Hitler telephoned again. Would Rommel leave at once?

He departed for Rome on the morning of October 25. "I knew," he wrote later, "there were no more laurels to be earned in Africa, for I had been told . . . that supplies had fallen far short of my minimum demands. But just how bad the supply situation really was I had yet to learn."

Reaching Rome around noon, he discovered that supply shipments to Africa had dwindled. Virtually no reserve stocks were available.

He crossed the Mediterranean in a small plane, arrived at his headquarters at dusk, and learned that the body of the Panzerarmee commander had been found — he had died of a heart attack at the front.

After a few hours of sleep Rommel made a tour of inspection. What he saw appalled him. The British had attained complete command of the air and the sea and were driving his forces from the battlefield. The new American Shermans appeared to be superior to the panzers.

He warned Kesselring, Mussolini, and Hitler to expect a disaster. His troops were exhausted and short of supplies. Lacking large numbers of motorized vehicles, they would probably be unable to escape the faster moving mechanized columns of the British.

But he had the uncomfortable feeling that the higher commands were misreading his reports and drawing their own conclusions.

"It is sometimes a misfortune," Rommel later wrote with a trace of self-pity, "to enjoy a certain military reputation. One knows one's own limits, but other people expect miracles."

North Africa, he felt, was probably already as good as lost. The most that could be done was to avoid the destruction of the Axis forces, particularly the German units. The only feasible course was to fight a sustained delaying action and withdraw across the northern shore of Africa. He would build up his strength while the British outran their supply lines, and finally he would counterattack when his forces were concentrated and the British, conversely, were dispersed.

The alternative was to abandon North Africa and move the Italo-German forces to Europe. Distasteful perhaps, but practical, he believed, in the long run.

At noon of November 3, the tenth day of the battle, having lost fifty thousand men, half of them taken prisoner, four hundred tanks, and one thousand guns, his Italian components falling apart, with acute shortages of fuel and ammunition threatening to turn into a rout a withdrawal that Rommel was keeping under control by sheer willpower, he received a message from Hitler that stunned him. Rommel, Hitler directed, was to have "no other thought but to stand fast and throw every gun and every man into the battle." He was to follow "no other road than that which led to victory or to death."

Rommel's initial shock had turned into quiet rage on the following day when Kesselring arrived to discuss with him what might best be done.

The conference started on a hostile note. "So far," Rommel said, "I've taken it for granted that the Fuehrer left the command of the army to me. This crazy order has come like a bombshell." He accused Kesselring of having misled Hitler. How else explain Hitler's directive? Kesselring must have sent optimistic reports that were farfetched if not altogether false. As Rommel later remembered the meeting, "some angry words passed between us."

Then both men calmed down. They had to reach agreement on what to do.

Kesselring favored stopping the withdrawal, and soon, at some defensible line. Rommel thought this would be impossible. What he wanted, he said, was complete confidence from his superiors and entire freedom to act as he judged best.

The demand was quite impractical. A commander in the field may suggest but can hardly himself determine the larger issues and aims of a campaign. His liberty to make tactical adjustments among his units in no way entitles him to make the decisions that rightly belong to the political leaders and the strategic planners. Complete freedom to Rommel would infringe upon Kesselring's authority, shunt aside and deny his policy-making role in the command structure. This was out of the question.

What Rommel really wanted was temporary authority in the critical emergency to save his forces from annihilation. Immobility and rigid adherence to preconceived orders, he felt, would be disastrous. Everything in the desert was open and incalculable; in the absence of natural obstructions, water obstacles, and woods for cover, a commander had to adapt and reorient himself daily, even hourly. He had to have freedom of tactical action.

Kesselring was not at all averse to this. The difference between the two men lay in their ideas of the method by which best to conserve the forces. Dig in somewhere and hold as long as possible was Kesselring's preference.

News coming during their conversation resolved the problem. The British had just broken through the front and captured the commander of the Afrika Korps. Rommel, with Kesselring's approval, immediately ordered the withdrawal to continue.

Returning to Rome, Kesselring persuaded Mussolini and Hitler to give Rommel the authority and discretion to act as he deemed best in the fluid conditions of crisis, which required instantaneous, on-the-spot tactical decisions. On the following morning, Comando Supremo issued the formal order authorizing retirement.

Mussolini had some reservations. He asked Comando Supremo to send a special emissary to Rommel to make known very discreetly a particular wish dear to the Duce's heart. Comando Supremo dispatched a diplomatic general who transmitted the Duce's desire: he hoped that the retrograde movement could be halted at the Egyptian border, for the loss of Italian territory would be painful to him.

Rommel was short with his visitor. A halt would be impossible, he said categorically. He could make no promises. The troops had incurred too many losses. He would try to get the Panzerarmee safely back across the Libyan border. He would probably have to give up much of Libya, painful though it might be.

The Italian general, Rommel noted, was "visibly shaken."

Two days later, on November 8, 1942, as his army was pulling out of Egypt and into Libya under the pressure of British pursuit, Rommel learned at 8 A.M. that an unidentified convoy had passed through the Strait of Gibraltar and was approaching the coast of northwest Africa. Three hours later he received word that Anglo-American forces had landed in French Morocco and Algeria, fifteen hundred miles behind him.

He still had plenty of room in which to maneuver. But eventually if the British continued to press him from the east and if the newly landed Allied forces turned against him from the west, the two were sure to trap him in Tunisia.

The Battle of Kasserine, though formless and unnamed, was conceived in that prospect.

3

BETWEEN the defeat of France in June, 1940, and the Allied landings in November, 1942, French North Africa was almost a forgotten corner of the earth. Except for the frantic refugees from Hitler's Europe who crowded the coastal cities, life continued as aimlessly as usual. Semi-nomadic Berbers followed their eternal pursuits, complacent *colons* tended their farms. The region occupied a position in limbo. The war had passed it by, and apparently so had the world. No German or Italian soldiers were present to disturb the quiet.

The French troops, who conducted training exercises and retreat parades as though nothing of importance had happened for half a century and nothing would for half a century to come, sank into desuetude. Their outmoded casernes decayed for lack of repairs. Their uniforms, once stirring to the sight, seemed old-fashioned and seedy. With limited responsibilities and curtailed means, they waited, like extras on a movie set, for the action to start.

The armistice of June, 1940, set all the conditions. The Germans occupied the northern part of France, while Marshal Henri Philippe Pétain established a government at Vichy for the other half of the country. Pétain abided strictly by the armistice terms imposed, though General Maxime Weygand issued secret instructions for conserving and concealing weapons and military stores for the day the French army would fight again.

A clandestine Resistance movement soon arose, generally sponsored and controlled by political parties that regarded Vichy as defeatist or, worse, pro-German. The British started to assist these underground forces morally and materially as early as November, 1940, and three years later the United States was also supplying instructors in sabotage and guerrilla warfare, ammunition, equipment, and radio operators.

The French army was reduced to a skeleton police force of about 100,000 men in metropolitan France and the same number in the North African territories, but the Germans promised to leave the powerful French navy undisturbed so long as France respected the armistice.

Distrust of the German promise and fear of French weakness led the British to a tragic step. To prevent the Germans from gaining possession of the French fleet, the British — less than two weeks after the armistice — seized French warships taking shelter in British harbors and in Alexandria, Egypt; and attacked and destroyed several vessels, the pride of the French nation, at Mers-el-Kebir near Oran, Algeria, and at Dakar. French casualties at Mers-el-Kebir alone totaled 1,297 men killed and missing, 351 wounded.

Franco-British amity had already suffered from mutual recrimination during the final phases of their coalition campaign in France — charges hurled on the one side that the French lacked moral fiber, on the other that the British would fight to the last Frenchman. But after the naval attacks, the friendship that had been traditional since the early years of the century went into a distinct decline.

Four days before the armistice had been signed, General Charles de Gaulle issued his radio appeal from England. Urging the people of France to continue the battle, he asked all able-bodied men to join him in a fighting force to be organized for action against the Germans. In August, 1940, Prime Minister Winston S. Churchill recognized De Gaulle as the "head of all free Frenchmen, wherever located, who rally around you to the support of the Allied cause."

About a year later, the Free French in London formed a National Committee under De Gaulle's presidency. Widely

1. "In a country strange and mysterious to most Americans, where . . . the civilization of a Roman province two thousand years earlier seemed resplendent," a light American M-3 tank, ungainly, awkward, and puny, captured and used by the Germans. *U.S. Army Photograph*

The flat, parched, and brush-covered plain of Sbeitla, with typical dry streambed wadi in foreground and barren mountain dorsale in background. *U.S. Army Photograph*

2. General Dwight D. Eisenhower, Supreme Allied Commander, who "fulfilled every expectation and more," and General Henri Giraud, who headed the French Government in North Africa even though he was "entirely non-political in his interests and outlook." *U.S. Army Photograph*

regarded as the legitimate successor, in embryo and in exile, to the Third Republic, the Committee received formal recognition from most Allied governments and active British support. The Americans gave only indirect assistance in the form of lend-lease supplies.

Authorities in several French overseas possessions who saw the Vichy government as an impostor organization, a fascist regime, and a puppet of the Germans, announced their allegiance to De Gaulle. By the end of 1942, these included French Equatorial Africa, the Cameroons, Syria, and others.

De Gaulle's military manpower produced a potential army of about 100,000 troops, and late in 1940 he began to create air, naval, and ground units. These became known as the Free French forces. Some, notably those commanded by Leclerc and Koenig, fought the Germans and Italians alongside the British in North Africa and the Middle East. Others clashed in Syria and Dakar with their compatriots, French units loyal to Pétain.

The United States established informal contact with De Gaulle, but maintained diplomatic representation at Vichy. The Americans wanted the armistice observed — Pétain to withhold from the Axis all privileges not pledged, the Axis powers to confine their demands to the concessions granted. Above all, the Axis was to have no control and use of the French fleet and colonial territories.

The colonial and overseas territories of principal interest and concern were French Morocco, Algeria, and Tunisia. Together with Libya and Spanish Morocco, they comprised the Barbary States, whose pirates had attacked Mediterranean shipping for three hundred years — until early in the nineteenth century British and American warships stopped the raids and the ransoms and the rest. Later in the last century, the lands were divided among France, Spain, and Italy.

Historically, the North Africans seemed incapable of grouping themselves around a chieftain or a common ideal, forming a durable state, and creating an original and lasting civilization. Overrun, conquered, and pillaged, they suffered successive incursion and invasion until the Europeans arrived and brought a certain measure of stability.

In their possessions, the French had developed ports, railroads, waterworks, power plants, and highways. The Navy had several bases, the Air Force occupied various airfields, and the Army had garrisons in the principal communities.

The French territories had a combined population of more than 16 million, all but a million or so either Berber or Arabic Moslem. Algeria was the most Europeanized, the maritime area having sent elected representatives to the national legislature in Paris before the war. Morocco and Tunisia were nominally governed by the absolute authority, both civil and religious, of native rulers, the Sultan of Morocco and the Bey of Tunis. But in the capital of each country, a French Resident General conducted all foreign relations and supervised, with a French staff, the civil administration handled by indigenous officials.

The Axis nations promised to send no armed forces there if the French themselves guaranteed to keep foreign powers out. Though the Italians believed that thirty thousand French troops would be enough, the French protested that an army of this size would be too weak to curb restless segments of the native populations. The strength of the military forces was then set, with German consent, at 100,000, later raised to 120,000, and finally augmented in 1942 to about 135,000. But the units were denied heavy artillery, antitank pieces, antiaircraft guns, and motorized infantry. Regiments were sharply restricted in composition, and divisions were permitted, for example, neither ordnance shops nor bridging equipment.

Pétain's military chiefs set out to rehabilitate the forces they were authorized. Their avowed purposes were to control the natives and to defend against invasion from any quarter by any force. Secretly, they hoped to fight the Axis again.

The troops, mostly natives, and their commanders, mostly French, were professional and well trained, yet lacked the major accoutrements of modern warfare, their weapons and equipment being obsolete.

The officials in North Africa, like the bulk of the people, followed a policy of what they called "unity of the French Union [the overseas empire] behind the Marshal [Pétain]." They opposed De Gaulle. Most had profound faith in Pétain and admired his authoritarianism. They felt that he held the Germans closely to the armistice terms and had the best interests of France at heart.

Devotion to Pétain was particularly strong among the military. The great majority of professional soldiers, with little interest in politics, saw De Gaulle dividing and weakening France and undermining the national leadership. At the instigation of Admiral Jean François Darlan, commander-in-chief of the armed forces and Pétain's designated successor, the Vichy government in 1942 replaced civilians with high-ranking military officers in almost all the leading administrative positions in French North Africa.

An invasion of North Africa would thus meet a dedicated force pledged to defend French soil — "*Défendre l'Afrique contre quiconque,*" as Weygand had put it. Even with their limited and outmoded weapons, the French were capable of putting up a fight. British components in a landing could anticipate only opposition deepened by rancor. De Gaullist Free French units could expect less than fraternal welcome. Only the Americans might hope for a friendly reception.

But a friendly reception would invalidate the armistice and bring swift Axis retaliation. The Germans would have no compunction about overrunning the defenseless unoccupied zone of metropolitan France, taking the Vichy government prisoner, seizing the bulk of the fleet tied up at Toulon, and holding, in effect, the entire population hostage.

The Allied governments were aware of the natural and understandable French concern over the German reaction. But surely, they figured, the French had more to gain from an Allied victory. And in that case, resisting Allied landings would be a useless, costly sacrifice contrary to the best interests of France.

To push aside the delicate as well as the hard obstacles in the way of an easy landing, the Allied leaders pursued three courses. They sought the help of a small group of pro-Allied elements in North Africa, hoping that a few bands of daring men might capture key military installations along the African shore to facilitate an invasion. This was why General Mark W. Clark traveled secretly by submarine to a hazardous rendezvous on an African beach a few weeks before the landings.

They also sought the help of General Henri Giraud, a national hero, who had twice escaped — once in World War I and again in World War II — from German prison camps. Affiliated with neither De Gaulle nor Vichy, he might unify North Africa behind his martial presence, form and head a new government dedicated to active Allied support, and open military operations against the Axis. But when he was secretly summoned to Gibraltar a few hours before the landings, he refused to take part. He had misunderstood the whole arrangement. Entirely non-political in his interests and outlook, a soldier who had no concerns beyond the battlefield, he had believed he was being called to become the commander-in-chief of the invasion expedition.

The third course of action was to give the landings an American character by selecting, over more experienced and senior British officers, General Dwight D. Eisenhower as commander-in-chief.

Eisenhower would fulfill every expectation and more. His great forte was getting individuals to perform together for the good of, as the cliché later became, the team. A rather junior officer compared to some of his British and American subordinates, he was not yet very sure of himself. He never, as a military commander, would show great talent for instantaneous and independent decision. Yet his supreme achievement in North Africa would be his capacity to deal successfully with the intricate aspects of a coalition venture in the midst of an involved political situation.

He would be aided immeasurably by his deputy, Clark, who had inexhaustible energy, vigor, and good sense and who could be direct and tough to the point of rudeness and charming and persuasive beyond the limit of larceny. Eisenhower's most intimate associate during the period of preparing for and executing the invasion, Clark was as close to being indispensable as any man can be.

Eisenhower was supposed to gain, together with the British Middle East forces, mastery of North Africa from the Atlantic Ocean to the Red Sea. After putting troops ashore, he was to extend control over the three French possessions and, since Generalissimo Francisco Franco was friendly to the Axis, be ready to seize Spanish Morocco. Then he was to thrust eastward to destroy the Axis army in Libya.

Because Tunisia was too close and too vulnerable to the Axis planes based on the islands of Pantelleria, Sicily, and Sardinia, and on the mainland of southern Italy, the Allies would land only in French Morocco and Algeria. American troops would come ashore at Casablanca and Oran; Americans and British at Algiers. All would be under American commanders — Patton at Casablanca, Fredendall at Oran, and Ryder at Algiers. As soon as Algiers came under Allied control, Ryder would give way to a British officer, Lieutenant General Sir Kenneth A. N. Anderson, who would launch a thrust eastward to seize Tunisia and bottle up Rommel.

Anderson, who represented the combat experience and knowledge of the British Army — in contrast with the untried Americans — was the third choice for the job. Alexander had been the initial selection, and there had been some question whether he would consent to serve under Eisenhower, who lacked battle experience and was his junior in rank. The two men met for the first time at lunch and liked each other at once. They would, it appeared certain, be able to work together in harmony. Then Alexander was sent to take command of the Middle East.

The British next chose Montgomery. On the day following his selection, the unfortunate death of General Gott prompted Montgomery's transfer.

The appointment went to Anderson, a tall, dour officer who had commanded a division in combat and whose performance had been judged competent. He was difficult to know and, it would turn out, difficult for Americans to deal with. He had a brusque manner and made a poor impression. Eisenhower's aide, who was inclined to be effusive in his praise of people he liked, was tight-lipped as he noted in his diary: "A Scotsman named Anderson has been assigned to Ike. Fine reputation."

Anderson would wait at Gibraltar until the landings at Algiers succeeded under American auspices. Then he would fly to North Africa and take command of the troops, mostly British but some Americans too, who would make a quick thrust along the coast to Bizerte and Tunis more than 550 miles away.

The invasion by 83,000 American and 26,000 British assault troops who came ashore on November 8, 1942, was facilitated by the presence in Algiers of Admiral Darlan, Pétain's deputy. Despite Pétain's insistence that the armistice of 1940 be honored and the invaders repulsed, Darlan agreed to a local cease-fire, began to negotiate for a broader understanding, and on November 10 ordered all resistance to stop. The clash of authority between Pétain and Darlan brought perplexity to North Africa, and the French military forces became passive.

Events moved swiftly. On midnight of November 10, more

than ten German divisions crossed the demarcation line in metropolitan France and six Italian divisions marched into eastern France. Overrunning the free zone governed by Vichy, they disarmed and disbanded the armistice army, occupied the entire country, and took Corsica. When the Germans attempted to seize the warships sheltered at Toulon, French naval authorities scuttled the vessels.

On the 13th, as Darlan established a provisional government in North Africa with himself at the head, President Franklin D. Roosevelt extended to him lend-lease. On the 14th, Darlan appointed Giraud, who had been brought to Algiers only to go into pouting seclusion, commander-in-chief of the French ground and air forces in North Africa. On the 15th, Giraud issued his first directive, instructing the French military forces to take up arms against the Axis. A week later, Darlan and Clark signed an agreement bringing French North Africa into the Allied camp.

Darlan's assumption of power was accepted by the Allies as a temporary expedient — to ameliorate the landings, to facilitate the establishment of military bases, and to keep the population in order. His efficiency and goodwill, despite his anti-British sentiment, embarrassed the Allies, for they needed him, yet his former ties with Pétain made it impossible to merge the Vichyite and De Gaullist forces of France. His assassination by a youthful Frenchman on the day before Christmas hardly helped matters. Giraud succeeded him as High Commissioner and commander-in-chief of all the armed forces. But in the following month, when Giraud and De Gaulle were reluctantly brought together by Roosevelt and Churchill, the two Frenchmen barely shook hands.

The political fragmentation and factionalism in French North Africa sharply divided loyalties for about ten days after the invasion. Junior officers in the military services generally favored the Allies, but many officers of senior rank hesitated to commit themselves. French civilians were apathetic,

Arabs indifferent or inclined to be hostile, and the civil authorities antagonistic. Many mayors, stationmasters, postmasters, and other key officials — for example, those in charge of the telephone and telegraph, which the Allies had to use — were lukewarm in their sympathies.

In this environment of suspicion and intrigue, the safety of the relatively small Allied forces concerned all commanders. If they suffered a setback, they might find the population turning against them. "Anything approaching failure," Eisenhower later wrote, "would have a most damaging effect upon the morale of all whose hopes had been buoyed by the entry of the United States into the war."

Then the atmosphere cleared. As the French joined in the common struggle, military considerations supplanted political reservations. Their leaders came to see their participation in the war as necessary — to overcome British skepticism, to win American confidence, and to restore faith in themselves.

But the French troops brought complications. Only in spirit could they pass muster. A handful of fine senior officers had nurtured the Army through the trying days of inactivity, and the young commanders were eager to prove their mettle.

Poorly equipped — "lamentably so," according to Anderson — they lacked radios, trucks, and boots; their rifles and cannons dated back to the era before World War I. Their material penury would handicap them and prevent effective action against the Germans except in mountainous regions, which denied access to mechanized equipment. Only there would the French have any chance of fighting the enemy on somewhat equal terms, and Americans and British would have to be alert always to buttress them.

There was also the question of command. The French flatly refused to serve under the British. They would take no orders from Anderson. Eisenhower was acceptable, but he was completely occupied with political and administrative matters, and his headquarters in Algiers was too far away for effective battlefield control. No other American immediately available had sufficient combat experience or prestige to be superimposed on Anderson. Thus, the enormous advantage of a unified direction supplied by a single commander was lost. Instead of an all-encompassing endeavor, the first step into Tunisia would be made by the British, helped by a few American units, and coordinated with the French. A hopeless intermingling of the three Allied forces would soon develop along the front, a thoroughly unsound military practice. Despite Anderson's "constant preoccupation to tidy up the mess and give each nation its own sector," he later explained, he found it impossible to do so until the Battle of Kasserine had driven that necessity home.

Though his troops, a few traveling by water, fewer still by air, most across the land, moved almost five hundred miles in a week, Anderson was pessimistic about reaching the northeastern corner of Tunisia unopposed. Sicily was too close, less than one hundred miles away, and the ports and airfields of Bizerte and Tunis were too tempting and too valuable for a passive acceptance by the Axis of the Allied eastward movement. Planes could transport Axis soldiers to Tunisia in a few hours, ships in less than a day.

Unless the French in Tunisia resisted the arrival of Axis forces.

On November 17, about forty-five miles from Bizerte, Allied elements ran into Axis troops. Some contingents would get as close as fifteen miles from Tunis at the end of the month, but the opportunity to gain Tunisia without combat slipped away. Axis troops had arrived in considerable numbers.

They had entered Tunisia freely. The French had offered no resistance, mainly because of mental anguish, agonizing doubts, and a paralysis of will.

4

FOLLOWING ORDERS is a military virtue, but in a time of confusion and conflicting loyalties may lead as easily to dishonor as to glory.

At the hour of the Allied invasions, General Georges Barré, who commanded the Army in Tunisia, and Admiral Louis Derrien, who commanded the naval forces, had wanted to give instant and unquestioning obedience to their superiors. Both wished only to serve their country. Yet their paths diverged. Judgment, conscience, and circumstances separated them.

When the Resident General, the supreme French official in Tunisia, learned around midnight of November 7 of the imminent invasion of Morocco and Algeria, he informed his chief military subordinates, Derrien and Barré.

Derrien, who commanded the naval base at Bizerte, immediately put his coastal batteries on combat alert, issued orders to call up reservists, and prepared to defend against what he termed Anglo-Saxon aggression.

Barré, who commanded the ground forces, did nothing. His troops were dispersed and difficult to assemble. He saw no way to offer effective opposition during the hours of darkness. And he wanted more information.

The information he wanted came at 9:45 A.M., November 8, in a message from the Government of France: "Profiting from our disarmament and from intelligence hypocritically obtained, the Anglo-Saxons have just attacked French North Africa. . . . The Marshal of France [Pétain], Chief of State, has replied in the only way the interest and honor of France permit: 'We are attacked. We shall defend ourselves. This is the order that I give.' "

Barré then issued an order to his troops: "The Marshal confirms our mission: defend the empire against no matter who will try to gain a foothold. Our duty as soldiers is simple and clear: execute the order of the Marshal."

By evening, the northern coast of Tunisia was prepared for defense against American and British incursion.

At midnight the German High Command informed Vichy that it was indispensable to oppose the invasion by allowing Axis air forces to be based in Tunisia and in the Constantine area of Algeria, and that such permission must be given in exactly an hour and a quarter.

Being unable to deny what the Germans could take by force, the French government acceded.

A message received in Tunis early November 9 announced the imminent arrival of German planes: "The French Government has had to accept the use of air bases in Constantine and Tunisia by German air forces destined to act against our aggressors. Technical discussions" — a French request that only German aircraft, no Italian planes, be sent — "are in process at Wiesbaden."

Darlan, not yet adjusted to the inevitable, sent confirmation: "The Americans having invaded Africa first are our adversaries and we must combat them alone or with help" — Axis help.

That morning Kesselring sent two German officers from Italy to North Africa by plane. Landing at an airfield in Algeria between Algiers and Constantine, they tried to reach Darlan by telephone in order to regulate the use of French military air bases. Unable to get in touch with him, they flew to Tunis, where Barré received them. He asked them to delay the arrival of German planes until he had specific instructions from Vichy. They agreed.

While he solicited instructions, the German officers called on the Resident General, who supported Barré's action.

At 12:30, before he had a reply to his request, the first German planes landed at Tunis. By three o'clock that afternoon, 103 aircraft were on the field.

As the initial planes were coming to earth, Barré telegraphed Vichy: "I have the duty to inform you of the emotion that is already being caused by this occupation . . . and the disturbing commentaries it is provoking among the majority of officers whose loyalty I will soon be unable to account for."

Derrien also made known his indignation and concern: "I have been told that tomorrow, November 10th, a convoy should arrive at Bizerte for the purpose of supplying the Axis air units. I inform you that these movements are of a nature to produce in the Army, Air, and Navy of Bizerte, which I hold perfectly in hand for the moment, an emotion of which I cannot foretell the results." What needed immediate rectification was the noxious presence at Tunis of German aircraft parked beside French planes.

"I understand your sentiments," Vichy replied that evening of November 9, "but it is impossible after the Anglo-Saxon aggression to prevent the German planes from coming. . . . Neither we nor the Germans carried the war to French North Africa. We can only submit." Then as an afterthought: "Have confidence."

The Resident General received much the same word: "Just as we could refuse access to our territories to all military forces before the Anglo-Saxon aggression, now it is impossible to prevent one or the other belligerent from carrying the war to our soil."

Barré had, meanwhile, placed several hundred soldiers around the airfield to guard the German planes. He also instructed his troops to defend the ports against Allied invasion from the sea and to resist Allied forces coming overland from Algeria.

By the morning of November 10 however, Darlan had had time to face reality. He dispatched two messages which changed everything. Announcing his assumption of authority over French North Africa, he ordered all hostilities suspended. All troops were to regain their camps and bases and show an "attitude of complete neutrality toward all belligerents."

That afternoon, when several British aircraft attacked the airfield at Tunis and destroyed six German planes — the first Allied bombardment of a series that would be launched every two or three days — the French units surrounding the air base retired to avoid being struck by bombs. After the air raid, they marched to their barracks.

When the Germans announced that planes would land on the following day at Bizerte and troops would arrive at Bizerte and Tunis, Vichy quickly instructed Barré and Derrien to permit their entry. But all contacts between German and French troops were to be avoided, and no units were to be intermingled.

On the morning of November 11, Derrien informed his subordinates: "In several hours sad events for French hearts are going to take place. . . . German troops are going to land on Tunisian soil. The Government of the Marshal has had to submit to these difficult exigencies. Our duty is to obey him. I count on everyone to keep his calm, his sang-froid, and his dignity."

Within a matter of minutes came the upsetting news that Pétain had disavowed Darlan's cease-fire. "I have given the order to defend against the aggressor," Pétain announced. "I maintain that order."

Did this mean, Derrien asked the Resident General, that he was to fire on the Anglo-Saxons?

The Resident General thought not, but he telephoned Darlan to find out. Learning that General Alphonse Juin now commanded the military forces in North Africa, he put in a call to him. According to Juin, Barré and Derrien were free to do as they thought best.

Derrien telephoned Barré. What did he think they ought to do?

In his opinion, Barré said, the best thing was to observe an absolute neutrality toward everyone, Axis and Anglo-Saxon alike, and this he ordered his troops to display.

Dissatisfied, Derrien cabled Vichy: "My point of view is as follows: 1) According to your message . . . , the landing of German troops is authorized. 2) The struggle continues against the Anglo-Saxons. General Barré, after having telephoned General Juin, estimates that the line of conduct to follow is strict neutrality toward all belligerents. I ask you to take all measures to clear up the confusion as soon as possible because it creates a dangerous trouble in all spirits."

The Minister of the Navy replied. Pétain had repudiated Darlan and had designated General Auguste Noguès, the commander in Morocco, to be his sole representative in North Africa. He added: "My personal advice since the events of this [past] night" — referring to the Axis occupation of the free zone of metropolitan France — "is passivity vis-à-vis all."

Seeking reassurance, Derrien telephoned the Resident General. Barré was there, and he came to the phone. He said that, according to Juin, the Germans and Italians, by occupying all of France, had broken the armistice. For that reason, Derrien and Barré decided to open fire on the Axis ships that were due to appear at Bizerte. They would permit Allied ships to enter freely.

Barré had a special request. Would Derrien hold his fire against Axis planes so long as no Axis ships appeared? Barré was moving his troops to the mountains immediately west of Tunis and Bizerte, and during that march they would be extremely vulnerable to air attack.

Derrien agreed. He instructed his subordinates to oppose

all Axis landings, to fire against Axis ships approaching the coast, to refrain from hostile acts against the Americans and their allies, and to observe until otherwise notified an attitude of neutrality toward Axis aircraft.

Carried away by his feelings, Derrien also issued a rousing order of the day: "After two long days of discussion and confusion, the order has just reached me formally and precisely, designating the enemy against whom you are going to have to fight. This enemy is the German and Italian. Soldiers, sailors, aviators of the defenses of Bizerte, you are now fixed. Go with full heart against the adversaries of 1940, for we have a revenge to take. *Vive la France.*"

Then he telephoned the Resident General and informed him of his action.

The Resident General was disturbed. What bothered him was the widespread distribution given to orders of the day. The emotional call, though restricted to military channels of communication, was indiscreet. It could have, he felt, not only serious but disastrous consequences. If the Germans somehow learned of it, they might move immediately against Barré, who was assembling his men in the hills.

It was a chastened Derrien who at once classified his order of the day "secret," thus imposing special handling procedures on its dissemination.

Forty minutes later, after uncomfortable indecision, he annulled the order. Neutrality was to be the order of the day.

But the message had already been read to the soldiers, sailors, marines, and airmen in the Bizerte area, and the call to arms had provoked great enthusiasm. The annulment brought consternation and heartbreak.

Six German ships and one Italian vessel that arrived at the port of Tunis with troops, weapons, and ammunition found no impediment raised against unloading.

During the night a message from Vichy informed Derrien that Pétain was continuing the struggle against Anglo-

Saxon aggression. "You should let pass without interference the Italo-German forces landing in Tunisia," he was instructed. "Follow the order of the Marshal."

Unable to bring himself to quite this position, Derrien ordered a strict neutrality toward all foreign forces.

About fifty miles west of Bizerte and Tunis, Barré was concentrating his ground forces. He awaited what he judged would be an inevitable opening of hostilities against the Axis. After a last visit with the Resident General, who raised no objection, he established his headquarters about seventy-five miles west of Tunis on the main road to Constantine.

Derrien spent a sleepless night. He was unable to obey Darlan, whom Pétain had repudiated. He had no instructions from Noguès, whom Pétain had appointed. And he estimated that his position at Bizerte was untenable without the support of Barré's troops.

Telephoning Algiers for help early on November 12, he found only confusion. Darlan would make no decision. Juin considered himself unqualified to exercise command. Everyone awaited Noguès, who was expected that afternoon.

Completely discouraged and depressed, Derrien told a colleague, "I have seven citations and forty-two years of service, and I shall be known as the admiral who delivered Bizerte to the Germans."

He had two alternatives: open hostilities against the Germans scheduled to debark at Bizerte — but this was against the orders of his government and appeared equally contrary to the Resident General's point of view; or take his naval garrison to join Barré's forces — but this meant abandoning the base, the arsenal, and the ships.

German planes landed at Bizerte that morning, bringing antiaircraft guns to defend the airfield. Then, all day long, air transports disgorged and deposited troops and materiel.

When two German officers announced the arrival of ships and asked Derrien to open the port and make available the unloading facilities, he requested instructions from Vichy: "discharge of their cargo requires accord of the Navy; should I accord it?" Yes, came the reply.

That evening Barré had a telephone call from Juin, who said that an immediate state of hostility against the Germans was desirable. Barré demurred. The Germans in Tunisia were too powerful, his own troops too vulnerable. Let the Germans open hostilities.

It was a helpless and harassed Derrien who set out by automobile on the morning of the 13th to meet with Barré along the road to Constantine. Was there some way out of the mess? Halfway to the meeting place, he was overtaken by a messenger. Urgent orders had arrived in Tunis for him.

Returning, he learned that the urgent orders were from Darlan, who had consolidated his authority in Algiers and who wanted Derrien to throw the Germans into the sea, bottle up the harbors of Bizerte and Tunis, and withdraw his naval forces overland to the southwest, to the Algerian border area near Tebessa and Kasserine.

How could he do all that? He no longer had the strength.

On the following day, the 14th, a message from Pétain to Darlan was transmitted to Tunisia for information: "You must defend North Africa against American aggression. Your decision violates my orders and is contrary to your mission. I order the army of Africa to exercise no action and in no circumstances against the Axis forces and to add nothing to the difficulties of the Fatherland."

The words struck home with Derrien. He made his decision. So far as he was concerned, Barré had passed "into dissidence." For while the influx of Axis troops at Bizerte and Tunis continued, Barré was deploying his troops across the interior of Tunisia, along a line from north to south, to bar an Axis advance to the west.

An emissary from Vichy arrived in Tunis on the 15th to reinforce the authority of the Marshal of France, Henri Pétain. He spoke with the Resident General and with Derrien, but he wished also to see Barré. The Resident General sent a letter by a Navy captain, who reached Barré's command post late in the afternoon. Would Barré come to Tunis for a conference?

He said he was unable to leave his troops.

The official from Vichy sent a second messenger that evening. "I beg General Barré," he had written, "to come see me immediately no matter what the hour of the night."

Barré confirmed in writing the response he had already made. He added that the official could come see him if he wished.

Pétain's emissary drove out on the morning of the 16th. When he approached the line of French troops and saw them turned facing the east, he decided to go no farther, for he feared that he might be seized and held. He turned back. At the first village that had a post office, he sent Barré a telegram: "General, I have the honor to confirm to you the order of the Marshal, Chief of State, to defend the territory of the Regency against the Anglo-Saxon invader."

Barré disregarded the message. His troops, who occupied a defensive line about forty-five miles west of Tunis and Bizerte, were under orders to oppose by force any Axis units that might approach.

Derrien, in contrast, was issuing another order of the day: "Foreign or dissident propagandists are trying to trouble our spirits. Conscious of my responsibilities, faithful to my vow to the Marshal of France, assured of the authenticity of his messages, I confirm to all troops placed under my command . . . 1) Oppose by force all American attack. 2) Abstain from all hostile action against Axis force."

Despite a personal letter from Darlan — "*Tu ne vas tout de même pas faire tirer des Français contre d'autres Français*" — Derrien was too far committed to change course. On his own initiative, at his own suggestion, accepted eagerly by the Germans, he signed an agreement with the German commander of Bizerte, promising to defend with his French forces certain sectors in the Bizerte area. He would, he assured the Germans, repulse all attempts of Anglo-American forces to debark.

With Derrien in their pocket, the Germans set out to get Barré. On the afternoon of November 18, the German Minister at Tunis sent his deputy to Barré's command post. Traveling by car, he was stopped about forty-five miles west of Tunis by French troops, who telephoned that a delegate of the German command wished to see Barré.

He sent a subordinate, a general officer, but the German insisted on seeing him personally. Agreeing, he fixed a rendezvous at a farm near the French line.

Around midnight, as Barré was driving toward the farm, he encountered the general who had met with the German and who gave him a letter.

The letter, written that day, was from the German commander in Tunis, who reminded Barré that the governments of Germany and France had decided to repulse Anglo-American aggression against the French Empire. To that end, it was necessary to have contact with Barré and his staff to regulate their collaboration. Could he have an immediate decision? What he wanted specifically was to have all the routes cleared of obstacles that might obstruct a German advance to the west — toward Algeria and a meeting with the Allied invaders. Would Barré therefore order his troops to act toward the Germans as toward allies? It appeared indispensable that they have an immediate talk in Tunis to straighten out the details.

There seemed little point in conferring with the German delegate. But he was waiting, and Barré had agreed to see him. So he continued to the farm and met the deputy minister as arranged. It was then 1 A.M., November 19.

The German insisted that the fate of the French people

depended on whether Barré rallied to Pétain and removed all obstructions in the path of the imminent advance to the west.

Barré said he would need first to confer with his chief, Juin, who was in Algiers. This would take several days at least.

That would be too long. Unless the German commander had a favorable response by seven o'clock that morning — in six hours — he would have to take action.

Barré made a gesture of regret. The meeting broke up. The deputy minister returned to Tunis, Barré to his command post.

At eleven o'clock that morning, German planes bombed the French positions and the farm where the meeting had taken place. Twenty minutes later, German artillery opened fire and infantry approached. When French soldiers returned the fire and drove the Germans off, they committed the French army in North Africa to active opposition against the Axis.

Marshal Pétain tried to reverse the course of events. "Frenchmen," he declared, "some general officers in the service of a foreign power have refused to obey my orders. Generals, officers, non-commissioned officers, and soldiers of the Army of Africa, do not obey these unworthy chiefs. I reiterate to you the order to resist the Anglo-Saxon aggression. We live in tragic hours, disorder reigns in our spirits. You hear news which has no other aim but to divide you and weaken you. But the truth is simple: failure to hold to the discipline which I require from each of you puts your country in danger. . . . Union [between France and Africa] is more than ever indispensable. I remain your guide. You have but one duty: obey. You have but one government: that which I have given the power to govern. You have but one country which I incarnate: France."

The rhetoric had no visible effect. The French forces in North Africa, with the exception of those trapped behind the

German lines in Tunisia, had opted in favor of the Allies.

Little more than two weeks later, on December 7, at six o'clock in the evening, a German liaison officer visited Derrien at his home. The German commanding the Bizerte sector was convoking a meeting of the important French officials. Would he be so good as to repair, with all his high-ranking staff members and commanders, to the tent of the Bizerte area commander at 9:30 the next morning?

Yes, of course. But he decided to take only three principal subordinates.

At the appointed time and in the designated place Derrien reported. As he entered the German compound, he noted the presence of what seemed to him to be an inordinate number of heavily armed guards. As he stepped into the tent, he noticed the arrival overhead of four squadrons of Junker 88 planes, which continued to fly menacingly over the well-defended and well-patrolled camp during the conference.

The German commander presented Derrien to General Alfred Gause, who had been sent by Hitler. After bowing stiffly, Gause handed Derrien a paper. It was an ultimatum that Derrien read in silence. The motors of the German aircraft sounded like a faint and accompanying drumroll.

The policy of collaboration with the enemy had reached its logical conclusion. Hitler had ordered the French forces in Tunisia to be disarmed. All troops were to be demobilized immediately. All weapons, military buildings, depots, mobile installations, radio stations, and other facilities, including vessels, were to be handed over intact. The scuttling of ships or destruction of equipment would be considered acts of sabotage, and the perpetrators would be tried by a German tribunal and executed immediately. Peaceful acceptance would mean repatriation to France for all personnel or, if they wished, eventual reconstitution into new units to fight alongside the Germans. Refusal would result in immediate attack by the Germans, who would take no prisoners but would kill all military personnel to "the last officer and soldier."

How much time did Derrien have to make up his mind? Thirty minutes.

"To you, Admiral," the paper concluded, "the decision! free return to France or death."

He and his three colleagues left the tent. Between lines of armed guards standing at attention, they walked a hundred steps. What could they do? Resistance was impossible. Opposition would serve no useful purpose. Why sacrifice lives hopelessly?

He would have to give up the coastal batteries, the arsenal, three torpedo boats, nine submarines, two dispatch vessels, some artillery, and the weapons of seven thousand Senegalese and three thousand other troops.

He waited until twenty minutes had passed. Perhaps he needed time to compose himself.

Then he returned to the tent and informed Gause of his submission.

Ten minutes before eleven o'clock, Derrien issued his final instruction: "Total demobilization order given in France has just reached me by German authorities. By terms of this order, all military materiel must be turned over intact to Axis troops. Axis troops will take all measures without pity against attempt to resist, to sabotage, to scuttle. I ask all to obey this sad order to avoid useless spilling of blood. This order to be executed without delay."

In contrast, Barré's soldiers, under the command of their own military chiefs, were fighting proudly beside the British and Americans.

5

HITLER WAS TRAVELING in a special train from his headquarters in Rastenburg, East Prussia, to Munich for his annual celebration with the "veteran fighters" of the National Socialist party when he heard the news of the Allied landings in North Africa. His first reaction was involuntary — he would have to calm the Italians. Then he decided he would have to send forces to Tunisia, diverting reinforcements scheduled for Rommel. When a message from Kesselring asked for authority to intervene and for additional troops, Hitler approved both requests.

While Kesselring dispatched planes to attack Allied vessels at Algiers, he started to assemble troops in Italy for transfer to Tunisia. The first ones he sent by air were his personal headquarters guards to protect the airfield. Despite the French request, that only German planes should be sent, Italian fighter planes landed on the 10th.

Men and equipment poured into Tunisia, arriving daily by air and every two or three days by sea. More than fifteen thousand soldiers were shipped by air alone during November. At the end of the month, seventeen thousand German and eleven thousand Italian troops were occupying the northeastern corner of the country, called the Tunisian bridgehead. In the south, several thousand Italian soldiers had crossed the border from Libya and had moved into the coastal region near the city of Gabes to fill the space along the eastern shore between the bridgehead and Rommel's withdrawing forces.

From the beginning, Kesselring instructed the bridgehead commander — initially an air force colonel, later an army colonel — to gather units and push to the west. Anglo-American columns were certain to come from Algeria, and the Axis forces had to be far enough into the interior to gain battlefield depth and to prevent getting hemmed in and besieged at the coastal cities.

Very quickly he decided he needed an experienced and senior officer in the bridgehead. Just the man he sought became available when General der Panzertruppen Walther Nehring unexpectedly appeared in Rome.

Nehring had commanded the Afrika Korps under Rommel. Wounded on the last day of August and sent to a hospital near Berlin, he was not yet fully recovered — the wound in his arm was still festering — when he received a phone call from Gause, who had been Rommel's chief of staff.

Gause too had been wounded and was on convalescent leave in Berlin. He had received a letter from Rommel, who asked him to find someone to take charge of building defensive positions behind his withdrawing forces. If he could back his troops into a prepared line, he might halt his retreat for a while.

Was Nehring well enough, Gause asked, to return to North Africa for this assignment?

Nehring said he was.

Gause having made the appropriate arrangements, Nehring flew to Rome. Before he could get a flight to Libya, he received orders to report to Kesselring. He learned that he was to undertake a mission more urgent than Rommel's — command of the Tunisian bridgehead. There, he was to execute an immediate and far-reaching thrust to the west, preferably to the Algerian border, to gain freedom of movement for the Germans in general and for Rommel in particular. He decided to make a one-day trip to look over the situation, then return to check his impressions with Kesselring.

The flight to Tunis, an hour and fifteen minutes, was uneventful until the plane descended. The pilot lost control, crash-landed, and wrecked the aircraft. No one was injured. Somewhat shaken, Nehring carried out his discussions, flew in a light plane to Bizerte for further meetings, and returned to Rome.

He was hardly cheered by his visit. He had seen considerable disorder and heard many complaints over shortages. His foremost impression, initiated by the unnerving crash-landing, was pessimistic.

Opening his command post in the bridgehead on November 14, he organized a drive to the west. It was he who had sent the ultimatum to Barré.

His initial contacts with Allied ground forces were somewhat unsettling. The French were stronger than he had bargained for, and the Allied units moving out of Algeria were closer to the bridgehead than he had expected. Already, it began to seem, he was compressed into the northeastern corner of Tunisia, without maneuver room or sufficient troops, and with no place to go except out.

To Nehring's military troubles was soon added a personal discomfort. The wound in his arm began to ache painfully.

When Kesselring came for a visit, he found Nehring gloomy. Trying to shake him out of his depression and to instill confidence and determination, he spoke sharply, but without effect. It became apparent that Nehring was not the man "to tie up the Allied forces in Africa," as he later wrote, and keep the war distant from the German homeland.

Part of Nehring's outlook came perhaps from his attachment to Rommel. Knowing Rommel's views, he probably shared them.

In the belief that the Axis nations lacked sufficient resources to support operations adequately in North Africa, Rommel favored leaving the continent altogether, salvaging as many troops and as much equipment as possible, and organizing a defense of Sicily and southern Italy at once.

But since the loss of prestige implicit in this course of action would probably prohibit its implementation, he felt that the Axis leaders ought to eliminate at least one of the two theaters of operation, Libya or Tunisia. Since they seemed to have chosen to fight in Tunisia, they should move him westward quickly out of Libya and into Tunisia and plan an attack to the west against the Anglo-Americans. But if they persisted in maintaining two theaters and if they expected him to hold Libya for an eventual counterattack eastward against Montgomery's British Eighth Army, they would have to send him reinforcements. How they would find additional forces was, of course, up to them. But otherwise it would be impossible to make even a temporary stand at Marsa el Brega, a naturally defensible area, about six hundred miles west of Alamein and five hundred miles east of the Tunisian border.

Trying to get a precise strategic statement from his superiors, he sent an aide to Hitler's headquarters in East Prussia. The aide returned with disappointing news. Hitler had bluntly said that Rommel should leave Tunisia out of his calculations, concern himself solely with Libya, and act on the assumption that other forces would hold the Tunisian bridgehead and protect his rear.

"What will become of the war if we lose North Africa?" he wrote his wife in despair. "How will it finish? I wish I could get free of these terrible thoughts."

He was making a distinction between a forcible ejection from North Africa, which meant the destruction of his army, and an intentional abandonment, which would insure his army's safety.

On November 20, Hitler and Mussolini came to a decision. It was not to Rommel's liking, but at least it was positive.

They would make their major effort in Tunisia, striking westward from Tunis and Bizerte. They would seize Tunisia, then Algeria, and force Spain to enter the war on the Axis side. But they wanted Libya too. Rommel was to defend as much of Libya as he could, for as long as he could, and to that end he was to construct and occupy a strongly fortified line at Marsa el Brega. He would get no reinforcements.

Rommel was hardly surprised. He doubted that he could hold for long with his seventy thousand troops. But what he "found really astonishing," he wrote later, "was to see the amount of materiel that they [his superiors] were suddenly able to ship to Tunisia, quantities out of all proportion to anything we had received in the past."

He continued to think of leaving Libya completely and withdrawing into Tunisia — to Gabes, 120 miles beyond the Tunisian border and midway between Tripoli and Tunis. Gabes was a magnificent place to establish and stabilize a defensive line. A chain of lakes and marshes only twelve miles inland from the coast created a narrow passage along the eastern shore that could be held with a handful of men. Leaving them to block Montgomery, who was bound to approach Gabes cautiously — "safety first," Kesselring called his tactics — Rommel would be able to shift his own excess forces against the Anglo-Americans. When they were defeated and driven westward into Algeria, he would return against Montgomery, throw him back into Libya, and pursue him into Egypt.

But this, he admitted, was a pipe dream. In the long run, he believed, neither Libya nor Tunisia could be held. The only feasible course was to gain time and get out of Africa as many battle-tried veterans as possible for subsequent use in Europe — and thus to rob the Allies of the fruits of their victory as the Germans had been robbed at Dunkirk.

To inform the Fuehrer of his thoughts, he sent another officer to Hitler's headquarters. He could hardly protest the strategic decision taken by the Axis leaders. But he could take exception to his own projected role. "Although a favorable turn in the situation is almost more than I dare hope for now," he wrote to his wife, "nevertheless miracles do sometimes happen."

Rommel's emissary described the difficulty of holding

Marsa el Brega without reinforcements, suggested a withdrawal of six hundred miles more to Gabes, recommended firm contact with Nehring's bridgehead, and proposed, after a consolidation of forces, a joint leap to the west to annihilate the Allied forces and gain Algeria.

Hitler dismissed the logic. Rommel, he believed, was simply too nervous after his defeat at El Alamein to stand fast and fight.

Trying still to obtain a change in his mission, Rommel persuaded Kesselring and the chief of Comando Supremo to meet him in Libya. His arguments again proved futile. According to Rommel, the chief of Comando Supremo "lived in a world of make-believe." According to the chief of Comando Supremo, Rommel wanted to retire into the "citadel of capitulation."

In desperation, Rommel flew to East Prussia himself — as he later said, "To put an end to the intolerable contrast between the mission assigned . . . and the means provided." He reached Hitler's headquarters on the 28th.

At 4 P.M. he had preliminary talks with Hitler's principal staff officers, whom he found "extremely wary and reserved."

At 5 P.M. he saw Hitler. There was, he remarked later, "a noticeable chill in the atmosphere from the outset."

Expecting a rational discussion, Rommel started to present his point of view.

Hitler interrupted. He would hear of no withdrawal.

After a violent outburst of denunciation, the Fuehrer became calm. He promised Rommel additional resources. He assured him that Comando Supremo would furnish him reinforcements. And he instructed Hermann Goering to go to Rome with him and talk with Mussolini about revitalizing the supply system for Libya.

Beyond that the matter was closed.

On the private train provided by Hitler, Rommel explained to Goering the plan he had been unable to present to the

Fuehrer. It was simplicity itself — consolidate in Tunisia and strike westward before the Allies could match the combined strength of his forces and those in the bridgehead; then turn eastward and eliminate the British.

Goering was hardly interested. He was thinking of the art treasures that awaited him in Italy.

In Rome, Rommel finally persuaded Kesselring of the validity of his viewpoint. The Tunisian bridgehead was by then under attack, and the advantage of combining the Axis forces became clear. Comando Supremo agreed that it was too late to give Rommel the strength to hold indefinitely at Marsa el Brega. And Mussolini became reconciled to the eventual loss of Libya on the basis that he would instead gain Tunisia.

* * * *

When Nehring received the first organized Allied ground attack on November 25, he outnumbered his adversaries about two to one. Containing the thrust, he launched an offensive of his own on December 1.

The Allies had to withdraw to defensible positions. Unbearably cold weather had come, together with an unceasing rain; the long journey from Algiers had been wearing on men and machines; and ammunition was in short supply. "I think the best way to describe our operations to date," Eisenhower wrote at the time, "is that they have violated every recognized principle of war, are in conflict with all operational and logistic methods laid down in textbooks, and will be condemned in their entirety by all Leavenworth and War College classes for the next twenty-five years."

They would try again in December to reach Bizerte and Tunis, but these efforts would fail too.

Despite Nehring's triumph, Kesselring's estimate of his abilities and the new and enlarged scope of activities determined by the strategic decision made another and more senior commander inevitable. Early in December, Hitler recalled from the Russian front a surly, sullen officer who walked with a slight limp, Juergen von Arnim. Promoting him to Generaloberst, he elevated him to command the Fifth Panzer Army in Tunisia. Generalleutnant Heinz Ziegler, also promoted, would be his deputy.

After meeting with Hitler, both officers reported to Kesselring in Rome, then went on to Tunisia. As Nehring departed for Germany and another assignment, Arnim assumed command of the bridgehead on December 9.

* * * *

In Libya, Rommel began to leave Marsa el Brega on December 6. Receiving little information, he was in what he termed a "continual state of anxiety about Tunisia." He feared that the Anglo-Americans might seize the Gabes bottleneck and drive a wedge between his army and the Tunisian bridgehead.

By the 15th, in little more than a week, Rommel drew back 250 miles to Buerat el Hsun.

Shocked by this rapid retrograde movement, the Italians applied the brakes. *Piano, piano,* they urged. The Duce was unwilling to abandon Libya in a single night. Or even a week. Stop a while at Buerat el Hsun, if for nothing more than the sake of appearances.

Rommel had to comply. But he chafed under the restriction, and he continued to press for permission to move into Tunisia. Yet while he argued vainly that it made little sense to keep his undernourished Panzerarmee at Buerat, he knew that Kesselring was assuring Arnim of an increasing flow of materiel.

Convinced that he would never have sufficient supplies to attack the British as long as Arnim was receiving the bulk of the shipments, Rommel came to a decision. On the 17th, he asked the Duce for authority to quit Libya at once. He said he had to arrive at Gabes before the Allies.

The proposal ran head-on into Mussolini's vested interests. There could be no swift flight from Libya for three reasons. First, the Italian people had to feel that Libya was being defended foot by foot and that final expulsion was the result of an overwhelming and irresistible British pressure that made further retention of Italian territory an unendurable sacrifice. Second, between Buerat el Hsun and Gabes was Tripoli, the major city in Libya. How could Mussolini allow Tripoli to be surrendered without at least the semblance of a struggle? More realistically, once the port of Tripoli was lost, Rommel would be completely dependent on shipments coming through Tunisia. Third, between Buerat and Gabes was also the Mareth Line, about eighty miles inside Tunisia. Constructed by the French before World War II to guard the Libyan frontier, the Mareth fortifications consisted of a series of antiquated blockhouses in a state of neglect. Though Rommel could see only the weakness of these defenses and wanted to go forty miles beyond to Gabes, Mussolini argued that they could be repaired. They provided enough protection for a temporary halt at least. Why permit the British to enter Tunisia without even a show of resistance at Mareth?

Mussolini told Rommel publicly to hold — stand fast and fight — at Buerat until the end, until not a single defender was left alive. "Resist to the uttermost, I repeat, resist to the uttermost," he thundered. At the same time, quietly admitting that Rommel could not run the risk of being encircled and destroyed, he gave him permission to fall back to Tripoli. But on one condition — that he take six weeks to make that withdrawal.

These were the contradictory facts of life.

Shortly thereafter, Hitler confirmed the policy. North Africa would be held. A bridgehead in Tunisia would be permanent. Reinforcements would be sent to raise the German strength in Tunisia to 130,000 or 140,000 men. But the Russian campaign, and specifically the battle for Stalingrad, which had started in mid-November, would interfere with his intent. The insatiable appetite of the Russian front would take the men promised for Africa.

On the last day of 1942, Mussolini authorized a conditional withdrawal out of Libya and into Tunisia. Rommel was to retire slowly, taking two months to move to the Mareth Line, which was to be repaired. To guarantee a deliberate rate of speed, he was to secure Italian approval for each step of his movement, a precaution designed to prevent the loss of Italian foot soldiers to motorized British envelopment.

Protesting that Montgomery or Eisenhower might have something to say about the duration of his withdrawal, convinced that the best way to save his non-motorized troops was to move them back at once, Rommel started them to the rear on January 2.

Faced with this disobedient act, Comando Supremo complained to Hitler, then ordered Rommel to be sure to defend Tripoli.

While Rommel moved his seventy thousand troops westward, Arnim was receiving a constant stream of men and materiel. By the end of January, 1943, he would have more than 100,000 men, three-quarters of them first-rate German troops. As his strength increased, he spread his bridgehead and his influence into southern Tunisia, into the Gabes area, which Rommel regarded as his own.

Arnim's star was in the ascendant. No longer Rommel but Arnim was the favorite son. Ambitious, stubborn, a man of iron will, he eclipsed Rommel in importance.

The fact that the Battle of Stalingrad was reaching its climax during January emphasized the critical primacy that Hitler and Mussolini attached to the bridgehead. Rommel's operations had become distinctly secondary.

Shortly after the turn of the year, to prevent the Anglo-American forces from coming between the two armies, Rommel was instructed to send one of his better divisions into

3. General Sir Harold R. L. Alexander, "sartorially splendid, quietly self-assured, ... an outstanding soldier," who took command of the Allied ground forces in Tunisia during the battle of Kasserine Pass. *U.S. Army Photograph*

4. Field Marshal Erwin Rommel, psychologist, master craftsman, captivating villain, and commander of the Italo-German Panzerarmee, later reluctant commander of Army Group Afrika. *From U.S. Army Files.*

southern Tunisia. This was heartening. But since he was too distant to control these troops, they passed under Arnim's command. The shift in emphasis stood out boldly. And this Rommel found galling.

When Rommel sent the 21st Panzer Division into southern Tunisia, the Battle of Kasserine began to take shape in his mind.

Unrecognized at the time was a preview of what was to come. In northern Tunisia during the end of November and early December, the meeting of American tanks and German panzers had foreshadowed what was soon to happen at Kasserine.

6

A GOOD SOLDIER is supposed to believe that he is part of the best platoon in the best company of the best battalion in the best regiment of the best division in the Army.

Second Lieutenant Freeland A. Daubin, Jr., really believed this about the platoon of tankers he commanded in Company A of the 1st Battalion in the 1st Armored Regiment of the 1st Armored Division of the United States Army. To Daubin they were the best — bar none.

He felt lucky to be in the outfit. From the moment he joined, he knew he belonged. He could conceive of no other assignment where he would have felt so much at home. Everything pleased him, the individuals from the division commander on down, the *esprit* of the team, and especially the light M-3 tanks he worked with — what a really great piece of equipment.

The division trained for more than a year before going to the United Kingdom in the spring of 1942. In the early autumn, the 1st Battalion of the 1st Armored Regiment, along with other units, moved to Scotland. The tankers put in several weeks of hard work to waterproof their vehicles, then went to the Firth of Clyde and boarded stubby, converted oil tankers flying the white ensign of the Royal Navy.

For twenty days, escorted by five armed trawlers, the men cruised the sea toward an unknown destination. They came ashore on November 8 at Oran, Algeria. During their short period of quasi-combat, as Daubin called it, they accomplished their missions with an exceptional verve and efficiency.

THE SETTING 57

The men had never lacked self-esteem. Now, like any body of troops experiencing a dashing and easy victory, they began to think quite highly of themselves. Self-confidence was desirable and healthy, but self-adoration led to carelessness. Seeing themselves as invincible heroes, they forgot that the French who had opposed them had been understrength, underequipped, and undermotivated. Really, the invasion had been simple, the battles nothing more than skirmishes, and the outcome never in doubt.

To puncture swelled heads, the battalion commander, Lieutenant Colonel John K. Waters, called his men together. "We did very well against the scrub team," he said. "Next week we hit German troops. Do not slack off in anything. When we make a showing against *them*, you may congratulate yourselves."

Congratulations, then, the men concluded, were only a week away.

The battalion moved to Tunisia, some men traveling by rail — their tanks and other tracked vehicles tied to flatcars; the others riding in or driving the wheeled vehicles. The trip through that peculiar land fascinated Daubin. French colonial troops who guarded key bridges, tunnels, and mountain passes waved at the Americans who passed. Daubin always waved back.

Joining Anderson's First Army, which was stabbing toward Tunis and Bizerte, Waters's battalion was to work closely with a British lancer regiment equipped with Crusader and Valentine tanks. In contrast with these, the American M-3 looked puny. But that was only the appearance, the men told themselves. The M-3 really packed a wallop. After months of range work, field maneuvers, action at Oran, constant maintenance, and loving care, the men were proud of their light tanks and had affection for them.

Love had not come at first sight. The M-3 was too ungainly, too awkward to inspire immediate admiration. The tank seemed as tall as it was long, with a chopped-off look that made it appear almost incomplete. The turret where the commander stood was extremely cramped. It could be rotated but only manually. Perched on the forward edge of the flat top deck, it reminded Daubin of a hatbox about to fall from the top shelf of the hall closet. Protruding from the turret was the 37-mm. cannon. Thin and needle-like, it resembled the bill of a woodpecker. But it was supposed to be a pretty good weapon, and the men believed in its prowess.

On hard ground the M-3 handled beautifully. It was agile and fast. Its 250-horsepower continental eight-cylinder radial air-cooled engine gave a high horsepower-weight ratio. Soft ground was something else. The eleven-inch track was too narrow for adequate flotation. Only fourteen tons in weight, the M-3 became hopelessly bellied in places where tanks four times heavier romped through with ease.

When the tank was buttoned up, the driver and bow gunner peered through narrow slits protected by prisms. The tank commander was even worse off — he looked through tiny peepholes in the so-called pistol ports along the sides and rear of the turret, and his forward vision depended on a low-powered telescopic gun sight. It was normal for a tank commander to go into battle with the overhead hatch open, for it was necessary, though risky, to raise his head out of the turret to see what was happening.

Very much aware of the deficiencies of the M-3 in visibility and flotation, the men had a great and abiding faith in the 37-mm. cannon. They were also confident that the 1½-inch armor plating on the front gave adequate protection against small-arms fire and high-explosive shell fragments.

Because of their beliefs and their unbounded enthusiasm, they would have protested the relegation of the light M-3 tanks to secondary and screening missions. They expected and usually received the same combat assignments as the better armed and heavier armored medium tanks. Why not?

They were tankers too, descendants of the dashing cavalrymen of derring-do, and they believed passionately in the doctrine of seeking out and destroying enemy armor. They could hardly wait to carry out the deep and furious thrust into the enemy rear and the fight to the finish of tank against tank.

As they looked forward eagerly to meeting the enemy, they heard and passed on some really wild rumors: the invasion had thrown the Germans and Italians into a panic; ten thousand enemy troops were being evacuated every day from Tunis and Bizerte; the only enemy armor in Tunisia consisted of a few obsolete panzers; most of the enemy forces were supply troops, rear-echelon types armed with rifles. What a cinch it would be to knock them off.

When the battalion bivouacked and the officers assembled for orders, a single fear was prevalent — the Germans might escape before the troops could punch their one-way tickets to Valhalla.

Waters had a bemused grin. He had received a quaintly phrased mission. His battalion was to establish what the British called a "tank infested area" about one hundred square miles in extent. How accomplish the infestation? That was left to his imagination.

Operations would go on a shoestring. The battalion had no artillery support — only its own mortar and assault gun platoons. Maintenance would be the responsibility of the troops — no ordnance shops were nearby. Infantrymen were simply not present. Air cover would come from a single understrength squadron of Royal Canadian Air Force planes brought forward hurriedly without ground crews; the pilots themselves would arm and repair their planes, fill by hand the bomb craters in the wheat fields and highways they would use as runways, and fly their ships on whatever fuel they could scrape together.

The center of the assigned infestation area was about thirty miles away, and at first light on the clear, crisp morning of

November 25, the vehicles started out, winding over goat tracks and sheep paths, past upland Arab shepherds that made Daubin think of biblical figures.

As the column descended into a valley, the men noticed about two dozen German planes in the distance, several ME-109 fighters covering a group of JU-88 bombers. When two Spitfires appeared and engaged the Germans, the men cheered as a Jerry fighter went down in flame. They became still when they saw a Spitfire trailing smoke, the pilot gliding down to try for a level landing. In silence they watched the Spit disappear behind a hill. They listened. The jarring crash and the explosion left no doubt.

Company A located enemy troops in a farmhouse that was actually a substantial stone and plaster fort built for defense against marauding Arab bandits. Connecting several buildings that formed a rectangle about a large tree-planted courtyard, a thick wall was loopholed for muskets and had a fighting parapet. The ground was flat, the only possible concealment coming from knee-high vineyards.

A firefight started. Mortars, assault guns, and tanks hammered away at the farm, but the shells only brought down terra-cotta tiles from the stoutly beamed roof.

Daubin's tank was quickly put out of action. Armor-piercing machine-gun bullets damaged his 37-mm. tube. When he examined his machine later, he found many small projectiles embedded in the armor plates that gave his tank the appearance of a three-day growth of beard.

In the midst of the firefight came sudden shouts — "Here they come. Take cover." A plane popped over a hill and buzzed low over the company. The roar of the plane was followed by a small earthquake and a shower of dirt clods. The JU-88 had laid an egg and was gone. Everyone felt foolish.

The plane had evidently tested the company's air defenses. For soon afterward a swarm of aircraft swooped over the valley.

With a glow of pride, Daubin noted that all the light machine guns designated for antiaircraft defense in his platoon were manned. With a shock of horror, he realized that the antiaircraft weapons were not worth, as he said, a tiddley damn.

The gun, in his words, was a misconceived abortion. Mounted on a spring-up cradle bracketed to the backside of the turret, it had metal belt boxes so loose that, even with a cardboard shim, the vibration worked loose every fifth or sixth bullet. The weapon jammed so frequently that it was useless. It could be loaded with a belt from inside the tank immediately before use, but air attacks were over and gone in a twink, too fast for prior loading.

Worst of all, the gunner was as exposed to aircraft as a fireplug to every passing dog. So far as Daubin was concerned, there was only one practical thing to do during an air attack. Stand on the back deck of the tank à la Humphrey Bogart, raise a clenched fist, and curse the Luftwaffe.

As the aircraft streaked over the valley in a long column, the lead plane peeled off and headed toward the tankers at five hundred feet.

Forget the noise of the strafing guns and the screaming brakes, Daubin said. The sight alone of a Stuka diving — the flexed appearance of its dihedral wings, its non-retractable landing gear thrust forward like the talons of a pouncing eagle — is enough to turn sporting blood into plasma.

If the men had had heavy machine guns adequately mounted, they could have talked back. But there was only one such gun in the company — on the command half-track — and its thin chatter hardly interrupted the German monologue.

Nine times the planes came over, fifteen of them, a mixed flock of ME-109's, Stukas, and twin-engined JU-88's. And when they were finally gone, the troopers of Company A picked themselves off the ground and discovered that one man had been killed and a few were slightly wounded. Not a single tank had been put out of commission.

The firefight against the farmhouse continued. But it was no go. Toward the end of the afternoon, Company A withdrew.

Company C, as Daubin learned that evening in the bivouac area, had also had an exciting day. The tankers had blasted several Volkswagens out of the road without even slowing down. They littered a village with the debris of destroyed trucks and motorcycles. They wiped out a guard detachment at a bridge.

Feeling that the Germans were by then alerted to their presence, they took to olive groves for cover and moved cautiously forward. When the olive trees petered out, the lead tank breasted a ridge to see what was ahead.

Down below was an airfield packed with parked planes. Fat geese on a pond.

It was too good to be true. But it was no mirage.

The company commander formed a line of foragers. Over the rise and down on the airfield charged seventeen light tanks, like cavalry troops of old. Enjoying themselves in a wild orgy of destruction, some tankers blasted the planes with high-explosive shells, riddled them with canister, set them afire with tracer bullets, while others physically crushed lined-up ships by running over tail assemblies.

Frenzied pilots trying to get their planes up and away taxied into each other or scudded off across the field with a tank in hot pursuit. Two got away. Eleven were destroyed.

The tankers turned their attention to hangars and shops, destroyed twenty-five more planes, and set gasoline stocks on fire. They lost two men, killed when the planes that had gotten off the ground strafed the field.

That evening the companies of the battalion came together and made camp. The troops looked forward to a Thanksgiving feast of British Compo mutton stew with hardtack biscuits. But first they had to gas up their tanks, replenish their ammunition stocks, check their weapons and engines, camouflage their vehicles, dig foxholes, and put out guards. They were highly conscious of the absence of artillery, infantry, and air support and well aware of how isolated they were from friendly forces.

Then they ate their rations and drank their concentrated British tea. They smoked leaves rolled in toilet paper, swapped their experiences of the day, and griped about how the base troops in Oran and Algiers had the soft life — they were having a meal of turkey, sweet potato, and cranberry sauce, and they were smoking cigarettes made of real tobacco.

The major test that Waters had warned about came several days later. Company A was in bivouac on a hill on one side of a pass, Company B on the other. The tanks were snuggled into the slope of a small ridge that overlooked the main road fifty to one hundred yards away. A mile distant was the walled farm that remained in German hands.

It was a bright, clear morning. The company commander was at the battalion headquarters. Daubin was sitting on the command half-track and chatting with the maintenance officer and the first sergeant, when a lookout yelled: Movement on the road!

Where? someone shouted.

Near the fortified farm.

Daubin looked through his GI binoculars and could see little. The sergeant handed over a set of powerful French naval glasses he had picked up in Oran. Through these he made out a column of dust. Raising the clouds of sand and dirt were large vehicles, each mounting a long protrusion that resembled the boom spar of a sailing ship.

He felt the excitement rising within him. What was a German engineer unit of mobile derrick equipment doing on that road? The machines were about to blunder into the company positions. They could be easily ambushed.

Several high-velocity shells came screaming in and dispelled the illusion.

Daubin gulped. Those were not engineer vehicles. They were German tanks, Mark IV Specials. The boom spars were long-barreled 75-mm. rifles. The Germans had apparently picked up movement in the company area and were approaching to make contact.

The men jumped to. Camouflage nets were jerked down, bedding rolls and musette bags tossed out, engines warmed. All extraneous gear — all the stuff that gets collected — was jettisoned. Cranked up and ready to roll, the troops awaited the return of the company commander from battalion headquarters.

While waiting, they watched a brilliant attack by the assault gun platoon — three snub-nosed 75-mm. howitzers mounted on half-tracks. Through a thinly planted olive grove, the guns moved in wedge formation across the valley floor to intercept the German tank column. About one thousand yards from the Germans, as they emerged from the olive trees into open ground, they halted. Section leaders quickly set out their aiming stakes by pacing and got their guns parallel; in a few seconds, all had ranged in with the center gun; then all three opened up, each firing ten shells as fast as the gunner could yank the lanyard.

Of the thirty rounds fired, all against the lead tank, many hit the target directly and all were close.

Figuring they had disposed of the lead tank, the gunners quickly shifted fires against the second and third tanks in column.

The hail of high-explosive shells stopped the Germans. But after an instant of hesitation, the panzers moved out of the dust and smoke unharmed. Seeing their tormentors, the tankers sent screaming bolts of steel that missed the American guns.

Realizing the futility of further action by the assault guns,

Waters called them back. The gunners threw smoke shells at the German column and, while the tankers were temporarily blinded, executed a classic disengagement without the loss of a man or gun.

The assault guns had only scratched the paint of the German tanks. But they had given the battalion time to mount an attack.

Waters ordered Company A to close diagonally against the German right flank, while Company B fired on the left flank and rear. The company commander having raced back, Company A boiled down the hill with Daubin's platoon on the right. Normally the company had seventeen tanks, but only twelve were in operating condition that day. Daubin had three instead of four tanks in his platoon. All headed for the column of what turned out to be thirteen Mark IV panzers.

Before emerging from the scattered olive trees that grew on the slope, Daubin spied an Italian light tank crawling along the valley floor several hundred yards off the German flank. He halted to dispatch this enemy. Two armor-piercing shells stopped the Italian cold. One round of explosive set him afire — "brewing," the British called it.

Daubin's crew cheered. "Look at the Ginzo burn!"

Their elation vanished when they noticed several tanks of Company A burning too.

In his state of high excitement, an irrelevant thought crossed Daubin's mind. A burning tank was an impersonal stage prop brought up from the bowels of hell to decorate a battlefield.

The sight exerted a morbid fascination over him, and he watched minutely, observing the phenomenon in detail. A tank that is mortally hit belches forth long searing tongues of orange flame from every hatch. As ammunition explodes in the interior, the hull is racked by violent convulsions and sparks erupt from the spout of the turret like the fireballs of a Roman candle. Silver rivulets of molten aluminum pour from the engine like tears, splashing to the ground, where they coagulate into shining reflecting pools. When the inferno subsides, gallons of lubricating oil in the power train and hundreds of pounds of rubber on the tracks and bogy wheels continue to burn, spewing dense clouds of black smoke over the funeral pyre.

Awareness of wicked rifles swinging toward him interrupted the reverie. The German tankers were disregarding Company B, which pecked away at the rear of the column. Instead, they were giving their undivided attention to Company A, which had swiftly executed the flanking maneuver.

Within gun range of the column, Daubin found partial cover in a small wadi, a dry stream bed that extended the protection of its low bank. Singling out one German tank as his own, he banged away, his cannon popping and snapping like a cap pistol.

Jerry seemed annoyed. Questing about, his turret rotating and turning with it the incredibly long and bell-snouted gun, the German soon spotted his heckler. Leisurely, he began to close the gap between himself and Daubin's light tank, keeping his thick sloping frontal plates turned squarely to the hail of Daubin's fire.

The crew of the M-3 redoubled their efforts. The loader crammed what suddenly appeared to be incredibly tiny projectiles into the breach, and Daubin, the commander who was also the gunner, squirted them at his foe. Ben Turpin could not have missed at that range. Tracer-tailed armor-piercing bolts streaked out of the muzzle and bounced like mashie shots off the hard plates of the Mark IV.

The German tank shed sparks like a power-driven grindstone. Yet he came on, 150 yards away, then one hundred, and seventy-five.

In a frenzy of desperation and fading faith in his highly touted weapon, Daubin pumped more than eighteen rounds at the German tank that continued to rumble toward him.

THE SETTING 67

Through the scope sight, Daubin could see the tracers hit, then glance straight up — popcorn balls, he thought, thrown by Little Bo Peep.

Fifty yards away, Jerry paused.

Daubin sensed what was coming and he braced himself.

The German loosed a round that screamed like an undernourished banshee. Ricocheting off the wadi bank a trifle short, the shell showered sand and gravel into Daubin's open turret hatch.

How had the German gunner missed? Was he addled? Was his gun useless at such short range?

Impassively the Mark IV continued to advance.

Daubin wondered wildly whether the tanker intended to use his gun tube to pry the M-3 out of its cozy terrain wrinkle. Was he planning to knock Daubin into a corner pocket with a three-cushion shot?

Instead, Jerry pulled to the right and mounted a small hummock of ground. This destroyed Daubin's slight advantage of defilade.

Now the German was only thirty yards away.

It was time for Daubin to go. Gracefully if possible. But go. Any way. If he could.

Having made an estimate of the situation and held a staff conference with himself, he decided that he was in a predicament known in the trade as "situation doubtful." A rapid retrograde movement to an alternate firing position was in order.

Because his driver was half buried in the brass of expended shells and unable to receive his foot and toe signals, Daubin crouched behind him and yelled into his ear. He wanted the driver to pull back with all possible speed, to zigzag while backing, and to keep the front of the tank facing Jerry.

"Yes, sir," the driver said clearly, without a trace of excitement in his voice.

Are people calm because they fail to understand what is

happening, because they lack imagination? The altogether normal, though unexpected, response encouraged him.

As the driver jockeyed his gears, Daubin began to feel that everything was going to be all right.

The M-3 lurched backward and across the wadi, then up the bank.

A distinct feeling of relief came over Daubin. He climbed into his turret and straightened up for a quick look out of the open hatch.

At that moment, death, inexplicably deferred, struck. The slug that was doubtlessly aimed at the turret struck the vertical surface of the armored doors and caved in the front of the tank. The driver was instantly killed.

Blown out of the turret by the concussion, Daubin was thrown to the ground. He lay dazed, only vaguely conscious of the fact that he had been wounded.

He saw the bow gunner, blind, stunned, and bleeding, crawl out of the tank and collapse. He watched the loader get out, jump to his feet, and run crazily toward cover until the German tank cut him down with machine-gun fire.

Then he became aware of his M-3. Sheathed in flame, the tank was still moving, backing out of the wadi, continuing to retire. He watched it go, backing slowly, until it was out of sight.

The panzer had already turned in search of another victim.

When Daubin could move, he pulled himself painfully into a ditch. As he waited for help, two thoughts kept recurring. How long would it be before a German tank swept past and finished him off with a single obliterating blast? And how was the battalion going to stand up to the Germans with only those measly little tanks and guns?

Captain Ben Cohen, the battalion surgeon, and Father Brock, the chaplain, found him. Heedless of the fires that fell about them, they were cruising around the battlefield in the medical half-track, removing men from knocked-out tanks and picking up the wounded. They lifted Daubin into the vehicle and carried him back to the battalion headquarters area.

While he waited for an ambulance to take him to the rear, he learned that the battalion had destroyed nine of the thirteen German tanks, not by setting them afire as the result of penetrating hits but rather by riddling their engine doors and knocking off their tracks — nibbling at them rather than smashing them.

He did not know, nor would anyone realize until a group of high-ranking officers visited the theater on an inspection tour at the end of December, that the troops had not yet received recently developed and highly effective armor-piercing ammunition. They had been using shells meant to be expended in training exercises.

Daubin learned that his company commander had been instantly killed when an enemy shell put a hole through the turret of his tank. His tank sergeant and devoted companion in combat, an Apache Indian, brought the body to the battalion headquarters area. Then, with tears streaking the dust on his dark face, the sergeant hastily replenished his ammunition and returned to the battle without a word.

Daubin would recover from his wounds, return to his outfit, and fight again in North Africa and also in Italy. But he would never forget his hundred-mile ride to a British field hospital in Tunisia.

There were four patients in the ambulance. One was an Oberleutnant whose Mark IV had been destroyed. Since he and the British medical orderly could speak French, Daubin had a brief exchange of conversation with the German, who was sure the Americans would lose the war.

Daubin asked him why he thought so.

Because, the German said confidently, the Americans built poor tanks.

How poor they were would become quite obvious at Kasserine.

Part II

FAID

7

ON CHRISTMAS EVE of 1942, Eisenhower admitted he had lost what he would later call the "pell-mell race for Tunisia." Addressing a group of officers, he and Anderson were unable to conceal their disappointment. To one listener, Anderson seemed "greatly depressed" as he spoke in a halting manner, groping for words. Eisenhower was "equally uninspiring."

Long distances, they explained, congested railroads, and insufficient trucks had reduced to a trickle the eastward flow of troops and supplies out of Algeria. As a result, there were shortages of reserve units in forward areas and of supplies, particularly spare parts, in forward depots. The absence of good airfields near the front also hurt.

But it was mainly the bad weather that dictated an indefinite postponement of offensive efforts and prolonged what had been hoped would be a swift seizure of Tunis and Bizerte and a quick conquest of Tunisia.

"Rain steadily all day," read the notes in a unit journal. "Personnel spent cold, miserable night in the rain and mud." The next day: "Still raining and ground is now sea of mud." On the next: "Rain has stopped. The mud is terrible." A week later: "Rain." Once more: "Rain." Christmas Day: "Still raining."

Not until the end of the rainy season, after two months, could the Allied leaders think of renewing full-scale activity.

Were any operations feasible in the meantime?

Eisenhower turned his attention toward southern Tunisia. His reasons were several: the geography of the country, the movements he expected Rommel to make, a desire to reinforce the French forces, and a wish to give American troops a front of their own.

He looked specifically to the border area between Tebessa and Kasserine, where the frontier separating Algeria and Tunisia follows almost exactly the line that marked the boundary between Numidia and Carthage after the Second Punic War.

* * * *

From Constantine, Algeria, one hundred miles west of the Tunisian border, a highway runs eastward along the coast for about 250 miles to Bizerte and Tunis. Turning south, the road follows the eastern shore of Tunisia for about 250 miles to Gabes. Between Gabes and Constantine, a distance of about three hundred miles, an interior route cuts across the arid land of Tunisia and the mountainous back country of Algeria.

Within the triangle formed by the roads connecting Constantine, Tunis, and Gabes would fall the Tunisian theater of operations. The area had once sustained a large and prosperous agricultural population. Now it was characterized by camel tracks and tarmac roads, dry roads and steel bridges, palm-fringed oases and treeless plains.

From the Allied viewpoint, the road leading to the southeast from Constantine to Gabes offered an exceptional opportunity. An advance through Tebessa, Feriana, and Gafsa to the coast at Gabes would block Rommel's retreat and separate him from Arnim's bridgehead.

Tebessa, one hundred miles from Constantine and just short of the Tunisian frontier: a town of twelve thousand people, with Roman columns and porticoes, a temple to Minerva, an arch of triumph, remains of a permanent camp garrisoned by the III Augusta Legion; an early Christian church; Byzantine fortifications; a golden-stoned wall built by Arabs; fine French buildings, houses, and gardens; camels,

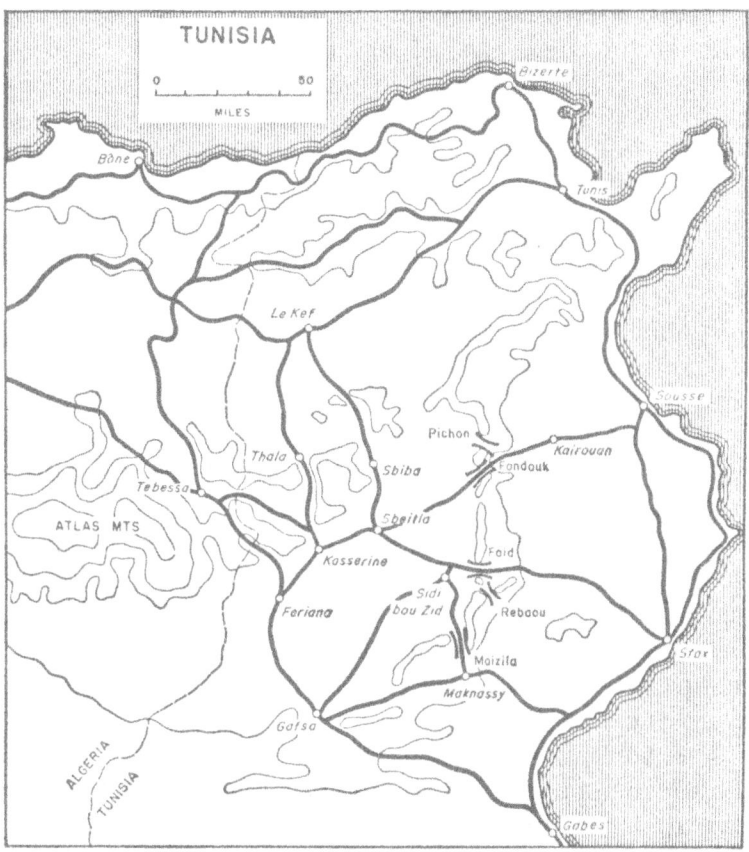

donkeys, herds of goats and sheep, and sheiks riding spirited horses; and mountains covered with a beautiful forest of fir trees.

Feriana: less than one thousand inhabitants, with olive groves, palms, oranges, and tangerines; white stucco houses with roofs of red tile; streets lined with eucalyptus and juniper trees. Nearby is Thelepte, a hamlet in the midst of Roman ruins.

Gafsa, ten thousand people: an oasis of tall palms, flowering gardens, pink buildings, and Roman baths.

Gabes, fifteen thousand inhabitants: superb beaches and a wall two thousand years old that faces south.

When Rommel entered Tunisia from the south and reached Gabes, he would have to choose between two routes. He could take that leading northwest through the oasis of Gafsa to Tebessa and beyond to Constantine — and strike deep into the Allied rear. Or he could set out along the coastal highway leading north to a junction with Arnim's bridgehead — through Sfax, an active port city of 100,000 inhabitants, and Sousse, which houses 25,000 living souls and an untold number of dead in extensive Christian catacombs.

If he chose the coastal route in order to consolidate his forces with those of Arnim, he would need to possess a series of mountain passes.

Stretching south from Tunis, a mountain chain reaches toward Gafsa. This high ground, with peaks about 4,500 feet high, overlooks the rich coastal plain of Sfax and Sousse. Called the Grande or Eastern Dorsale, the range rises rather brusquely from the adjacent plain and is particularly abrupt along its eastern face.

The best places to traverse the barrier of the Eastern Dorsale are openings in the mountain wall. A traveler going west from Sfax would take the Maknassy Gap or the Faid Pass; going west from Sousse, he would cross at Fondouk or Pichon.

If Rommel wished to occupy the coastal plain along the eastern shore of Tunisia, he would need to control these passes.

A smaller mountain range called the Petite or Western Dorsale detaches itself from the larger mass up north and moves away to join the Atlas Mountains near Tebessa. In this chain of hills, two of the major passes are those of Kasserine and Sbiba.

Between the Faid Pass in the Eastern Dorsale and the Kasserine Pass in the Western, a road runs like a causeway for fifty miles across the flat and semi-arid plain of Sbeitla. It is straight as a tautly stretched string for thirty miles between the tiny oasis of Faid and the ancient Roman town of Sbeitla. After a slight hook, the road straightens and rushes twenty miles to the village of Kasserine.

* * * *

Kasserine, during antiquity, was a border town, situated between untamed tribes on the south and the successive imperial civilizations of Carthage and Rome on the north. Located on the seam that separated pacified zone from unconquered territory, sedentary and peaceful natives from restless and nomadic bands, the Kasserine Pass provided access for the forays and inroads of turbulent and pillaging Berbers and for the punitive expeditions of the Carthaginians and, later, the Romans. More than a place of combat, the Kasserine region was a place of encounter, a frontier where the uncouth jostled the cultured, where a vortex of agitation and brutality attracted soldiers, traders, and adventurers in search of excitement and fortune.

When the Berber allies of Jugurtha, King of Numidia, raided the Kasserine region in 107 B.C., the Proconsul Marius took to the field. Unable to gain a decisive success in the Constantine area, he set out to destroy the important oasis of Gafsa, a refuge for the insurgents. He sent a group of cohorts under the Legate Manlius eastward as a measure of deception, while he marched southeastward to the bank of the river Hatab, where he camped briefly. Going through the Kasserine Pass, he reached Gafsa in the middle of the night, took the town by surprise at dawn, and broke the power of Jugurtha and the Berbers.

One hundred years later, the Romans, having established a military post at Haidra, constructed a major highway to Gabes. The road ran southeast from Haidra about twenty-five miles to the Kasserine Pass — the roadbed, straight as a ruler, is utilized today by a narrow-gauge railway — then across the desert to the sea. Marking the line between pacified zone and wilderness, the road, together with a chain of forts along it, served the III Augusta Legion as a route for their patrols.

Early in the first century A.D., Tacfarinas, a deserter from the Roman army, where he had commanded a contingent of auxiliary troops, assembled a group of nomadic Musulames from Tebessa, some attracted by booty, others impatient with Roman rule, and made war with Numidian support. Defeated in A.D. 17 and again in 21, he mounted a supreme effort in 23, appealing, according to Tacitus, "to those who prefer liberty to slavery."

The Proconsul Q. Junius Blaesus concentrated his forces around Tebessa. He placed troops at the pass of El Ma el Abiod to guard against incursion from the south. He sent the Legate Publius Cornelius Lentulus Scipio and the IX Hispana Legion to block the Kasserine Pass. Then he methodically cleared the Kasserine region, breaking the power of Tacfarinas and stabilizing the populations in the area.

As the frontier moved south, the Romans shifted their main garrison from Haidra to Tebessa. They built a new road to Gabes, this one through Thelepte — twenty miles south of and parallel to the older Haidra-Kasserine road.

The newly pacified zone was a pentagonal area marked by Tebessa, Haidra, Thala, Kasserine, and Thelepte at the corners. On this ground in February, 1943, the final phase of the Battle of Kasserine would culminate.

* * * *

Under Giraud, who headed all the French military forces, Juin controlled the ground forces. He had a detachment deep in the Sahara region of Algeria and the XIX Corps in eastern Algeria and Tunisia. The XIX Corps was commanded by General Louis-Marie Koeltz, who directed two forces — Barré's troops in northern Tunisia and General Joseph E. Welvert's "Constantine" Division around Tebessa.

That Welvert's division could function at all was somewhat miraculous. The troops had received no vehicles for three years. They had few spare parts. Gasoline was so scarce that many trucks had been converted to motors that burned alcohol and charcoal. Their weapons were ridiculously outmoded.

Yet Welvert had moved in mid-November, 1942, to menace Rommel's withdrawal route. From Tebessa he dispatched two hundred men in antiquated trucks and cars, some requisitioned from civilians, to the eastern shore. One column advanced through Sbeitla and the Faid Pass to Sfax; the other went through Gafsa to Gabes. In the coastal region, these few troops played hide-and-seek with incoming Axis contingents. They drove off a dozen transport planes trying to land at Gabes, derailed a German troop train, destroyed bridges, and generally harassed the forces trying to establish control over southern Tunisia. Upon learning that substantial enemy units were about to arrive, the French withdrew behind the Eastern Dorsale to Gafsa and Sbeitla.

Lacking the means to take secure possession of southern Tunisia, Giraud asked for help. Eisenhower was putting everything into Anderson's drive, and he could spare only a parachute battalion. Dropped on the airfield at Youks-les-Bains, a Berber village ten miles west of Tebessa, the paratroopers marched eastward to Gafsa. During the next few months, these few Americans, bolstered eventually by some infantry and tank destroyers, worked together with the French in a cordial relationship of mutual goodwill. Their hit-and-run tactics, raids, and ambushes kept the Axis command in perpetual agitation over the possibility that the Allies might drive a wedge between the armies of Arnim and Rommel.

With both sides lacking the strength for decisive control, Koeltz sent French troops to occupy the Faid, Fondouk, and Pichon gaps in the Eastern Dorsale and back-up forces to the defiles in the Western Dorsale. Though carrying out a defensive mission, he emphasized that he wanted no stagnation or phony war. French troops were to annoy the enemy, harry him, kill his troops, take prisoners, capture materiel; in short, wage a kind of guerrilla warfare. "That we must hold," he wrote in mid-December, "I am profoundly convinced, but knowing the mentality of the German command, I know also that we must not give him the least indication of weakness or fatigue, for he would take advantage to push in strength."

The Germans were well aware of the truth. As Eisenhower was canceling the offensive in the north, Arnim made his first overt threat. On Christmas Day he attacked the French troops holding the Pichon Gap and drove them out.

In retrospect, this opened the series of operations that would conclude at Kasserine.

Though the French heroically stabilized the front at Pichon, the weakness of their tragically obsolescent equipment became more than clear.

Where were the Americans? Almost two months had gone by since the landings, and the French had seen in southern Tunisia only *"le commando fugitif"* of paratroopers, as Koeltz put it. *"C'était peu."*

If Axis troops appeared in strength, they could push aside the French and pry open the roads to Tebessa. West of Tebessa, there were no natural features on which to anchor a defensive line. The Germans could drive virtually unopposed into Algeria, to Constantine.

Why not send American forces to Tebessa?

For two reasons: Eisenhower was keeping strong contingents in Morocco and near Oran to counter possible German intervention in Spain and Spanish Morocco. And he doubted that his supply system was capable of supporting a larger number of troops in Tunisia — those in the north were already straining the logistical structure.

Was it possible at least to assemble a strategic reserve near Tebessa?

He had been considering this for some time. Airfields were being opened in the Tebessa area — at Youks-les-Bains and Thelepte — and they required protection. An American force, equipped with modern weapons and concentrated behind the thin screen of French, could destroy Axis penetrations. Beyond that, American troops might possibly move against Rommel's rear, perhaps even seize Sfax on the eastern coast and sever contact between Arnim and Rommel. If Rommel were cut off, he would have to surrender. Or Arnim would have to move south to help him. In this case, Bizerte and Tunis would be open for a decisive blow by Anderson.

The American force designated to move into southern Tunisia was the 1st Armored Division. A powerful organization of more than 15,000 men who operated almost 3,500 vehicles — 158 light tanks, 232 medium tanks, almost 100 armored cars, 730 half-tracks, and 2,100 trucks and other vehicles — the armored division was designed to fight with two fists: combat commands named A and B. Each combat command normally fought as a balanced force of tanks, infantry, artillery, tank destroyers, signal, engineer, quartermaster, ordnance, and medical units.

Only Combat Command B (CCB) had participated in the North African landings and in the subsequent battles in northern Tunisia — Daubin's platoon, for example, in the battalion commanded by Waters. CCA had arrived in Oran later. Though CCB had the advantage of experience, CCA brought somewhat better equipment — radios, for example, obtained in the United Kingdom. One battalion had turned in its Grant medium tanks armed with short-barreled, low-velocity 75-mm. guns and had received new Shermans mounting long, high-velocity guns.

With the commitment of the division in the Tebessa area, it was reasonable to assume that the seasoned units would be consolidated with the newly arrived elements, not only to spread the experience of combat but also to concentrate the whole weight of the inherent striking power. Instead, the process of fragmentation was to continue.

The division commander, Major General Orlando Ward, had fought with Pershing in Mexico and in France. A graduate of West Point and of the Army's advanced schools, he had served as Secretary of the General Staff in Washington, where his intelligence, competence, and balance had been remarked. A spare man who was quiet in speech and manner, with a rose-tinted complexion that caused him to be called "Pinky," he had something of the ascetic and the intellectual in his appearance. Methodical and thorough, he had trained his division well. His men held him in high esteem. His dignity and soldierly bearing gave confidence. What he lacked in fire he made up in fairness and integrity.

Eisenhower briefly considered sending Clark and his newly activated Fifth Army headquarters to Tunisia, then dispatched them to Morocco.

Designated the senior American commander in Tunisia, Ward flew from Oran to Constantine, then traveled by jeep for three days over long and tiring distances to visit his future area of operations. He became acquainted with the localities of Tebessa, Kasserine, Sbeitla, and Faid, places that would become an ineradicable part of his life.

When he returned to Algiers, he learned that Eisenhower had changed his mind. Since the British possessed an army command in Tunisia and the French a corps, why should the senior American be only a division commander? He named Fredendall, who commanded the II Corps, and sent the corps headquarters to Tunisia. Ward then would serve under Fredendall. Between the two commanders would soon develop, in one observer's understated words, a "most unusual" antipathy. Fredendall openly detested Ward, and Ward, in his quiet manner, had no use for Fredendall.

The mutual dislike would have serious repercussions.

8

MAJOR GENERAL LLOYD R. FREDENDALL was fifty-eight years old, though his unlined face made him look younger. Of medium height, he was solidly built, almost chunky. He moved vigorously, spoke loudly, and had a firm opinion on every subject.

He had arrived in London a month before the North African landings, and, as was customary, reported promptly to Eisenhower. On the following day, he committed a *gaffe*.

It was Saturday, and Eisenhower telephoned and asked him to dinner. According to the custom of the service, an invitation from the commanding general is tantamount to an order.

Instead of accepting the invitation at once, Fredendall said that he had just made another dinner appointment that he would be glad to cancel.

Eisenhower, of course, refused to hear of it. His action was gracious, but he had reason to feel uncomfortable. Younger than Fredendall, junior to him in point of service, sensitive to the prerogatives of his position and title, he had been rebuffed.

Had Fredendall acted thoughtlessly? Or had he subtly tried to put Eisenhower in his place? No matter.

During the invasion Fredendall commanded the troops who landed at Oran. They performed superbly and seized their objectives in less than three days, the only Allied units to win a decision wholly by force of arms. Though Fredendall had remained in his command post aboard ship offshore, he gained his reputation as a forceful commander who had succeeded. In an army lacking experienced commanders, success was a virtue highly esteemed.

When he went ashore on November 10, it was to confer with the French on an armistice. Yet the citation for the Distinguished Service Medal awarded by Eisenhower spoke of his "exceptionally meritorious service," his "brilliant leadership and resolute force," and his having "demonstrated the highest qualities of leadership."

Concerned solely with the military features of the operation, Fredendall was uninterested in political questions which he dismissed as irrelevant. He permitted all civilian officials to retain their positions no matter what their party affiliation, made no effort to identify and restrain Axis sympathizers or to locate and help those French who had been pro-American, and adopted a policy of what was later generously called "very mild arrangements." It was much simpler that way.

Fredendall and his staff moved into the Grand Hotel, the best in Oran, and in that elegant continental establishment the headquarters took on the trappings and the pageantry, as well as the spit and polish, of a rather swanky garrison life. Leggings and unbuttoned khaki shirts were definitely out, officers' blouses and pinks in.

When the routine duties began to pall, Fredendall became impatient. The war was going to be won in Tunisia, and he wanted to be in on the kill. Eisenhower could hardly refuse him, for during the landings he had said, "Clean up that situation today and write your own ticket." Fredendall had cleaned it up.

Already Fredendall was known for his picturesque language. It gave his personality a certain flair. The journal of one combat unit recorded the striking contrast between normal military communications and Fredendall's mannerisms. The entries were matter of fact, without excitement, completely businesslike in tone — for example: "ALL GREEN assault wave is proceeding to final objectives. Your reserves released to you." Or again: "Roads and bridges to top of hairpin turn are OK. Beach roadway material urgently required" — until suddenly a message came from Fredendall: "Go get 'em at once.... Go smash 'em." The details be damned.

"Everything is rosy," he had radioed from his ship during the invasion. The troops "went to town."

The commander stamps his temperament on his subordinates, and Fredendall's permeated the command. The password established and changed each day to enable troops to recognize friend from foe consisted of two words, a challenge given by the guard and a response returned by the unknown. They were usually innocuous, something like "SAN FRANCISCO — CALIFORNIA," or "POPEYE — SAILORMAN," and the soldiers were required to know them. The password in the II Corps one day consisted of "SNAFU — DAMN RIGHT." Maybe it was good for morale.

Slipping into slang deprived Fredendall's speech of precision. What he said was sometimes incomprehensible because it embodied only a half-formed and vague impulse rather than a thoroughly formulated idea. Using the slogan as a substitute for thought, he failed to communicate his wishes clearly. If a subordinate asked for clarification, he responded with a hostility that stemmed from an improper assumption. The subordinate was stupid or trying to make him look foolish.

Sometimes the lack of clarity worked the other way. For example, the XII Air Support Command had the task of giving air support to the II Corps. To insure close cooperation between air and ground components, the air commander set up his headquarters near the corps command post on the basis that men who were in close association would work together better. The theory was fine, but the practice, in this case, was somewhat deficient. He and Fredendall got along so well that Fredendall told him, "Don't wait for us to order air missions, you know what the situation is, just keep pounding them." While this reflected great confidence, it also represented the abdication of responsibility to make known clearly the requirements of the troops on the ground. Unless the air commander is specifically requested or directed to carry out definite missions in a changing situation, he can never be fully responsive to ground force needs.

Loud and brassy, Fredendall was outspoken in his opinions and inclined to be critical of superiors and subordinates alike. Somewhat ponderous in action, overbearing in attitude, he often jumped to conclusions. When he spoke, it was with an air of finality. He knew best, and there was little anyone could tell him. His humor was not always funny or in the best of taste.

In short, he considered himself a rough, tough customer who was going to let nothing stand in the way of winning the war, even if it took all kinds of flailing of arms and bearing down.

Yet whoever visited his command post near Tebessa had a twinge of doubt. Commanders usually try to establish their headquarters near a road, adjacent to existing communications facilities and close enough to the combat units for convenient visits. Fredendall's was distant from the front and far up a canyon, a gulch that could be entered only by a barely passable road constructed by his corps engineers. Though towering mountains and wooded hillsides concealed his presence, he had underground shelters dug and blasted for himself and his staff. Two hundred engineers would work for more than three weeks on this project, then abandon it unfinished under the German threat at Kasserine.

The command post was cold, cheerless, even gloomy, despite what one visitor called "exceedingly military" behavior by the personnel. Everyone wore helmets and pistols despite the rear-area location. And this gave an unfortunate impression, as someone remarked, of an "excessive emphasis on security and safety."

To those who asked, Fredendall explained that German aircraft were active over the area and that they made special

5. Generaloberst Juergen von Arnim, commander of the Fifth Panzer Army, surly, sullen, ambitious, and less than cooperative. *U.S. Army Photograph*

6. Lt. General Sir Kenneth A. N. Anderson, First Army commander, "who represented the combat experience and knowledge of the British Army." *U.S. Army Photograph*

efforts to destroy command posts. He had gone underground because he had no intention of having his activities disrupted. Though sixty or seventy miles behind the front was rather far for frequent visits to the combat units, he saw no need to be closer. He would run the battle by telephone and radio.

"Most American officers who saw this command post for the first time," an observer later wrote, "were somewhat embarrassed, and their comments were usually caustic." For nothing can take the place of personal visits by a commander to his troops, and nothing can substitute for personal reconnaissance, the actual sight of the ground, which often erases the pessimism created by grease pencils tracing dispositions on a map far to the rear of the action.

Rarely leaving his command post, Fredendall would be impatient with the recommendations of those who were familiar with the terrain and the other vital conditions on the front, while the units serving under him would come to believe that the corps headquarters was looking out for itself above all and had little interest in or knowledge of the actual situation as it was known to the troops on the ground.

Rommel put it this way: "There are always moments when the commander's place is not back with his staff but up with the troops. It is sheer nonsense to say that maintenance of the men's morale is the job of the battalion commander alone. The higher the rank, the greater the effect of the example. The men tend to feel no kind of contact with a commander who, they know, is sitting somewhere in headquarters. What they want is what might be termed a physical contact with him. In moments of panic, fatigue or disorganization, or when something out of the ordinary has to be demanded from them, the personal example of the commander works wonders, especially if he has had the wit to create some sort of legend around himself."

The legend that Fredendall tried to create would soon fall apart.

9

EISENHOWER desired a truly Allied command, with a real unity of direction and a centralized administrative responsibility. What he had in Tunisia was a loose coalition.

"Alliances in the past," he wrote after the war, "have often done no more than to name the common foe, and 'unity of command' has been a pious aspiration thinly disguising the national jealousies, ambitions and recriminations of high ranking officers, unwilling to subordinate themselves or their forces to a commander of different nationality."

Had he been a bitter man, he might have thus described the situation in Tunisia.

He had erased national distinctions in his own headquarters by creating an integrated Anglo-American staff and by insisting that its members work in harmony. It was well and widely known that he sent home an American who had called an associate a *British* son of a bitch. Unlike the close-knit men in his own official family, the field commanders grappled with insoluble problems.

Having little control over these problems, the field commanders were beset with frustration, and some began to squabble among themselves. In part their clashes stemmed from differences in national interest and outlook. Others arose from simple diversity of character and behavior. For the exercise of command is not only a matter of organizational structure, doctrine, and authority; it is also a matter of personality — each commander commands in a personal manner. In times of tactical success, frictions among men tend to be overlooked or minimized; in times of operational adversity, annoyances develop into irritations and contribute their own influences on a deteriorating situation.

Rommel was well aware of the difficulties of coalition warfare and, drawing from his own experience, he shrewdly guessed that the several nationalities bred dissension — the Army, he noted, "probably lacks cohesion and suffers from the inherent weakness of an Allied command."

Preinvasion planning had projected Tunisia as a British theater of operations, and this alone produced a measure of grief. The entire line of supply was British in concept, organization, and control. Since British officers were generally unacquainted with American methods and Americans were similarly unfamiliar with British practices, American units employed with the First Army encountered unexpected difficulties getting support.

Troops had on occasion been employed piecemeal, without respect for unit integrity, and intermixed with British elements, and some American commanders believed that the British were being favored in the choice of missions, equipment, and supplies. Some Americans, who tended to be less reserved and more outspoken than the British, rubbed their cousins the wrong way. And some British soldiers impressed Americans as being supercilious and conceited.

When the French joined the team, the complexities increased. Political considerations provoked some difficulties, but most came from the comparatively strange procedures, national characteristics, and interests of the French, differences accentuated by the barrier of language.

Anderson had the impression that the French were unduly sensitive and suspicious. He felt he needed always to conciliate them, even at the expense of combat efficiency. And, like the Americans, he could not help feeling a lack of confidence in their performance because of their poor equipment.

When Eisenhower proposed that the French forces, like the Americans, go under Anderson's command, Giraud refused. The two men then formulated a vague oral agreement:

all the troops in northern Tunisia, mostly British, some French, and a few Americans, would fight under British command; those in the south, mostly French, some Americans, and a few British, would fight under the French. Eisenhower himself would exercise direct command of the trinational force in Tunisia even though he was in Algiers, 400 miles from the front, two far for effective direction and control.

But then, where did Juin, who commanded all the French forces in Tunisia, fit into this structure? How were Juin and Anderson to regulate their command relations? Juin was responsible to Giraud, while Anderson reported to Eisenhower.

In Algiers, Eisenhower and Giraud met but little. Their relationship was courteous, formal, and rather distant. Absorbed by political and economic questions, both men had time for only brief visits to the front, and Algiers was too far to permit instant decisions in time of emergency. As a result, Allied cooperation would result from agreements made hastily in the midst of crisis.

The insertion of the II Corps into the command structure dislocated the arrangements. It was easy enough for Koeltz to retain an independent front with his XIX Corps, but what was to be the status of Welvert's "Constantine" Division, which was in the II Corps area? Was Welvert responsible to Fredendall, Koeltz, or Juin? And to whom in the Anglo-American structure was Juin responsible?

A distinguished soldier whose reputation was well known to the British and Americans, Juin had great personal charm and military ability. He was unfailingly cooperative and loyal. He did much to tie the command together.

To give Juin, as Giraud's representative, a firmer point of contact with the Allied command structure, and to achieve closer supervision himself, Eisenhower established a forward command post at Constantine and appointed Major General Lucian K. Truscott, Jr., his deputy chief of staff and representative for operations in Tunisia. Through Truscott, he would coordinate the parallel activities of the three national forces.

Truscott, though extremely competent, was a relatively junior officer, and at Constantine he would be two hundred miles from the front. No matter how rapidly, accurately, and completely he learned about developments and transmitted the information to Eisenhower, he would be unable to regulate affairs effectively, particularly in an emergency. Furthermore, regulation or coordination was hardly the same as command.

The Allied structure became somewhat shaky as the Germans nibbled away at the passes in the Eastern Dorsale. Having gobbled up Pichon on December 25, Arnim grabbed Fondouk on January 3. Though the Germans now menaced the Sbeitla plain from the northeast, the threat failed to develop. For Arnim had made what was essentially a defensive move. He was interested only in protecting the Tunisian eastern shore.

So that the Allied command could react more quickly, Eisenhower made Anderson his "advisor" for the entire Tunisian front. Precisely what that meant was unclear. Anderson was already acting in an advisory capacity, for his army was providing most of the signal communications for all the troops, and by that service he was monitoring and coordinating the front.

But he never quite took hold. Though personally bold and fearless, he inspired Americans with little confidence. He was too reserved and reticent. And he usually took a dark view of operations. His chief of staff was even more dour, silent, and pessimistic. Both officers believed in wide margins to compensate for error and chance, and looked with disfavor on the movement of American forces into southern Tunisia. They believed that the resources being shifted to Fredendall detracted from the more important job of building up the First Army for the eventual drive to Tunis.

Fredendall did little to simplify the problems of interallied cooperation and command. He turned out to be an anglophobe in general, and he disliked Anderson in particular. He had no confidence in and little patience with the French. He never understood the pathetic nature of their mule-drawn carts, ancient trucks, and obsolete guns, or the wretched condition of their battered light tanks. Nor did he appreciate the frustration of men who were denied the weapons they needed to fight. Had he observed the scene, he would have dismissed its significance — French soldiers who stood in delight at a road junction as American tanks passed and who watched in the way that children gape at fire engines.

Welvert, the commander of the French "Constantine" Division, was already at Tebessa when Fredendall arrived, and his troops occupied key points along the Eastern Dorsale. With the help of American and British units, a French detachment surveyed and blocked the western exit of the Fondouk Pass. Farther south, a group held the Faid Pass and, ten miles to the south, the Rebaou defile.

A dozen miles west of Faid and Rebaou, a garrison of Welvert's troops occupied Sidi bou Zid, a village of five hundred Arabs and a handful of French, with Gendarmerie and PTT — *Postes, Télégraphes, et Téléphones* — the principal buildings of what had formerly been an important camel market. Two roads from the south converge at Sidi bou Zid — one coming through the Maizila Pass from the village of Maknassy, the other from the town of Gafsa — and the garrison sent out periodic patrols to keep the Maizila Pass under surveillance, while French troops at Gafsa, reinforced by Americans, barred the main road from Gabes.

Welvert thus watched over the southern and eastern approaches to the heart of Tunisia and Algeria, and he welcomed the arrival of Fredendall's forces, which promised to strengthen his defenses. Instead, Fredendall had been instructed to prepare an attack toward Sfax.

When President Roosevelt, Prime Minister Churchill, and their principal military advisors met at Casablanca for ten days in mid-January, 1943, to determine their global strategy, they summoned Eisenhower to report on operations in Tunisia. He spoke of the contemplated action against Sfax.

Alexander, who had come from Cairo for the meetings, quickly questioned the risks. He pointed out that Montgomery would probably reach Tripoli as the Sfax attack was starting. Since he would lack fuel until he could open the port of Tripoli, he would be unable to lend a hand. The Americans would face Rommel alone. If, however, they waited until Montgomery took Tripoli, the British would be able to help. Together, they might corner the Desert Fox.

Eisenhower accepted the advice. He canceled the thrust to Sfax. If he undertook the operation later, he promised, he would integrate it carefully with Montgomery's plans.

To coordinate the two Allied forces in North Africa — the British army pursuing Rommel across Libya and the Allied army facing Arnim and awaiting Rommel in Tunisia — the leaders at Casablanca decided to establish a single, overall command. When Montgomery crossed the border into Tunisia, probably in February, he was to go under Eisenhower's control. At that time, Alexander was to come to Constantine as Eisenhower's deputy commander-in-chief in charge of all the ground forces.

When Eisenhower returned to Algiers, he instructed Fredendall to be defensively minded, to hold the 1st Armored Division in reserve, and to protect the forward airfields being opened near Tebessa. By calling off the Sfax operation, he made inevitable the consolidation of Arnim's and Rommel's armies.

Arnim again seized the initiative. Having taken the passes of Pichon and Fondouk, he attacked the French farther north on January 18. Completely dislocating Barré's sector, he cut up a French division and threatened to get behind the Eastern Dorsale.

Juin appealed for reinforcement, and Eisenhower told Fredendall to send a suitable force to help stabilize the front.

The normal procedure would have been for Fredendall to consult with Ward, his major subordinate commander. Instead, he bypassed the 1st Armored Division commander with what Ward considered to be a contemptuous disregard of his own prerogatives. Fredendall telephoned directly to CCB, one of Ward's two principal subordinate commands.

"Move your command," Fredendall told a staff officer, "that is, the walking boys, pop guns, Baker's outfit and the outfit which is the reverse of Baker's outfit and the big fellow to M, which is due north of where you are now, as soon as possible. Have your boss report to the French gentleman whose name begins with J at a place which begins with D which is five grid squares [on the map] to the left of M."

The unmilitary manner of the order and the eccentricity of the language could be excused only on the ground that Fredendall was endeavoring to guarantee the security of his telephone.

The commander of CCB, Brigadier General Paul M. Robinett, was a short and cocky American who believed that he had a better grasp of the situation, both tactical and strategic, than anyone else in the Allied camp. Having participated in the fighting in northern Tunisia and having thus acquired knowledge of German tactics, he was sure he knew more about combat than Fredendall and Ward. Having attended the Ecole de Guerre and the cavalry school at Saumur before the war, he felt he knew the French army and its methods of operation. Having been Secretary of the War Department General Staff, he was certain he understood the point of view at Washington. In command of a relatively powerful force of about thirty-five hundred men, he liked being separated from his parent organization, welcomed an independent role, and enjoyed dealing directly with the top commanders. An excellent combat officer, he had a well-trained and spirited command, a grasp of terrain that gave him an eerie prescience, and energy as well as thoroughness.

Moving quickly north, his CCB performed splendidly and,

together with British forces sent from the north toward the threatened sector, helped to stabilize the front.

Fredendall, it appeared, was getting the job done. But he had complicated Robinett's mission. By telling him to keep in touch with the corps headquarters, he detached him from Ward's control. And Tebessa was too far away for Fredendall to exercise competent direction. During much of his week of combat, Robinett was unable to determine whether he was under the command of Eisenhower, Anderson, Fredendall, Truscott, Koeltz, or Juin, all of whom made their presence, weight, and superior rank felt.

The mixture of Allied units — each with its own distinctive organization, training, doctrine, communications, supply arrangements, and staff procedures — gave each commander a feeling of helplessness, particularly since higher headquarters were too far away to exercise the control and guidance required.

Arnim's attack did more than temporarily disrupt the front. It exposed again the weakness of the French. When Anderson confided that no reliance could be placed on them unless they were strongly reinforced by British or Americans or both, Eisenhower decided that Americans and British would have to operate toward a common boundary in order to buttress the French. When Fredendall was ordered to help the French retake the Fondouk Pass, he reported his inability to "pull off Fondouk" because the French were on the verge of collapse.

To gain a better view of what might be done, Anderson visited all the major commanders in Tunisia. Judging the distances too large to rely on radio messages, ordinary telegraph, or the telephone, hampered by the bad weather that made air travel erratic, and feeling that coordination required personal discussion and compromise, he motored more than one thousand miles in the course of several days, a fatiguing journey on the Tunisian roads. He became increasingly impressed by the weariness of the French troops. They were feeling the strain of sustained combat. Their supplies and equipment were becoming exhausted. Their few trucks were worn out.

If the British and Americans, who were already spread thinly, could no longer count on the French, how were they going to build up power for the eventual and culminating thrust to Tunis? Could Eisenhower, he asked, find more forces? Could he bring forward the 1st and 34th U.S. Infantry Divisions, which were scattered along the line of communications, and assemble them in Tunisia? Could he move the 9th Division from Morocco?

Perhaps. But until additional forces arrived, Anderson would have to dispose his units economically. To that end, Eisenhower placed the entire front under his command and told him to supplant the French forces gradually with Americans and British. The French would have to withdraw for rest and refitting, though some were to remain for political reasons. But the fighting would be done by the national forces that had the weapons and equipment to meet the enemy on equal terms.

Late in January, while Eisenhower exercised control through Truscott, Anderson's First British Army headquarters supervised three national commands. In the north a British corps under Lt. General Sir C. W. Allfrey faced Bizerte and Tunis. In the center, in a mountainous area where the underequipped French would be least disadvantaged and where the British and Americans could maintain close watch on the flanks, was Koeltz's XIX Corps. In the south was Fredendall's II Corps. All were holding defensively while they prepared for the decisive strike to be launched at the end of the rainy season, some time in March.

Meanwhile, Anderson decided that as soon as enough American troops of the 1st and 34th Divisions arrived, he would pull the French units out of the line and send them to the rear to receive better equipment and weapons.

That was the time the Battle of Kasserine started.

10

ROMMEL HAD every intention of retiring slowly and of holding Tripoli until mid-February. During the first two weeks of January he moved his forces back 130 miles to Homs. There, he was only sixty-five miles east of Tripoli, and Tripoli was little more than one hundred miles from the Tunisian frontier. When the British outflanked his defenses, he had to accelerate his movement. Threatened by encirclement, he started the last stage of his retreat into southern Tunisia.

To Italian protests that he was abandoning Libya precipitously, Rommel was short. "You can either hold on to Tripoli a few more days and lose the army," he said, "or lose Tripoli a few days earlier and save the army for Tunis. Make up your minds."

Against this intransigeance there was no reply save drastic action. This would come shortly.

On January 23, three months to the day after the attack at El Alamein, after a pursuit of fourteen hundred miles, Montgomery's army entered Tripoli. The troops found the city destroyed, its military installations, including the harbor and the airfield, demolished by the Axis forces.

Despite its sustained back-pedaling, Rommel's army had escaped serious harm. Except for the inevitable troop exhaustion and worn-out equipment, as well as the loss of relatively light casualties in screening his retrograde movement, he had preserved his forces intact.

Three days after abandoning Tripoli, he moved his headquarters across the Tunisian border to Ben Gardane, the first important town. Now Gabes was only eighty miles away.

The weariness and the humiliation of the constant retreat were about over. The opportunity to reverse the situation was at hand.

The 21st Panzer Division that Rommel had detached in compliance with instructions and sent to Sfax to become part of Arnim's army was receiving, from Arnim's resources, new equipment and troops. It was scheduled to attack Gafsa to keep the Allies at arm's length from the Eastern Dorsale. In Rommel's opinion, this was a defensive concept and unsatisfactory. Why not attack through Sbeitla as well as through Gafsa? Why not drive to Tebessa? Why not think ultimately of Constantine?

If he could improve the defenses of the Mareth Line to guarantee with a few troops the southern flank against the British, or, better still, if he could get permission to move to Gabes and that short defensive line, he could envision virtually limitless prospects of wreaking havoc on the Allies. But first, the two armies had to be joined in a solid mass from Bizerte to Gabes.

As the possibility of offensive action began to fill Rommel with exhilaration, the drastic blow fell. On the same day that he established his headquarters at Ben Gardane, on the 26th of January, he received word that he was to be relieved from his army command because of his bad health.

It was true that he was not altogether well. He had severe headaches. His nerves were strained. His old circulatory trouble had reappeared. He suffered from insomnia.

But he was feeling no worse than usual. The excuse was transparent.

Furthermore, he learned, when his army was completely withdrawn into the Mareth Line, the Italo-German Panzerarmee was to be redesignated the First Italian Army and put under an Italian commander. Mussolini had already selected General Giovanni Messe to take his place. With two armies operating in Tunisia under Messe and Arnim, the Axis would eventually create a superior command to be known as Army Group Afrika. Until the activation of that headquarters and the appointment of an army group commander, Arnim was to be in charge of coordinating the operations in Tunisia.

The blow struck home, particularly the last point.

Rommel's first reaction to the news was that he had had enough. He would give up command of his army as soon as Messe arrived.

By the 31st his mood had changed. Messe arrived with considerable enthusiasm, started to familiarize himself with the duties he was about to assume, and waited impatiently for Rommel to depart. But Rommel had decided to hand over his command only when he felt that the Army, which was then withdrawing into the Mareth Line, was reasonably secure.

This was his rationalization. What actually excited him was an attack that Arnim had just launched against the Faid Pass.

The prelude had opened, and Rommel had no inclination to give up his command quite yet. A week later he fortified his resolution. Regardless of the state of his health, he would depart only when he received a direct order to do so. Would they have the nerve to issue him an order of that sort?

If he dealt the Allies a severe blow, if he gained a great victory, if he played his cards right, he might yet retrieve some measure of glory and reputation from the debasing circumstances of the retreat across Libya.

* * * *

Like Rommel, Fredendall dreamed of glory. Instructed to protect the growing supply base at Tebessa, the increasingly important airfields at Thelepte, and the southern flank of Koeltz's French sector, Fredendall had several choices: he could bolster the French garrisons at the passes in the Eastern Dorsale; retake Fondouk; hold his troops concentrated in a central location; or try to keep the Germans off balance by striking sharp blows in the Gafsa and Gabes areas.

The last attracted him. Eager to show his aggressiveness, he decided to launch a series of hit-and-run raids around Gafsa. Not only would he upset the Germans but he would also give his inexperienced American units a taste of combat.

To fulfill his defensive instructions, he sent CCA to Sbeitla — about one hundred tanks, eighteen artillery pieces, and a dozen tank destroyers — plus one thousand infantrymen, there to intercept enemy thrusts coming from Fondouk in the northeast, Faid in the east, or Maknassy in the southeast. Then he turned his attention to the village of Maknassy, fifty miles east of Gafsa and halfway to Sfax. If a triumph at Maknassy lured the Allied command into a full-scale offensive to Sfax, Fredendall in the south, rather than Anderson in the north, would lead the decisive attack that would destroy the Axis armies in Tunisia.

Maknassy seemed ripe for picking. A month before, eighty Americans had made a night raid from Gafsa, swooping into town, taking the garrison of 164 Italian troops by surprise, shooting up the place for two and a half hours, killing an estimated twenty soldiers, wounding thirty or forty, destroying enemy equipment and vehicles, capturing twenty-one prisoners, and making their getaway before daylight. Two Americans had been very slightly wounded, one jeep had been struck by enemy fire and abandoned. According to the reports of the exuberant attackers, the Italians had been terrified by Indian warwhoops and Lone Ranger yells of "Hi Ho, Silver!"

But since the Axis had probably reinforced the Maknassy garrison, Fredendall decided to go only halfway — to the village of Sened.

Ward, the 1st Armored Division commander, protested, and so did Welvert, the commander of the "Constantine" Division. The two officers preferred to have the Americans reinforce the poorly equipped French at the passes, particularly the opening at Faid.

Fredendall saw no necessity to change his plans.

Colonel Robert I. Stack took about two thousand men from Gafsa about four o'clock on the morning of January 24, struck Sened, overwhelmed the defenders, and returned at 6 P.M. with ninety-six prisoners. The cost of what was a highly successful raid designed principally as a morale exercise was slight — two Americans had been wounded, one tank had been damaged by a mine, another hit by gunfire.

The Germans were unconcerned. They correctly diagnosed the attack as a distraction, and they refused to be distracted.

Fredendall was overjoyed by his success. Telephoning Eisenhower's representative, Truscott, in the middle of the day, he positively crowed. "Remember that force I sent toward Maknassy looking for trouble? They ran into some stuff and smeared it. I can't give you the details. . . . They were very cheerful about what they had done — our trouble is to get them back. They are coming back tonight. . . . Whatever it was, they smacked the hell out of them. I thought you might like to have a little cheerful information from down here."

Later that evening he was flying high as he reported the details. "I told them to go on and get contact," and the troops had located the enemy and "ran them all out of town. . . . Trump that if you can, damn it! . . . There is a splendid note of cheer down here. We must have killed a hell of a lot but could not stay to find out."

Hoping that he was satisfied with his adventure, the French Army commander, Juin, visited him and raised again the idea of using American troops to bolster the French, particularly at Faid.

Fredendall knew better. He now wanted a stronger force for a two-pronged attack converging on Maknassy. More American troops were available: CCB had been released from the north and was near Tebessa for rest; a battalion of the 34th Division had arrived at Tebessa; and two battalions of the 1st Infantry Division were at hand — one at Gafsa, the other blocking the road from Fondouk to Sbeitla.

While Ward busied himself preparing the attack to Maknassy, Fredendall suddenly phoned Stack, the hero of the Sened raid, at 1 P.M., January 30 and told him to move out at once from Gafsa — not eastward to Maknassy but northeastward toward Sidi bou Zid, fifty miles away. The Germans had attacked the Faid Pass and the Rebaou defile that morning, and Stack was to help restore the situation.

After checking with Ward, his immediate superior, Stack set out. His progress was slow, for the road was poor, he had only occasional radio contact with Ward, and he had no desire to rush headlong into a battlefield about which he knew nothing. When night came he had covered about twenty-five miles. He halted and bivouacked to give his troops several hours' rest. Up ahead in the distance, the faint sounds and winking flashes of gunfire told him little except that a battle was under way.

An hour or so before dawn, he learned that he was to continue toward Sidi bou Zid while other formations carried out the attack on Maknassy. The whole thing seemed queer. If a battle had developed at Faid, why was Fredendall insisting on Maknassy? It made better sense to concentrate at Faid.

He asked by radio whether his orders had been changed. The reply was blunt: "Comply early and vigorously with orders you now have."

He marched his troops to the northeast. As he neared Sidi bou Zid on the afternoon of January 31, he received word from Ward at Gafsa, who had received instructions from Fredendall at Tebessa, who had received a directive from Anderson in northern Tunisia. "Stack," Ward now radioed, "turn [south] and join in concentrated effort . . . on Maknassy."

Somewhat bewildered, he followed instructions. He turned toward the Maizila Pass, blocked the northern mouth of the defile, and prepared to attack through the opening to Maknassy in the morning.

During the night Welvert arrived in a surprise visit. He was quite upset. The French, he said, had suffered a defeat at Faid, and Stack's men were sorely needed. Continuing to Maknassy had no meaning. Would Stack do him the courtesy to check his orders with Ward?

He did so, and Ward, after making contact with Fredendall, confirmed that Stack was to advance to Maknassy. Other troops would handle affairs at Faid.

It was a bitter Welvert who departed. He was convinced that the Americans knew nothing about waging war and had neither understanding of nor compassion for allies in need of help.

Early on the morning of February 1, just as Stack was about to assault the Maizila Pass, a message came from Ward: "You will remain in present position and prepare for attack on Maknassy on our order."

Stack waited. Perhaps he was needed, after all, at Faid.

Meanwhile, the attack from Gafsa toward Maknassy was under way and making little headway. "Use your tanks and shove," Fredendall bellowed.

Ward then told Stack to go ahead and take the Maizila Pass.

He had no luck. "Ground soft," he explained by radio, "hard going for tanks. . . . Will attack tomorrow unless otherwise ordered."

An hour later Ward told him to abandon his effort: "Disengage, move via Sidi bou Zid to Sbeitla."

Stack turned around and marched northward during the night. In the dark both literally and figuratively, he had no idea of what was going on. In a useless action without discernible result save the fatigue of his command, he had lost three men killed, twenty wounded, and forty-three missing and presumably captured. He could well have wondered what his operations had accomplished.

When the Maknassy attack was called off, Arnim decided he no longer had to be concerned about the approaches to Sfax. The Americans were not about to threaten the coastal region of the eastern shore.

The vital point in Tunisia had suddenly shifted to Faid, where the Battle of Kasserine had begun.

11

ARNIM HAD the substantial forces of two panzer divisions gathered in the coastal area of southern Tunisia — the 21st, detached from Rommel's army and now near Gabes, and the 10th, behind the passes of Pichon and Fondouk — when Comando Supremo, on January 28, approved a cautious push through the defiles of Pichon in the north and Faid in the center and an advance to Gafsa in the south. Once these movements gave him secure control of the Eastern Dorsale, Arnim might perhaps, depending on the circumstances, drive west toward Tebessa.

Essentially, this was Rommel's concept. But while he continued to backtrack toward the Mareth Line, Arnim would carry out the idea.

In a characteristic action, Arnim decided to execute only part of the instruction. Pichon particularly and Faid to a lesser extent interested him. Gafsa, too far south, he ignored. Attracted, like Anderson, his British counterpart, to northern Tunisia, where he envisaged the decisive battle eventually would be waged, Arnim set up a preliminary attack at Faid to divert the Allies and a major effort at Pichon. He saw no need to inform his superiors, Comando Supremo and Kesselring, of the change he was making in the program.

At four o'clock on the morning of January 30, about thirty tanks of the 21st Panzer Division came out of the darkness from the direction of Sfax and struck the one thousand French troops who held the Faid Pass.

French artillery fire stopped them.

Ten miles to the south, German tanks and infantry rolled through the Rebaou defile, overwhelmed the handful of

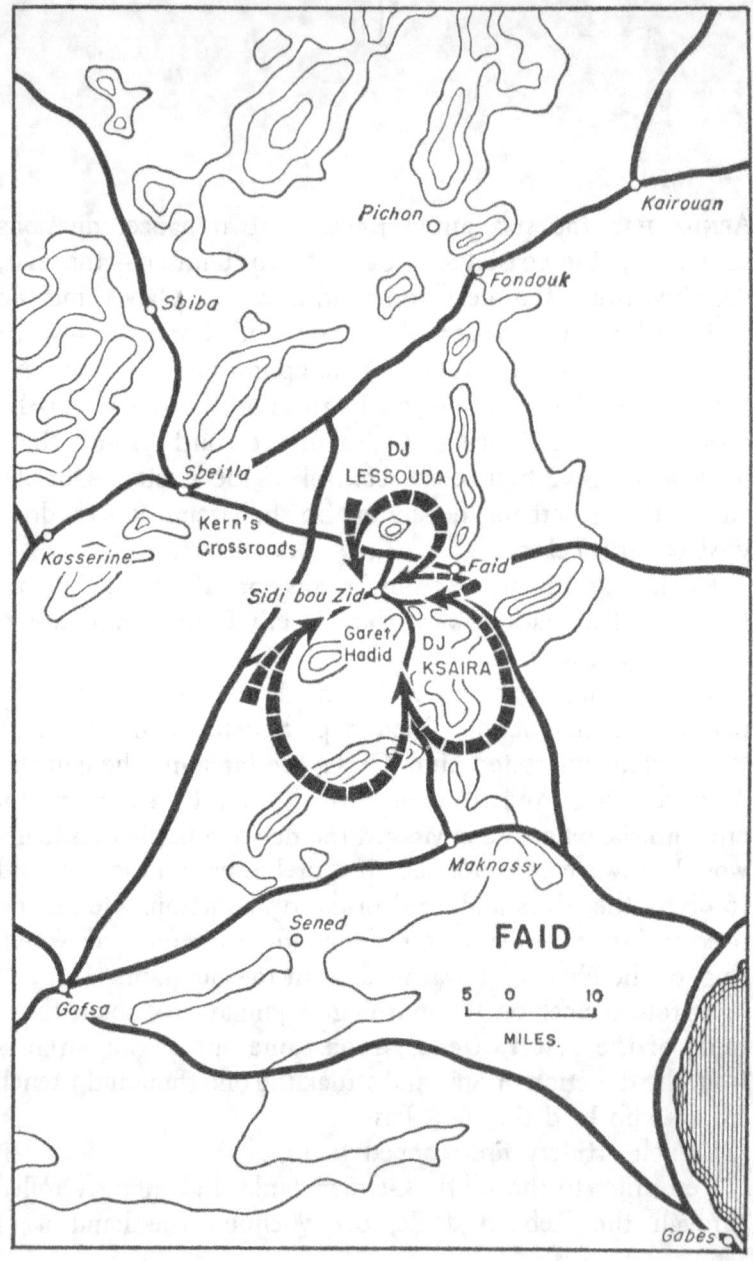

defenders, and came up on the rear of those still holding Faid.

Encircled by noontime, hopelessly outnumbered, the French continued to fight. Unless reinforced quickly, they were doomed to death or capture.

As soon as Welvert received word of the attack, he drove to Sidi bou Zid for firsthand information. Learning that his troops were about to go under, he went to Sbeitla, where CCA was supposed to be ready to launch a counterthrust in support of the French. He asked for assistance.

The trouble was that he had no authority over CCA. Brigadier General Raymond E. McQuillin, the CCA commander, a mild, gentlemanly soldier of the old school, felt constrained to wait for orders from his immediate superior, Ward, who was sixty miles away at Gafsa, or from his next higher commander, Fredendall, who was seventy miles away at Tebessa.

Welvert appealed to Fredendall, who said he would first have to check with his superior, Anderson.

In despair Welvert radioed Juin.

Around nine o'clock that morning, five hours after the German attack started, Anderson sent instructions "to restore the situation at Faid." Fredendall then assured Welvert that he would order McQuillin to take immediate action.

The directive he dispatched, unfortunately, was based on an inadequate knowledge of the enemy strength, an incomplete understanding of the Allied dispositions, and an insufficient appreciation of the terrain. He told McQuillin to move to Faid at once but without weakening his defenses at Sbeitla. How could he advance to Faid, thirty miles to the east, without reducing his strength at Sbeitla? He was to leave substantial forces in case the Faid attack was only a diversion. This meant restoring the situation at Faid with small forces.

McQuillin issued his orders rapidly, thirty minutes after receiving his instructions. A model of caution and good sense who operated by the book, he sent out two small reconnaissance units — one to the east to discover what was happening around Lessouda, about halfway to Faid; the other southeast to Sidi bou Zid, toward Rebaou. Around noontime, eight hours after the German attack had begun, they reported that strong enemy forces had control of the Eastern Dorsale between Faid and Rebaou.

It was then that Fredendall telephoned Stack and ordered him to march from Gafsa to Sidi bou Zid.

When McQuillin's assault forces got under way, they came under severe air attack. It was impossible for them to proceed. Calls for air support had no effect. The few Allied craft sent from Thelepte were unable to clear the skies.

Already, in the initial combat action of CCA, confusion had arisen. After American antiaircraft gunners shot down a P-40 by mistake, American planes returning from a mission against Faid dropped bombs on the CCA command post, killing one man and wounding four.

McQuillin decided to postpone his counterattack. He would wait for nightfall to move his assault forces forward. While he waited, the Germans conquered Faid.

Around midnight, when Welvert received word that some French troops were still resisting at Faid, he telephoned Fredendall. "It would be shameful, *mon Général*," he said, "to let a battalion of French be captured after fighting all day long with derisive arms against more than fifty tanks."

The corps commander could only express his regret.

McQuillin was planning to attack eastward with two battalions of infantry. One under Colonel Alexander N. Stark, Jr., was to advance from Lessouda to Faid, the other under Lieutenant Colonel William B. Kern from Sidi bou Zid to Rebaou.

To Welvert, who was at the CCA command post early on the morning of January 31, the second day, the Americans were fumbling. The attack was several hours late. And only weak forces were being committed, a common mistake of amateurs. The effort, he was sure, was bound to fail.

Eisenhower's representative, Truscott, had left Constantine that morning. He went to Tebessa and picked up Ward, and the two generals drove to the CCA command post, through the sparsely settled desert country that reminded them of New Mexico and Arizona. They found nothing amiss.

Except for Colonel Stark, who was unhappy. He doubted McQuillin's capacity. Less than forty-eight hours earlier, on a bitterly cold night, he had unnecessarily and unpardonably kept Stark's infantrymen sitting in trucks for three hours. Now he had issued an attack order that was both complicated and senseless.

Look, he showed Truscott. Here was his own plan, and McQuillin had disapproved it. How could he, a tanker, thus question Stark's ability as an infantryman?

Stark and McQuillin were much alike. Both were mild in manner and somewhat slow-moving. "Old Stark," his associates referred to him, as McQuillin's colleagues called him "Old Mac." And as is sometimes the case, each lacked confidence in the other, perhaps because each saw in the other a reflection of his own shortcomings.

By exposing his disapproved plan, Stark committed a faux pas, for Truscott had no use for those who went out of command channels. He believed passionately in personal loyalty between superiors and subordinates. More than likely, he nodded as he glanced at Stark's paper, meaning that he had noted it — and the implicit complaint. Stark took this to mean, as he later said, that Truscott "sanctioned" his scheme of maneuver.

In any event, Truscott refused to interfere. McQuillin was the responsible commander, and he was running the show.

To observe the attack, Truscott and Ward climbed Djebel Lessouda, a hill mass thrusting up from the Sbeitla plain. From the top of this rugged, jagged height, they could see the oasis of Sidi bou Zid in the distance and, farther, rimming the flat, brush-covered desert, the barren mountain of the Eastern Dorsale. They watched as untidy bands of skirmishers ventured out and dropped to the ground at the first sound of fire. Tanks lumbered toward Faid, crawling uncertainly like ungainly beetles, stopping now and then to shoot, their guns sending out short stabs of flame and raising small tornadoes of dust that enveloped and momentarily blotted out the details of the far-off and somewhat impersonal landscape. A filmy haze of earth particles and smoke soon covered the field, rendering objects indistinct. The foot troops became lost and wandered in all directions. As confusion and fright spread, some began to run wildly. Several tanks were hit, each that was struck by a shell coming to an abrupt and jolting halt followed by a transitory quiver that might burst into a searing sheet of flame.

As Welvert had predicted, the attack petered out. The terrain was surprisingly rough — dried-out stream beds and ditches cut routes of advance. The defensive fires were heavy. And bombing and strafing Stukas and ME-109's spread terror and destruction.

It was not long before McQuillin admitted his inability to take Faid and Rebaou.

While the Americans were meeting defeat at Faid, a new threat arose at Pichon. Shortly after dawn on that day, January 31, his diversion at Faid having attracted the desired Allied attention, Arnim struck with the 10th Panzer Division farther north. The attack soon disrupted the French defense and threatened to tear open the front.

As Anderson sent British troops from the north to buttress the French, he asked Fredendall to send Americans from the south.

The only unit at hand was Robinett's CCB, which had just returned to Tebessa. Fredendall had thought of bringing CCB forward to Sbeitla to help CCA, but now he had to order the troops to take to the road for Pichon.

Though Arnim was about to gain a decisive success, he called off the Pichon attack for two reasons. The 10th Panzer Division commander had been killed when his automobile ran over and detonated a mine. And the attack at Faid had disclosed more American tanks at Sbeitla than he had anticipated. Hesitating to overextend himself, he ordered the 10th Panzer Division to go over on the defensive at Pichon and the 21st Panzer Division to do the same at Faid.

McQuillin tried once more on February 1 to reach the Faid Pass but to no avail. Acknowledging candidly that he had failed to accomplish his mission, the cardinal sin of a commander in combat, he gave as the principal reason the disgraceful performance of Stark's infantry.

Anderson was profoundly disturbed. Seeing Arnim's attacks as having been provoked by Fredendall's dispersed dispositions, he began to feel that the scattered forces in the south would continue to invite German thrusts. And this would prevent him from ever stockpiling the resources he needed for his eventual thrust to Tunis.

Giraud was deeply angered. He saw no excuse for the inept American intervention at Faid, the ineffective counterattack, the general lack of vigor.

Eisenhower began to question Fredendall's ability. Had he expended men, ammunition, and other supplies in useless operations at Sened and Maknassy? Had he broken his units into too many small detachments? Was he exerting sufficient control? Was he being rash?

With Eisenhower's approval, Anderson told Fredendall to pull in his horns. To his instructions to suspend all offensive action, he added a gratuitous insult. Inexperienced troops, he tactlessly said, were often unduly affected by exaggerated reports of enemy ground and air strength. In other words, the Americans, in Anderson's opinion, had looked bad against relatively weak Axis elements.

As both sides renounced further offensive operations, a calm came to the Tunisian front.

The lull was to be only temporary. The American failure at Faid would soon develop into disaster.

Part III

SIDI BOU ZID

12

ANDERSON, ever mindful of his eventual drive to Tunis and Bizerte, worried over the weakness of the French in the center, which opened his northern sector to a flanking effort by the Germans. Happily, a large part of Major General Terry Allen's 1st U.S. Infantry Division was coming into the French area early in February and part of Major General Charles W. Ryder's 34th U.S. Infantry Division would soon bring additional strength. Each of these divisions had a regiment with the II Corps in the south — Stark's 26th Infantry had fought at Faid, and Colonel Thomas D. Drake's 168th Infantry had seen action below Gafsa at Sened.

Despite the growing power in the center, Anderson feared that the French were altogether too poorly equipped and the Americans insufficiently trained to withstand an Axis attack. The best course would be to wheel back the forces in the south and center in order to solidify the positions in the north. This he told his subordinates. Koeltz was to be ready to withdraw from the Eastern to the Western Dorsale, swinging back to cover the forces in the north. And Fredendall was to move back too if the enemy attacked. Though this would put the II Corps near Feriana and Kasserine, uncomfortably close to the supply complex at Tebessa, there seemed to be no way to avoid the risk.

Giraud paid little attention to the north. He was bothered by Rommel's presence in the south, which, he said, "appears to be serious. The month of February could bring us disagreeable surprises. . . . Rommel must be placed where he cannot attack."

But no one saw a way of crushing Rommel until the end of the rainy season, some time in March.

Ward, who had the task of containing the enemy along a front of fifty miles, from the Fondouk Pass to the Maizila Pass, instructed his subordinates to block enemy thrusts from Fondouk, Faid, and Maizila "by the quick reinforcement of French troops where the situation indicates by active reconnaissance and patrols, by artillery, and the use of mobile striking forces to counterattack enemy penetrations." If the wording was rather fuzzy, the intent was unmistakable. He hoped to counter enemy probes without getting seriously involved in a major battle, a desire that stemmed from the dispersal of his forces. Robinett's CCB was one hundred miles up north and out of his direct control. Stack was about twenty miles away near Fondouk and, like McQuillin's CCA at Sbeitla and Sidi bou Zid, under Fredendall's heavy hand. The only troops Ward really controlled were some small reserve elements.

The other units in the II Corps area were few and far-flung: a battalion of Drake's 168 Infantry at Tebessa; the other two battalions of Drake's regiment at Sbeitla; and Stark's 26th Infantry at Feriana blocking the Gafsa-Tebessa road and protecting the Thelepte airfields. All had fared badly in their initial combat experience. Stark's infantry had taken a raking at Faid, and the regiment was short ten officers and 110 enlisted men lost in action. Drake's infantry had also taken heavy casualties at Sened. Though more units were arriving early in February — a Ranger battalion, more artillery and tank destroyers, and part of the 1st Derbyshire Yeomanry — they were relatively small and they lacked the cohesive solidity that an additional division would have given.

The men also lacked battle hardening, initiation into the unnerving mystique of combat, learning the sights and sounds of warfare, coming to distinguish between incoming and outgoing artillery rounds, how to tell the location of fire, when to take cover and when to be bold, how to advance and communicate and keep direction and shoot. It took experience to understand the complicated business of fighting. Eventually the hesitancy, the uncertainty, and the frightful feeling of helplessness would vanish. Perhaps in time for the next enemy onslaught.

The German attacks along the Eastern Dorsale produced an increasing tension at every echelon and among all Allied units. By the second week of February everyone was on edge. Where would the Germans strike next? And when?

Suddenly, Eisenhower's intelligence officer had definite word. Whether Allied monitors had intercepted an enemy message or received information from an agent highly placed in the enemy camp has since remained a mystery. In any event, there was now reason to doubt neither the imminence of an attack nor its location. The Germans would attack through Fondouk, go northwestward, rip through the defenses of the French in the center, and plow into the flank of the British forces in the north.

Anderson acted immediately. Since the enemy was likely to launch diversionary activity in the south to mask the major thrust, he instructed Fredendall categorically to abandon Gafsa at the first sign of enemy action. Along with Koeltz, he was to move to the rear, evacuate the Eastern Dorsale, and take up positions in the defensible high ground of the Western range in order to preserve the forces in northern Tunisia.

As the uneasiness deepened, Giraud asked why the 2d U.S. Armored Division could not be shifted to Tunisia. "It has nothing to do in Morocco," he suggested. Why not have it "moved to the Tebessa region" instead? The reason for his anxiety, he added, was simple: "One never feels too strong facing an adversary like Rommel."

Eisenhower shared his sentiment, but his logisticians had informed him that additional combat forces could not be supported in Tunisia by the relatively few service troops and the small supply complex established in the theater.

* * * *

Obtaining a proper balance of manpower resources between the troops who fight and those who sustain and support them has always been a troublesome problem for armies in the field. The military forces of the major powers, particularly the highly industrialized nations of the West, have seen their logistical establishments expand enormously and inexorably for at least a century.

By the 1940's, an army had far more men in technical and non-divisional units than in the combat formations. In an overseas theater of operations, about twenty-five thousand men were required to service and support a combat division of fifteen thousand, and almost half the troops in every division were also engaged in supporting activities.

In 1899, Churchill wrote of Kitchener's Nile campaign and described victory as "the beautiful, bright-coloured flower," but acknowledged that transportation was "the stem without which it could never have blossomed." Forty years later, he had forgotten his observation, and the demands exerted by mechanized warfare — for service troops, a vast organization of workshops and repair units, supply and ordnance depots, road, railway, and dock complexes — seemed altogether exorbitant. They had created, he believed, an administrative and logistical tail of "fluff and flummery" behind the fighting front. The army in North Africa, Churchill remarked, was "like a peacock — nearly all tail." The Chief of the Imperial General Staff had an apt reply. "The peacock would be a very badly balanced bird without its tail," he said.

Though Churchill insisted that the armies "have less fat and more muscle . . . a smaller tail and larger teeth," the requirements continued to mount for troops who served but did not fight, and the field commanders kept calling for

7. General Louis-Marie Koeltz, commander of the French XX Corps, who understood the requirements of coalition warfare. *U.S. Army Photograph*

8. Djebel Lessouda, "island of resistance marooned in a sea of enemy troops."
U.S. Army Photograph

Djebel Ksaira. They wrote off the defenders because there was "no use prolonging the agony." *U.S. Army Photograph*

additional support and service units. "Sharpen your teeth," Churchill again advised, "and cut off the tail."

But in a primitive and arid land, remote from the sources of supply and lacking base installations and modern transportation, the trend toward an evergrowing supply and service organization continued irresistibly. The disproportionately low ratio of service to combat troops during the first three months of the campaign had made supply, according to Truscott, "the absorbing problem in every headquarters in North Africa."

A basic deficiency was transportation. The narrow-gauge railroad between Constantine and Tebessa, the main supply depot for the American troops in Tunisia, could carry only about one-third of the daily requirements of the II Corps. Truck convoys supplemented the railway shipments. But by the end of January, the trucks were giving out, mechanically worn by constant use or deadlined for lack of spare parts. At least seventy-five were urgently needed for the Constantine-Tebessa run alone, and the loss of a single vehicle became "almost a tragedy" to the logistical planners.

During the Casablanca Conference, Eisenhower had requested and been promised additional transport. A shipment of more than five thousand trucks, two thousand trailers, and several hundred railway freight cars would leave the United States on February 15, but reach North Africa in March, too late for an immediate solution to the problem.

At the end of January, the II Corps was suffering acute shortages in all types of equipment. There were only thirty-five spare tanks on hand, and of these twenty were light M-3's, already regarded as too weak for effective use against the Germans. Binoculars, machine guns, and spare parts for all kinds of weapons and vehicles were badly needed.

The shortage of automotive spare parts was exceptionally severe. Carrying ammunition, weapons, fuel, food, and other supplies forward of Tebessa were six thousand trucks about to fall apart from overuse. If they broke down, the tactical situation would disintegrate. They needed repair work and replacements of engines, clutches, generators, starters, spark plugs, fan belts, and carburetors. Nuts, bolts, headlight bulbs, and tire patches were precious items.

The lack of adequate base shop facilities and depots in the rear and of support and service had resulted in a deterioration of vehicles and tanks at the front, a starvation in spare parts, and an absence of tools and men to keep the combat troops armed and mobile.

At the beginning of February, Eisenhower created an organization to handle for the American forces all the complicated aspects of logistics and administration on a more professional, less haphazard basis. At Algiers, in a city already crowded with the varied and extensive fixtures of a modern army headquarters — American, British, and French installations, hotels and other buildings converted to office space and billets, antiaircraft batteries, smoke projector units, car and truck companies, hospitals, military policemen, signal communications personnel, postal and radio censorship units, all performing tasks directly or indirectly related to nourishing the men at the front — the new Services of Supply started to organize more effectively the multiplicity of activities required. But not until March would the supply network be effective enough to service additional combat troops in Tunisia.

The Battle of Kasserine would be fought on a slender stem incapable of supporting the bright flower of victory.

* * * *

Despite the prevalent belief that the next German thrust would come somewhere in the north, Fredendall's intelligence officer gathered an impressive body of evidence indicating an enemy buildup in the south. Arab laborers had quite suddenly and for no apparent reason vanished from the scene.

SIDI BOU ZID 121

Reconnaissance patrols met stiffened resistance. Sounds of increasing vehicular movements were heard. These signs, plus information gained from the interrogation of occasional prisoners of war, the observation of German artillery fires, and the reports of reconnaissance flights, all added up to preparations for an enemy attack.

Heeding the warning, Fredendall drew up a detailed directive, prescribing exactly the defensive measures he wished Ward to carry out. "You will take immediate steps," he wrote, "to see that the following steps concerning the defense of the Faid positions are put into effect."

The key terrain features just west of Faid are two hills flanking the road to Sbeitla. North of the road is Djebel Lessouda. On the south is Djebel Ksaira. Fredendall wanted these heights held firmly, with mobile reserves at Sidi bou Zid in support.

But this was not enough. Continuing his precise instructions, he lectured Ward in a tone that was as unflattering as it was inappropriate, covering subjects that all junior officers are supposed to have mastered — the proper employment of patrols, wire, mines, the importance of aerial photography, the function of artillery, and other similar topics.

"I desire that a copy of this directive, together with your own comments, be sent to McQuillin," Fredendall added. "You will inform me when the instructions enumerated in this directive have been complied with."

There was one more thought, this one contained in a handwritten postscript at the bottom of the paper: "In other words I want a very strong active defense and not just a passive one. The enemy must be harassed at every opportunity. Reconnaissance must never be relaxed — especially at night. Positions [I have] indicated *must* be wired and mined NOW. L.R.F."

These instructions were contrary to normal American practice. According to American military doctrine, when a commander assigns a mission, he gives the subordinate the initiative and the authority to carry out the mission in his own way. Fredendall had, in effect, done Ward's job — he had placed Ward's units in specific locations and he had given them specific tasks to perform.

In part this reflected his lack of confidence in Ward. In part it followed and conformed with Anderson's practice. Since Anderson was giving Fredendall's affairs a rather close and detailed supervision, Fredendall saw no reason why he should not adopt a similar method with Ward.

There were two significant differences. British army doctrine permitted a far closer command supervision over subordinates. In addition, Anderson moved around the front constantly and knew the situation firsthand, while Fredendall tarried well to the rear and was in no position to challenge Anderson's detailed orders.

Though Fredendall had made only one short visit to Sbeitla, he as much as took command of Ward's division. Ward, in effect, became a supernumerary, his headquarters taking on the complexion of a message center that transmitted communications from corps down to the units and informational reports from the smaller units up to corps.

Ward's close associates who knew of the ill-feeling between him and Fredendall appreciated the insulting nature of the instructions and found that Ward had an amazing capacity for remaining calm and cheerful.

Quite apart from the personality conflict, Fredendall's scheme of defense was defective. Placing troops on the hills of Lessouda and Ksaira created islands of resistance on high ground that was vulnerable to encirclement. Though the positions appeared excellent on a map, they were not mutually supporting, that is, the troops on one height could not aid those on the other. Senior officers in the 1st Armored Division recognized the error of Fredendall's dispositions, but they could persuade neither him nor his staff members to make the personal reconnaissance that would have quickly showed how easily the forces on Lessouda and Ksaira could be marooned.

Furthermore, Fredendall's meticulous placement of Ward's units froze the defense. Ward would be unable to react quickly in a crisis. He would first have to secure permission from a commander who was far to the rear and who doubted Ward's military capacity. "The inevitable consequence of these arrangements," in the words of the division historian, "was rigidity and delay in meeting the unforeseen." Ward would lack the freedom to maneuver his units that characterizes the successful management of battlefield tactics.

13

VAGUE BUT disquieting rumors of the bad blood between Fredendall and Ward having reached Eisenhower, he decided to make an inspection tour of the American front. At the end of his working day on Friday, February 12, he traveled from Algiers to Constantine and spent the evening discussing a variety of subjects with Truscott.

The most important topic, according to Truscott's recollections, was the question of whether to hold or give up Gafsa and Sidi bou Zid in the event of an enemy attack. Unlike Anderson, Truscott believed they should be retained if possible, particularly to protect the airfields.

On the following morning, Saturday, the 13th, the weather that had been miserable during the past several days, with snow flurries and violent winds, suddenly improved. Though the sky remained half covered with heavy clouds, though the high winds persisted and the temperature stayed cold, the atmospheric conditions became favorable for offensive operations.

As Anderson was warning his subordinate commanders all along the front that the change in the weather increased the chances of the expected enemy attack, Eisenhower and Truscott left Constantine for Tebessa. The location of Fredendall's command post in the canyon and the tunneling still in progress surprised and dismayed Eisenhower. They indicated an expectation of a static situation rather than a readiness for offensive action.

Anderson had come to Tebessa too in order to review for the Allied commander the disposition of forces along the front. At the hour scheduled for the conference, Eisenhower, Truscott, and Fredendall gathered. They waited fifteen minutes for Anderson, who was somewhere in the headquarters, to appear. Since his manner with Eisenhower was never very respectful, everyone was somewhat uncomfortable. Finally, someone telephoned to find out where he was.

He was listening to Fredendall's intelligence officer, who guessed that an enemy attack was coming in the Gafsa area and perhaps in the Faid sector too.

After asking penetrating questions, Anderson said, "Well, young man, I can't shake you." But he remained convinced that the attack would be in the north. For he later told Fredendall that he had a "jumpy" staff officer.

Joining the others who were waiting for him, Anderson described the front. He detailed the British units in the north, under Allfrey, spoke of the increasing American elements entering Koeltz's sector, and pointed out the interspersal of national forces in the south, where Welvert's "Constantine" Division, the bulk of Ward's 1st Armored Division, two infantry regiments, a Ranger battalion, and part of a British armored car regiment were located under Fredendall's command.

Eisenhower was satisfied. The positions, he said, were "as good as could be made pending the development of an actual [enemy] attack and in view of the great value of holding the forward regions, if it could possibly be done."

By the latter part of this statement, he seemed to have accepted Truscott's point of view — that it was better to retain the forward positions. But if he now believed this, he failed to rescind his earlier agreement with Anderson to abandon them. The ambiguity would remain.

If responsibility on the corps level was rather well understood, the delineation of command below was not always firm. Welvert's "Constantine" Division, for example, was spread out alongside the American units: an armored regiment together with Stack's force guarded Fondouk; a mixed group occupied positions near McQuillin's CCA in the Sbeitla region; other units were at Gafsa and Feriana; and French troops manned the desert posts of Metlaoui and Tozeur. Despite the close proximity of the French and American units, Fredendall had never defined Welvert's mission. As a consequence, Welvert had no specific role in the defense of southern Tunisia. In effect, he was an advisor on the use of the French forces in the II Corps area. In that capacity, he had clearly expressed his predilections — opposing all thought of evacuating Gafsa at the first sign of enemy activity, doubting in principle that troops should withdraw simply from a threat, stating that abandoning Gafsa under enemy pressure would be a disaster for the French troops who lacked enough vehicles for a motorized withdrawal and would be overrun and cut to pieces, and believing that the rallying position at Feriana was worthless because it could be too easily outflanked. But advice was free and could, of course, be disregarded.

The conference at Tebessa was barely over when a telephone call came for Anderson. It was additional confirmation that the enemy was about to attack in the north. Anderson departed at once. In the event of a full-scale enemy effort, which now seemed indisputable, his place was at his command post.

Koeltz had alerted his troops early that morning of February 13, but everything remained calm along his front. He saw nothing abnormal. Late in the afternoon he received a phone call informing him that an attack against the French on the following morning was firmly expected.

The information hardly jibed with occurrences around Faid. At 1:30 that afternoon, a forward observer on the height of Djebel Ksaira reported a disturbing sight. He saw about one hundred enemy trucks moving in the area east of Faid; traveling from north to south, they appeared to be loaded with troops.

The location of this lucrative target was quickly transmitted, and before long American planes flew across the Eastern Dorsale and bombed the enemy trucks. The pilots claimed the destruction of about twenty vehicles. They also verified the nature of the cargo — the trucks were, as reported, filled with soldiers.

Later that afternoon, German artillery began a sporadic shelling of the American positions around Lessouda. The slow rate of fire continued intermittently into the evening.

At Sidi bou Zid, McQuillin warned his troops to expect an enemy attack. He sent his supply and maintenance elements to the rear to Sbeitla.

Up in the north, where CCB was stationed, Robinett was puzzled. Everyone looked for an enemy attack, but the only evidence he could see was a growing nervousness among the staff members of higher headquarters. Unable to judge the validity of the warnings, he drove to Sbeitla on the afternoon of February 13. Perhaps Ward would know what was going on.

Ward was upset. Expecting at least a flurry of enemy activity to the east around Sidi bou Zid, he was concerned because his troops were dispersed and because Fredendall kept injecting himself into Ward's affairs, making Ward's decisions. Would Robinett stay that evening, he asked, and give Eisenhower, who was coming, an estimate of the situation? It would be unseemly, he explained, to make any semblance of complaint.

Eisenhower and Truscott, after some sightseeing around Tebessa, came to Ward's command post after dark. Ward showed the defensive dispositions of his division, then asked Robinett to speak. He said he believed that the troops occupying Djebels Lessouda and Ksaira were too far apart to be mutually supporting and that the troops stationed near Sidi bou Zid were too weak to provide adequate reserve support. If additional forces were unavailable, he would suggest abandoning the forward positions in order to save the units from useless destruction.

To Robinett, Eisenhower appeared impressed by the presentation and "really seeking the facts," while Truscott's face registered his disapproval of the recommendation to evacuate the forward positions.

During the evening, another message of warning came from Anderson, who was quite positive and precise: the enemy would attack the next morning. Though he expected the main blow somewhere in the north, he looked also for a diversionary effort, and where that would strike was anybody's guess.

Robinett decided to return to his troops, while Eisenhower and his party went to the CCA command post at Sidi bou Zid. As word was flashing all along the front of the expected enemy attack, Eisenhower, at 11 P.M., was listening to a description of the situation from McQuillin. Except for asking why so few mines had been set out to strengthen the defenses — there was no satisfactory answer — he had no comments. That he "formulated no observation regarding the defensive dispositions," Koeltz later wrote, struck the French commander as strange. But Eisenhower was conforming to the American tradition that kept a senior commander from interfering with the local arrangements of a subordinate. All he did was to pin a Silver Star on Drake, the commander of the 168th Infantry, decorating him for gallantry at Sened.

About this time, Fredendall drove from his command post in Tebessa to Welvert's headquarters nearby. He wanted to be sure that Welvert had received the attack warning and had alerted his troops. Also, having concluded from Eisenhower's rather turgid statement earlier in the day that the forces at Gafsa were expected "to resist at all costs," he passed this on.

Close to midnight, Eisenhower went for a short walk into the desert at Sidi bou Zid. The wind had quieted. The moon had appeared. All was calm. As he stood in the darkness on that St. Valentine's eve, he could discern on the left the looming height of Lessouda and a dozen miles on the right the indistinct shape of Djebel Ksaira. As he peered eastward toward the gap in the black mountain mass that marked the Faid Pass, he had little idea that the Germans were preparing to deliver a bloody valentine at dawn.

Eisenhower and Truscott returned to Tebessa during the early morning hours of Sunday, February 14. At 5:30 A.M. they learned that German forces had launched an attack at Sidi bou Zid an hour and a half before. The operation seemed like a local effort. There was no cause for alarm. All the indications were good. The Americans would be able to hold.

Departing Tebessa, Eisenhower and Truscott turned off the main road to visit the famous Roman ruins at Timgad. In the middle of the afternoon they reached Constantine. There they found word that the American defensive action had not gone so well as anticipated. Fierce fighting was in progress.

That evening the news turned bad. The Germans, they learned, had destroyed an American tank battalion, overrun a battalion of artillery, and driven the remainder of McQuillin's force back from Sidi bou Zid toward Sbeitla. The men on the djebels of Lessouda and Ksaira had been surrounded. Fredendall's islands of resistance were marooned in a sea of enemy troops.

14

THE GERMAN BLOW on Sunday, February 14, a carefully conceived operation involving Kesselring, Arnim, and Rommel, had its ambiguous aspects.

If at the beginning of the month Arnim was pleased with his success at the passes of the Eastern Dorsale, Rommel, who was backing his Panzerarmee into the Mareth positions, and Kesselring, who was coordinating the armies in Tunisia, were less than satisfied.

The presence of American tanks around Sbeitla and Gafsa bothered Rommel. Since the leading elements of Montgomery's British Eighth Army were arriving near the southern border of Tunisia and were likely soon to attack the Mareth Line, Rommel would be better able to fight if he were rid of the anxiety of the Americans on his right flank and rear. If he could destroy the American tanks before the bulk of Montgomery's army reached southern Tunisia, he would be free to turn his entire resources against the British.

Kesselring agreed. Since the Russian front, and particularly the Battle of Stalingrad, was depriving him of the reinforcements he had been promised, the only forces available for a strike against the American armor were the 10th and 21st Panzer Divisions, assembled around Sfax.

Ever since November, when Rommel had pointed out the advantage of combining the two armies in Tunisia for a subsequent westward drive into Algeria, Comando Supremo had been cautiously entertaining the idea. Rommel had presented the concept again in December and once more in mid-January, this time more specifically suggesting a blow through

Gafsa and Sbeitla toward Tebessa. Convinced finally that the suggestion had merit and that the Axis forces were strong enough to try, Comando Supremo, on January 28, had authorized Arnim to probe beyond the Eastern Dorsale.

In February, after Arnim's success at Faid and Pichon, Rommel returned to his idea. In a memorandum dated February 4 and addressed to Kesselring for Comando Supremo, he proposed that he attack the Americans at Gafsa while Arnim struck at Sbeitla. Reasoning that time favored the Allies, he recommended a swift and surprising attack by superior forces under a unified command. Implicit was the thought that he would exercise that single and overall control.

Kesselring transmitted the memo to Comando Supremo for decision. He added a note of his own, stating his belief that the Allies were still unable to deliver a decisive blow and that it was thus possible to profit from what was bound to be only a temporary advantage. An attack against the Americans and an advance toward Tebessa would remove the threat against Rommel's flank, prevent a thrust toward Tunis and Bizerte, and bring into immediate prospect the capture of objectives as far distant as Bone on the north coast and Tozeur in the desert. Finally, a striking victory in North Africa would partially compensate for the surrender of Paulus and his Sixth Army at Stalingrad on February 2.

On February 8, Comando Supremo gave approval for further offensive operations but specified that they should be concerned primarily with destroying Allied forces, not with gaining territory.

To lay out the operation with the field commanders, Kesselring went to Africa on February 9 and met with Arnim and Rommel near Gabes.

Arnim opposed an attack toward Tebessa. Like Comando Supremo, he believed that the Axis forces lacked sufficient troops, ammunition, and gasoline for so ambitious an operation, and he favored a limited maneuver restricted to the goal of inflicting on the Allies losses of men and materiel. He proposed a blow in the Pichon area and a short advance to the west to force the Americans and the French to pull back to the Western Dorsale. Thrown off balance and forced to withdraw, the Americans would be unable to threaten Rommel during the approaching battle at the Mareth Line.

Somewhat regretfully, Kesselring recognized the merit in Arnim's estimate. Yet he looked wistfully on the larger opportunity in the south. "We should not lose from sight," he said, "the large operation envisaged toward Tebessa, which, if circumstances are favorable, would enable us to attain the distant objectives" — Tozeur and Bone.

The upshot of the conversation was a decision to execute a small operation. There would be two attacks, both limited in nature. Arnim was to launch the first, code-named "Fruehlingswind," against Sidi bou Zid, using the 10th and 21st Panzer Divisions. Rommel was to trigger the second, code-named "Morgenlust," against Gafsa, using part of the Afrika Korps and some Italian units, plus whatever part of the 21st Panzer Division Arnim could make available upon the conclusion of his venture.

It remained then to regulate the question of command. Though Comando Supremo planned to create an army group headquarters in Tunisia to control the two armies, no commander had been appointed. Kesselring wished to name Rommel the acting commander — as a field marshal, he was senior to Arnim — but Comando Supremo demurred on several grounds: Rommel had retreated too quickly across Libya, he had hazarded audacious operations without due consideration of Italian interests, and he was scheduled to leave Africa as soon as Messe was ready to take over his army.

The two operations, then, would be independent, though the army commanders would be expected to coordinate their endeavors.

After the conference, Kesselring told Rommel privately

that if the armies attained a success that lured them into the "big operation" toward Tebessa, he would see to it that Rommel received the overall command. Should Rommel gain a spectacular success rapidly, he was sure he could persuade Comando Supremo to subordinate Arnim to Rommel's control.

He hoped thus to excite Rommel's ambition and improve his efficiency. Rommel had been magnificent in carrying out the withdrawal across Libya, but he had an aversion to this type of warfare, which required careful and meticulous arrangements ill-suited to his style. "Rommel opposed it [the retrograde movement] in his soul," he later said. The audacious gamble, the bold offensive strike interested him. If he had "an opportunity . . . to conclude the damaging period of retreats by a successful series of offensives," the Desert Fox might be revitalized. "After the nerve-wracking retreat" from El Alamein, he deserved the chance to ignite a blaze of glory for himself.

A revived and reinvigorated Rommel, wrested from his pessimism, restored to ebullient optimism, would advance the Axis strategy of remaining in North Africa. For he might apply his military genius to finding a highly imaginative and brilliant conception that could entirely reverse the situation in Tunisia.

In contrast with Kesselring's motivation and reasoning, Arnim intended to do no more than complete and strengthen his hold on the Eastern Dorsale from the Pichon defile to the Maizila Pass. If he pushed the Allied forces back from Sbeitla in the process, so much the better. He understood Rommel's role as only to destroy the Allies around Gafsa. Though he was to relinquish part of the 21st Panzer Division upon the completion of his own attack, he was under the impression that this would enable Rommel to pull back the bulk of his troops to await the British at Mareth. At that point, Arnim would move as much of the 10th Panzer Division as possible to expand his control over the area west of the Fondouk and Pichon gaps. Far more interested in his own area in the north, he conceived of Fruehlingswind and Morgenlust as fundamentally defensive operations. He expected the assault forces to take Sidi bou Zid and Gafsa, then engage in reconnaissance toward Sbeitla and Feriana, respectively, in order to stabilize the front in the south and gain security for Rommel's Mareth Line operations.

On Saturday, February 13, at an airfield halfway between Sfax and Faid, the German field commanders came together to make the last-minute arrangements — Rommel, Arnim, and his deputy, Ziegler, who was to be in direct command of Fruehlingswind.

With more than two hundred tanks, half-tracks, and guns, Ziegler hoped to deal the Americans a sharp setback. After going to the top of a hill near Faid to inspect the terrain, he issued his order for a double pincer movement designed to surround Lessouda and Sidi bou Zid. First, the 10th Panzer Division was to assemble east of the Dorsale and move through the Faid Pass at dawn of February 14 in two groups; Group Gerhardt was to sweep around the northern tip of Djebel Lessouda, drive south along its western face, and cut the road to Sbeitla to prevent the arrival of American reinforcements; Group Reimann was to drive straight down the road from Faid to the southern tip of Lessouda, destroying whatever Allied forces got in the way. Second, the non-motorized elements of the 21st Panzer Division, which were holding the Faid Pass, were to attack westward to Sidi bou Zid. Third, the mobile elements of the 21st Panzer Division were to go through the Maizila Pass and split into two groups to surround Sidi bou Zid; Group Schutte was to push northward along the road from Maknassy to outflank Sidi bou Zid on the south; Group Stenkhoff was to push westward, then turn north on the road from Gafsa to take Sidi bou Zid from the rear.

While Ziegler's divisions took their places for the attack, Colonel Freiherr Kurt von Liebenstein, the acting commander of the Afrika Korps who was in charge of Operation Morgenlust against Gafsa and Tozeur, started to assemble his units: a mixed detachment from the Afrika Korps and a mobile group of the Italian Centauro Division already concealed nearby. His composite Italo-German force had about 160 tanks, half-tracks, and guns, but it was to be augmented at the end of Fruehlingswind by part of the 21st Panzer Division. How much he would get would depend on how the action developed.

Though Liebenstein understood he was to conduct only a limited attack to Gafsa, Rommel had in mind going beyond, as far as Tebessa. But he was inclined toward a pessimistic evaluation of his chances. Figuring Tebessa as a long shot, he emphasized that he wanted no risks taken at Gafsa. Since there were no reserves, a reverse would have a catastrophic effect on the overall situation. Thus, he fixed no further operational objectives for the moment.

Liebenstein thought that Rommel intended, after capturing Gafsa, to fall back to cover Gabes. The operation, then, according to his interpretation, was to be little more than a raid. And on this basis he readied his forces for a jump-off any time after the afternoon of February 15.

Unlike Rommel, Arnim was full of confidence. He began to feel that the attack beyond Faid would draw most of the American forces away from Gafsa. In that case, Rommel would need no help, and Arnim could keep all of the 21st Panzer Division in the Sbeitla area and move all of the 10th to the north.

But then, Arnim was unaware of the big operation that interested Rommel and Kesselring.

Yet some inexplicable and intangible prescience bothered him. Unable to identify or dispel the nagging tug, he decided he would not inform Kesselring or Comando Supremo of the date he planned to start Ziegler's attack. His reason, he later said, was his desire to preserve operational secrecy from Italian gossipers.

Without the slightest inkling that the operation was about to start, Kesselring left Rome that evening of the 13th — only a few hours before the opening of the attack — to visit Hitler in East Prussia.

With these untidy strings marring what might have been a neat operational package, the attack began to unfold at four o'clock on the Sunday morning of February 14. As a violent wind rather than a Fruehlingswind blew through the Faid Pass and stirred up a sandstorm, the head of the 10th Panzer Division started through the Eastern Dorsale and moved slowly through the predawn darkness toward Lessouda.

No one knew that the second phase of the Battle of Kasserine was under way.

15

THE MEN on Djebel Lessouda were under Waters, who had been placed in charge two days earlier. With a single staff officer and two drivers, one for a half-track command vehicle, the other a jeep, he set up his command post in a wadi-ravine that gave him concealment on the south slope of the hill.

His troops consisted of most of the 2d Battalion of the 168th Infantry, a company of tanks, some reconnaissance elements, a platoon of tank destroyers, and a battery of self-propelled 105-mm. howitzers. Engineers had helped to fortify the hill with mines and barbed wire. Except for the infantry battalion commander, a young officer who seemed unsure of himself, except for a certain vagueness in the assigned mission, and except for a desire to have additional resources, Waters was reasonably satisfied with the setup.

Ward came to Lessouda on the 13th for a brief visit. He showed Waters a letter from Fredendall, who directed the precise manner of employing the units. Though Ward said nothing of his problems, Waters was aware of his seething frustration.

On Saturday evening, February 13, Waters was called to McQuillin's headquarters in Sidi bou Zid for a final briefing before the expected German attack. McQuillin emphasized that nothing was supposed to happen in his area, but he wanted everyone to be alert for a German thrust out of the north, from Fondouk or Pichon. Someone said that Ernie Pyle and Jack Thompson, war correspondents, had left Sbeitla and gone north to be close to the battle.

Waters left Sidi bou Zid and passed Eisenhower and his party. He reached Lessouda shortly before midnight.

While his tanks remained close to the djebel during the night, protected by antitank defenses and in turn helping to cover the approaches from Faid, patrols roved through the area between the height and the pass to give warning of German movements. During the daylight hours, a force of tanks and infantry screened Lessouda by manning an outpost line on the plain. These men were to delay and break up a German attack.

After making certain that the night patrols were out and that the tank-infantry group was ready to move out at daylight, Waters called the commander of the 2d Battalion, 168th Infantry, and told him to notify his company commanders that a German attack was imminent. Then he turned in for a few hours of sleep.

According to the scheme of defense devised by Fredendall, Waters was to block and tie down Germans coming through the Faid Pass in order to give Lieutenant Colonel Louis V. Hightower time to launch a counterattack from Sidi bou Zid with a mobile armored reserve force of about forty tanks and a dozen tank destroyers, supported by two artillery battalions.

Much the same arrangement was in effect for Djebel Ksaira, occupied by the 3d Battalion of the 168th Infantry, some engineers, a few antiaircraft guns, and several artillery pieces. They were under Drake, who had been promoted to colonel and placed in command of the regiment at the turn of the year. He had his command post in a small olive grove about two miles east of Sidi bou Zid. A mile farther east, on a hill called Garet Hadid, was a company of the 2d Battalion, 168th Infantry. Two miles still farther east and across the Maknassy road was Djebel Ksaira.

A shipment of two hundred replacement troops had arrived on Friday, the 12th, each man carrying two heavy barracks bags full of clothing and personal belongings. Some lacked weapons, some had never fired a rifle, none had entrenching tools or bayonets, and many were not even trained infantrymen. Drake sent them to Ksaira, where they were parceled out among the companies.

On Saturday afternoon, Drake received several truckloads of ammunition and some brand-new bazookas that no one had ever fired. Distributing the bazookas at once, he intended to schedule instruction on the next day.

In the same way that Waters was to block an enemy thrust from the east, Drake was to protect the approach to Sidi bou Zid from the south — the road coming up from Maknassy and through the Maizila Pass. At the northern exit of the pass, fifteen miles away, was the reconnaissance battalion of the 1st Armored Division.

Called to McQuillin's headquarters on Saturday night, Drake was awarded the Silver Star by Eisenhower and was alerted to a possible enemy sortie through the Maizila Pass. Prepared for that eventuality, he was concerned by his vulnerability to encirclement from Faid. "General," he asked McQuillin, "what will we do if the enemy attacks from the pass in the east?"

"Don't bring that up," McQuillin said, closing the conversation.

Where Hightower was to launch his counterattack if the Germans came through both passes and attacked Lessouda and Ksaira simultaneously had not been decided.

Behind Lessouda and Ksaira, twenty miles to the west at Sbeitla, was Ward's division reserve — a battalion of infantry, one of tanks, and a company of tank destroyers. Forty miles west of Sbeitla, near Tebessa, was Fredendall's corps reserve — a few artillery and tank destroyer battalions and one of infantry. At Feriana was a mixed group built around Stark's infantry. These elements were ready to move to meet an enemy thrust wherever it might appear, but whether they were close enough to the front to render immediate assistance was another matter.

On Sunday, February 14, as daylight touched the morning

with dirty, gray fingers, Waters arose. He climbed the slope of Djebel Lessouda to an observation post and looked toward the Faid Pass. A strong wind was kicking up the sand so bitterly that it was impossible to see or hear much. When a dim sun started to rise bravely directly behind the Faid Pass, Waters descended the hill to his tent. The phone rang. Colonel Peter C. Hains, III, was calling from the CCA command post in Sidi bou Zid.

A dapper officer who looked like Broadway's stereotype of an English teacher, Hains commanded the 1st Armored Regiment, which was split into segments divided among Waters, Hightower, and Robinett. Acting as McQuillin's second in command, he asked Waters what the shooting was all about.

What shooting?

Somewhere along the road between Faid and Lessouda.

Waters said he would find out. By radio, he tried to make contact with the covering force that presumably had departed at daylight. There was no answer.

Had the cover force left?

He sent his jeep driver to the tent of the major in charge. The officer was in his sack; he had overslept. The force had left on schedule. The men had a radio network that gave them internal communications; but in the absence of the command tank they lacked the means to be in touch with Waters.

The major dressed hurriedly, got into his tank, and moved out to join his men. No one knew that the cover force had already been overrun by German tanks. The major too would be taken.

Waters again climbed to an escarpment to see what was happening. He could see and hear nothing. The wind howled across Lessouda, and sand particles filled the air.

Returning to his command post, Waters called Hains, who said that Lessouda seemed to be under attack.

Waters moved back up the hill. This time he heard the

sound of tanks firing in the east. He regained his command post and ordered his artillery to open fire on prearranged targets in the pass. The enemy was already too close, he was informed. Pull back, Waters said, so you can shoot. Before they could do so, the artillerymen were overrun.

At Sidi bou Zid, where the sandstorm was less violent, McQuillin's headquarters guessed that a German attack had started. "It appeared," a notation in the CCA journal stated, "that an envelopment of our northern flank was in progress." But exactly what was going on was far from clear. Had the "hostile debouchment," as the clerk at the headquarters recorded it, been made through the Faid Pass or another defile farther north?

McQuillin had set up several listening posts, but no word had come from them. Had they been taken by surprise and overrun, or had they simply failed to perform as directed? No one called for the strong concentrations of artillery fire that had been specially prepared to blast the western exit of the Faid Pass.

Because of the whirling sand and a heavy ground haze, McQuillin's headquarters could follow the action only by the sight of gun flashes. A tank duel seemed to be going on somewhere between Lessouda and Faid, but no one knew for sure.

Waters dissolved some of the uncertainty at 6:50. Lessouda, he reported, was being attacked by tanks and infantry. Other than that, he could tell little; visibility was still limited. He had sent his company of fifteen tanks out to block and delay the enemy.

The act was a futile gesture. Close to eight o'clock, thirty German tanks were making a wide turn around the northern part of Djebel Lessouda. They had swept away Waters's defenses around the base of the height.

McQuillin had already put the defensive plan into effect. At 7:30, he had told Hightower to "clear up the situation."

About that time enemy aircraft struck Sidi bou Zid and

blew the village apart. The air attack was the first of a series of raids that would harass the Americans all day long. Except for a flight of four planes that came into the area and left quickly around 10:30, not a single American aircraft would appear all morning despite repeated requests for support.

As the wind died down during the morning and visibility improved, reports from Lessouda became more detailed and ominous. By 8:30, Waters counted twenty enemy tanks passing along the western side of Lessouda and cutting the road between Lessouda and Sbeitla. Seven minutes later the number of hostile tanks west of Lessouda had risen to thirty-nine. When he ticked off eighty enemy vehicles behind Lessouda, about sixty of them tanks, he realized that his forces on the djebel were completely surrounded. Those on the hill were safe from armored attack — the panzers were unable to climb into the mountain mass — but he was concerned by a swarm of Arabs he saw moving into the area taken by the Germans. They knew the routes of access into the djebel.

He moved his command post — his half-track and jeep — up into the hill to escape detection. In doing so, he lost contact with his infantry. Then he phoned Hains at Sidi bou Zid. Don't worry about us, he said; we'll be all right. You get on with the war.

Now it would be up to McQuillin to drive the Germans back to Faid. If he could. If he couldn't, perhaps Waters could get his men off the hill and back to safety during the night. In that case, it was going to be a long day's wait. The time was barely 10 A.M.

* * * *

While Hightower's tanks rolled across the desert toward Lessouda, McQuillin telephoned for help. Since he had no reserves to establish blocking positions, could Ward send part of his reserves, at least the infantry battalion, down the road east of Sbeitla to bar a possible enemy advance from

SIDI BOU ZID

Lessouda? Otherwise, the enemy armor might roam unopposed into Sbeitla and beyond.

At the division command post in Sbeitla, Ward received only fragmentary reports. Though his first inclination was to depreciate the enemy effort as only a local attack, he acceded to the request. He directed Kern to take his battalion of infantry eleven miles east of Sbeitla to a road intersection. There, about seven miles west of Lessouda, Kern was to set up blocking positions and a rally point.

When Hightower saw the number of hostile tanks around Lessouda, he advised McQuillin that there were too many for anything but a delaying attack. On that despondent note, he courageously went into battle. By 10:15, his tanks were heavily engaged in a firefight about four miles northeast of Sidi bou Zid. He met the forces of Gerhardt, who had passed around the northern and western sides of Lessouda, and of Reimann, who had struck from Faid directly toward the djebel. His action was futile. His tanks were outnumbered and outgunned.

As Hightower battled in the northern portion of McQuillin's zone, the leading elements of the 21st Panzer Division came through the Maizila Pass in the south and split according to their plan. While Schutte drove directly toward Sidi bou Zid, aiming to thrust between Djebel Ksaira and Garet Hadid, Stenkhoff started a long westward flanking march designed to cut the road from Gafsa and to take Sidi bou Zid from the rear.

Ten minutes after these tanks were first reported coming through the pass, they captured a company of Ward's reconnaissance battalion.

On the heels of this news came word from Drake, who had counted eighty-three German tanks around Lessouda and who could see Hightower's force being crushed. He reported the artillery support beginning to crumble, the men leaving their positions and fleeing the battlefield in panic.

"You don't know what you're saying," McQuillin told him on the telephone. "They're only shifting positions."

"Shifting positions, hell," Drake said. "I know panic when I see it."

The reply was less than respectful, but McQuillin let it go. He told Drake to look the other way. German tanks were coming through the Maizila Pass and would soon threaten him.

Then he phoned Ward and asked whether division and corps reserves could be sent forward to relieve the pressure the Germans were exerting on Sidi bou Zid.

While Ward was checking with Fredendall, McQuillin learned that at least thirty German tanks, probably more, were coming toward his command post. They were still far away, more than ten miles, but they advanced inexorably, sweeping aside the light vehicles of the American reconnaissance battalion.

"Enemy tanks closing in and threatening both flanks and cut off Drake," McQuillin reported to Ward close to eleven o'clock. "Any orders?"

"Wait," came the reply.

Ward again checked with Fredendall, who said there was to be no change in orders. Everyone was to hold tight.

"Continue on your mission," Ward told McQuillin.

Schutte and Stenkhoff, hampered by poor visibility, moved slowly. It would be noontime before Schutte could get a sizable body of troops near Ksaira, two o'clock before Stenkhoff could terminate his wide flanking march to the west. But long before they brought their maneuvers to completion, they squeezed the defenses at Sidi bou Zid.

Shortly before the noon hour, Ward began to realize the scope and the strength of the enemy attack. Hightower had by then lost about half his tanks. Waters was surrounded on Lessouda. Drake was being encircled on Ksaira. And McQuillin's forces around Sidi bou Zid would soon have to move to avoid being trapped or overrun.

McQuillin had already sent most of his command post out of Sidi bou Zid, retaining only the command elements, a handful of officers and two or three enlisted clerks. Exactly at noon he informed his subordinate units that he would probably have to withdraw to Sbeitla.

Drake's executive officer went to the observation post where Drake was watching the battlefield through his field glasses. "General McQuillin is on the telephone," he said. "He is pulling out and you are to stay here."

Drake rushed to the field telephone. The line was dead.

At 12:08, a clerk in the CCA headquarters recorded a short notation: the enemy was right on top of the command post.

Stenkhoff's tanks, making the long flanking march to the Gafsa road, were coming within range of Sidi bou Zid, and they began to shell the village as they approached.

As American artillery units started to leave to avoid being overrun, dive bombers harassed them.

At 12:40, McQuillin told Ward that he no longer had effective communications with his subordinate units. Ten minutes later he took the last part of his command post out of Sidi bou Zid and traveled cross-country to get out of range of the German fires. At two o'clock, he set up a temporary command post about five miles west of the village. Almost immediately he received a message from Drake, who requested permission to withdraw his men from Djebel Ksaira. McQuillin transmitted the communication to Ward, who passed it on to Fredendall. Eight minutes later CCA received an answer: "Too early to give Drake permission to withdraw." McQuillin relayed the message to Drake: "Continue to hold your position."

* * * *

Drake had already acted to improve his situation. As soon as he lost telephonic communication with McQuillin, he decided to consolidate his forces. With Lessouda surrounded and CCA pulling out, with enemy tanks and trucks coming up from the south to outflank Djebel Ksaira and his own command post in the olive grove, he decided that Ksaira was now too far forward and far too exposed for a sound defense unless it was reinforced. To provide that additional strength he would move his headquarters and miscellaneous elements around him forward to the high ground of Garet Hadid, a defensible feature. Closer to the 3d Battalion on Ksaira, he too would be overlooking the road coming up from Maknassy. Together, the troops on Ksaira and Garet Hadid would be able to block further German advance along the road that came across the flat and open ground between the hills.

He would, he realized, be putting his head into a noose. But he could not abandon his troops on Ksaira. And he had been ordered to stay and fight.

Having collected a force of various troops — infantrymen, engineers, artillerymen, tankers, reconnaissance troopers — he ordered them forward. They occupied Garet Hadid just as the Germans coming up from the south appeared within rifle range. At the same time, he received McQuillin's message to hold his position.

He acknowledged receipt, then counted his troops. He discovered that he had 10 officers of the regimental headquarters, 3 officers and 11 men of the medical detachment, a single officer and 53 men of an attached platoon of engineers, 39 members of the regimental band, 7 officers and 201 men of Company E, 168th Infantry, an officer and 40 machine gunners and mortarmen of Company H, and 4 officers and 89 men of the attached Cannon Company of the 39th Infantry. He gathered in about 150 engineers who were guarding a mine field across the Maknassy road and 40 men of the 1st Armored Division reconnaissance battalion. Altogether, he had about 650 men on Garet Hadid; across the road several miles to the east, the 3d Battalion on Ksaira numbered close to 1,000 troops.

With this substantial strength, he could hold out, he was sure, for quite a while. But not without help. And ultimately, higher commanders had to know without any doubt that he would need a counterattack launched from the rear to make possible an evacuation from Ksaira and Hadid.

Having lost confidence in McQuillin, Drake wrote a message to Ward. On British-issue toilet tissue, the only paper he had, he wrote hastily and under some stress: "Enemy surrounds 2d Battalion [168th Infantry] located on Mt. Lessouda since 0730 this morning. Forty tanks known to be around them. Shelled, divebombed, and tank attack. All artillery pulled out at 1300 [1 P.M.], still trying to locate them. McQuillin's headquarters pulled out at 1100 [eleven o'clock] to southwest, did not notify except by message. Talked to McQuillin once by radio and he said help had been requested. Germans have absolute superiority, ground and air. Have stopped retreating tank destroyer unit and am attempting to hold my command post position. Unless help from air and armor comes immediately, infantry will lose immeasurably."

He gave the message to a young lieutenant named Marvin E. Williams and told him to take it to Ward's headquarters. Feeling like an Indian scout carrying a message from Custer, Williams slipped off the hill and started walking cross-country toward Sbeitla.

* * * *

In the midst of the desert west of Sidi bou Zid, McQuillin was unable to keep his temporary command post open for more than half an hour. When dive bombers and long-range tank fire blasted and hurt a nearby battalion of infantry and when Stenkhoff's tanks eluded American reconnaissance elements on the south flank and started menacingly toward Sidi bou Zid, he had to move again to escape destruction.

Together with a mass of withdrawing units, including the remnants of Hightower's tank force, the CCA command post moved northwest across the desert, with long-range enemy tank and artillery fire, plus the inevitable dive bombers, harassing and hurrying the vehicles and foot soldiers. There was considerable disorganization, though no great congestion, as artillery pieces, tank destroyers, engineer trucks, tanks, and infantry moved in open formation across the flat ground.

Hains, McQuillin's second in command, had been begging division headquarters all morning long for permission to get the forces under Waters and Drake off the hills of Lessouda and Ksaira. Distraught and despairing, his concern mixed with rage, he drove to the division command post that afternoon and saw Ward. Choked with emotion, almost in tears, he reiterated the need to get the troops off the heights. How could they be left there to perish?

Ward tried to calm him. The forces had to remain on the hills, he said, because that was the order from higher headquarters. But a counterattack was already being planned for the next day to restore the situation and regain contact with the isolated elements.

Hains was not altogether reassured. Too much time had already passed. What had happened to the military tradition that one never abandoned one's companions in distress?

Kern's battalion of infantry, supported by a company of light tanks, took positions at the designated intersection on the main road, eleven miles east of Sbeitla and seven miles northwest of Sidi bou Zid. The place would soon become known as Kern's Crossroads.

Passing through Kern's troops, McQuillin re-established his command post just east of Sbeitla at 5 P.M. and began at once to reassemble and reorganize the units that had escaped the German pincers.

The initial estimates of losses were staggering: fifty-two officers and 1,536 men were unaccounted for. Of these, more than five hundred were missing from CCA alone. Later, as men straggled in, the final casualties for February 14 were set at six men killed, twenty-two wounded, and 134 missing, a high enough total.

Just before nightfall, young Williams reached Ward's headquarters and delivered Drake's message. Ward reassured him that plans were being prepared for a counterattack to get the troops off the djebels.

At about the same time, the German forces on the extreme flanks, Gerhardt's, which had come around Lessouda, and Stenkhoff's which had come up the Gafsa road, made contact just west of Sidi bou Zid. They sealed off the troops located on Lessouda, Ksaira, and Garet Hadid.

The extent of the German victory was plain to see. Between Faid and Kern's Crossroads, on the plain of Sbeitla, forty-four tanks, fifty-nine half-tracks, twenty-six artillery pieces, and at least twenty-two trucks lay abandoned, wrecked, or burning.

* * * *

Life had been good for Sergeant Clarence W. Coley and the other men who were bivouacked in a cactus patch near Sidi bou Zid. For a week there was not much for Coley to do. Eat, sleep, hope for mail, and keep the radios in Hightower's command tank in operating shape.

Shortly after daybreak of what Coley later called "that fatal morning" of February 14, he crawled out of his foxhole and, together with the other crew members, started the daily routine inspection of equipment — motor, guns, and radios. Coley climbed into the turret and made sure that the radio there was working. In the assistant driver's seat, he checked out the other one. The driver, Clark, had barely started the engine, when Hightower unexpectedly appeared, Coley noted, "with brief case in hand." Getting into the turret, he told Clark to take off for Sidi bou Zid and the tent where McQuillin had set up the CCA headquarters.

While Hightower conferred at the command post, Coley and the others wondered what was happening. There was a faint rumble of what sounded like thunder in the distance, but it hardly seemed serious. They noticed the two companies under Hightower's command moving out toward Lessouda, and about that time, from the radio traffic, Coley learned that the Germans had attacked.

Hightower soon emerged from the tent, mounted the tank, and told Clark to follow the companies heading toward Lessouda. Coley was too busy with his radio to see very much, but he sensed that the battalion was running into what he later called "blistering fire from many guns."

He heard Hightower tell Clark to back the tank in zigzags, keeping the front, where the armor was thickest, facing the enemy until he reached a place where he could "turn fast and get going."

Moving in reverse was an intolerably slow process, not only to Coley but also to two soldiers who had survived the destruction of their tank and had leaped aboard the deck of Hightower's vehicle. The passengers dismounted and made better time on foot.

After Clark turned the tank around, Hightower told him to make for Sidi bou Zid. There they stopped again, and Hightower went into a building.

It was then about noon. They had had no breakfast that morning, so Coley and Clark and the other two men, Agee and Bayer, warmed up some C rations and ate. They felt played out, and the food was tasteless.

When Hightower returned, everyone got in and Clark moved the tank out into the desert. Coley had no idea where they were going. He had the impression that Hightower's command had been all but wiped out.

The afternoon turned hot, and the whole area was smoky. Other vehicles were driving in the same general direction, half-tracks, jeeps, motorcycles, and trucks spread out over the

9.

Major General Lloyd R. Fredendall (left), commander of the II Corps, who "moved vigorously, spoke loudly, and had a firm opinion on every subject." *U.S. Army Photograph*

Major General Orlando Ward (below), "something of the ascetic and the intellectual," commander of the 1st Armored Division. *U.S. Army Photograph*

10. Sbeitla, "on a remote, windswept, sun-parched plain . . . the crumbling ruins of a Roman city." *U.S. Army Photograph*

plain. Occasionally, a German plane roared over, dropping bombs or strafing the mass movement. Sometimes a stray shell fired at long range dropped nearby.

A radio message from CCA headquarters alerted Coley to "a bunch of German tanks" coming up from the south and "shooting up the column." Coley wrote the comunication on a message blank and passed it up into the turret to Hightower.

Hightower tried to make radio contact with some of his tanks up ahead and had no luck. So he decided to take on the enemy alone.

Rotating the turret until the 75-mm. cannon "was pointing over the left rear fender at the German tanks," Hightower told Clark to halt. Bayer, the gunner, started firing. Agee, the loader, was busy passing up the shells. Clark, the driver, "was craning his neck trying to see the action."

The tank received several hits. They were glancing blows. Coley felt the shock each time a projectile bounced off. But he paid little attention to the nearness of death. It was as though all this was happening to someone else.

When the rounds began to run out in the turret racks, Coley took off his headphones. He removed the back of his assistant driver's seat and placed it up front under the .30-caliber machine gun. Sitting backward on his seat, with his feet on the escape hatch, he began to pull reserve shells from the racks underneath the turret and to pass them over to Agee, the loader. Before this, when he had had to take ammunition from those racks, he had done so gingerly, for he had been afraid of hurting his fingers. Now "those rounds came out easy." His fingers were the least of his worries. But he was rather surprised that he had no sensation of fright. As long as he was busy he had no time to think.

They had only about three shells left, lying on the turret floor, when their luck ran out. A round became stuck in the gun, and it would neither go in nor come out.

F

Hightower told Clark to move on out. Coley straightened up, turned around on his seat, and put on his headphones.

About that time, an enemy shell penetrated the tank. The projectile came in the left side, passed through the gas tank, ricocheted with a terrifying clatter around the inside of the tank without hitting anyone, and wound up on the escape hatch just behind Coley's seat, the place where, thirty seconds earlier, he had been bent over pulling ammunition from the racks.

Sitting transfixed with surprise, petrified, his emotions numb, Coley watched the shell standing on end, spinning like a top, with fire flying out of the upper part.

He heard Hightower say, "Let's get the hell out of here." And he realized that the inside of the tank was on fire.

Everyone piled out, everyone but Coley.

Coley was stuck. Three times he tried to raise his escape hatch, and three times he failed.

He finally gave up.

Slithering across the transmission and into the driver's seat like a snake, he wriggled up through the driver's hatch and dived headfirst out of the burning vehicle.

Coley hit the ground on his shoulders. He rolled over before getting to his feet. He noticed that the tank tracks were also burning.

Taking off like a shot to get away from the tank, he ran as fast as he could. While he was running, he heard an explosion. He looked back. The tank had blown up, and flames were shooting into the sky.

After Hightower made sure that his men were all right, he instructed them to scatter out a little and move across the desert on foot.

Coley was wearing a tank helmet, a pair of coveralls, and a combat jacket that had "a busted zipper." He realized that he had forgotten his pistol that morning; it was lying in his foxhole. He almost felt like laughing. He had been in combat without a weapon.

In half an hour or so, after walking and running, the crew came across two half-tracks. One was disabled. A soldier had a nasty wound in his side, but someone had treated him with sulfa powder and put on a bandage, and he seemed to be all right.

Hightower suggested that everyone pile into the single working half-track and take off. After stripping the broken-down track of its machine guns and transferring the crew's personal belongings to the other vehicle, everybody climbed aboard and started off.

They reached Kern's Crossroads about dusk and passed through the infantry guarding the road.

That night Coley learned that Hightower and his crew, before losing their own tank, had knocked out at least four panzers. He wished he could have seen at least one of the others go up in flames.

They had done fine. Great. But of Hightower's original complement of fifty-one tanks, four had been deadlined in Sidi bou Zid for repairs before the attack and were now demolished and abandoned, while forty had been destroyed in action. Hightower's battalion now consisted of a total of seven serviceable tanks.

16

McQuillin tried to pick up the pieces. At six o'clock on Sunday evening, February 14, he instructed all units to recover during the hours of darkness as many vehicles as possible from the battle area. The order was virtually meaningless. The troops were too battered, exhausted, and despondent to venture into no man's land.

An exception was Lieutenant Colonel Charles P. Summerall, Jr., an artillery battalion commander, who took his men out to the desert, where they picked up abandoned guns, trucks, and ambulances. On the following morning his battalion, which had been destroyed, would have eight instead of twenty-four guns, but these would be in firing positions bolstering Kern's force at the crossroads.

Though the Americans had every expectation that the Germans would press their advantage, Ziegler stayed at Sidi bou Zid. Convinced that he had more than fulfilled his mission, unaware of how complete his victory was, and figuring that the Americans would counterattack on the following day to relieve the troops on Lessouda and Ksaira, he decided to lie in wait for the rescue forces.

When Rommel learned of Ziegler's success, he urged Arnim to keep up the pressure and go on to Sbeitla. Push during the night, he suggested, keep the enemy on the run; don't forget, he said, "tactical successes must be ruthlessly exploited."

Arnim, who preferred to press farther north against Fondouk and Pichon and who was thinking of recovering the 10th Panzer Division, approved Ziegler's caution.

Ward, who was preparing to counterattack on the follow

ing day, had finally prevailed upon Fredendall to recognize the danger. In grudging acquiescence to what he at first considered to be Ward's excessive concern, Fredendall dispatched some artillery and tank destroyers from Feriana to Sbeitla. Ward then asked for Robinett's CCB. With the passes of Fondouk and Pichon quiet, he began to suspect that the Germans had massed the bulk of their strength at Faid. What, then, was to be feared in the north? Fredendall supported Ward's request.

Anderson was sure that the action was only a diversion. As evidence for his belief, he pointed to the fact that the 10th Panzer Division had not appeared at Sidi bou Zid.

His information was, of course, erroneous. Had the 10th Panzer Division been identified at Lessouda, he would have realized at once that the Germans had no substantial forces available for an attack farther north. The Battle of Kasserine might have been over before really getting started.

But he was not altogether deaf to the American appeal, and he instructed Robinett to send one of his tank battalions to Sbeitla.

Lieutenant Colonel James D. Alger's battalion took to the road and arrived in Sbeitla on Sunday evening. But he would hardly augment Ward's forces. His tanks would only replace Hightower's destroyed battalion.

Those in the Sidi bou Zid area who knew the degree of the German strength and the extent of the American losses felt that all of CCB was needed at Sbeitla. Since Anderson refused to release the whole combat command, Fredendall, now alive to the full force of the German threat, ordered Lieutenant Colonel Ben Crosby to move his battalion of tanks from the Thelepte airfields to Sbeitla during the night.

As reports of the American casualties in men and materiel filtered back to Anderson, he became concerned over Gafsa. Though everything was calm in that area, he believed it might be time to evacuate the town. Phoning Eisenhower, he obtained permission to abandon Gafsa to make possible a better concentration of the Allied forces in the south. Eisenhower asked that the withdrawal be gradual, that it take place, if possible, over two successive nights. Later, when the situation became more stable, he suggested, perhaps the forces pulled out might be combined with the mixed force built around Stark's infantry at Feriana for a counterattack to regain the town.

Passing on the order, Anderson told Fredendall to move the French troops out of Gafsa that night, the Americans on the following night.

Fredendall objected because the absence of the French would make the remaining Americans too weak to resist a German attack. Why not have all the forces retire at once?

Anderson turned him down, then had his chief of staff transmit a formal order that was characterized by a peculiar wordiness and a precious niceness: "Based on information regarding information on your front given verbally by you to him this afternoon and in conformity with his previous decision not to risk heavy loss in attempt to retain Gafsa, the army commander has decided that the first steps to evacuate Gafsa will be begun during night 14/15 February, in accordance with your prearranged plan. Although enemy concentrations are taking place in evident preparation for an assault on Gafsa, it is not believed likely that such assault will take place for at least another 36 hours. There is therefore time to make an orderly withdrawal, removing all stores and supplies, placing booby traps, etc., under cover of vigorous patrolling and rearguard action which will continue until at least night 15/16 and longer if enemy does not press. As regards action in Sidi bou Zid area, concentrate tomorrow on clearing up situation there and destroying enemy. Thereafter collect strong mobile force in Sbeitla area ready for action in any direction. . . . Army commander deeply regrets losses suffered by CCA, but he congratulates them on their fine fight, is confident they will decisively defeat the enemy tomorrow, and is sure the enemy must have suffered losses at least as heavy as their own."

It started to rain that night as engineers laid mines on roads entering Gafsa, demolished a railroad bridge, and helped destroy supply dumps. The French troops marched out of the town, followed by most of the civilians and a miscellany of American supply and service units. The narrow road leading to Feriana, forty miles away, soon became choked with vehicles of all sorts, tanks, trucks, jeeps, horse-drawn carts, guns; with animals, camels, goats, jackasses, sheep; and with Arab and French families, including crying children; all making the exodus in blackout conditions that intensified a widespread expectation of even more dolorous calamities to come.

Around midnight, as the mass movement produced increasing congestion and confusion, approval came for the entire withdrawal to be completed that night. The Americans then departed hastily, an ordnance detachment bringing up the rear to pull tanks, carts, and vehicles out of ditches.

As the vanguard of the withdrawing tide washed into Feriana, the troops manning rear-area installations became nervous. Fear had already spread to nearby Thelepte and its two airfields, for a Service Squadron preparing a forward airstrip at Sbeitla had stopped work during the German attack on Sidi bou Zid and had returned to Thelepte, taking most of their equipment and supplies, destroying what they could not carry, and bringing rumors of disaster that inflamed the fires of panic. The retirement from Gafsa seemed to bear out the wild stories of catastrophe, and some troops who anticipated a continuing pullback to Tebessa began to destroy stockpiles of materiel in the Feriana-Thelepte area.

The withdrawal from Gafsa strengthened Fredendall's right flank, but the loss of Sidi bou Zid prompted Anderson to consider the possible loss of Sbeitla. If Sbeitla fell, the Sbiba Gap, twenty miles to the northwest, would be endangered.

Looking ahead to this contingency, he told Koeltz to cover the Sbiba Pass not only with French troops but also with the 34th U.S. Division.

Koeltz was disgusted. This meant, he felt, that Anderson was ready to abandon Sbeitla and move back to Kasserine without a struggle.

If he had known that an American cannon company at Oran had been ordered to start that day for Kasserine, he would have been virtually certain that his intuitive feeling was correct. The cannon company would need several days to get to Kasserine, but that night Fredendall sent some engineers to the Kasserine Pass to start building defensive works thirty miles west of Kern's Crossroads.

In contrast with these preparations for the worst, Ward had no thought of withdrawal. He exuded confidence. He was sure he could re-establish the situation at Sidi bou Zid by a counterattack in the morning.

17

FOR HIS counterattack, Ward called upon Stack, who was to move his troops south from Fondouk to Kern's Crossroads, pick up Alger's tank battalion, push through Sidi bou Zid to help Drake's men get off Ksaira and Garet Hadid, then assist Waters in bringing his forces back from Lessouda.

The whole thing seemed relatively simple. With a sizable force of infantry, tanks, artillery, tank destroyers, and engineers, Stack seemed far stronger than the Germans, who probably had no more than forty tanks around Lessouda and perhaps another fifteen or twenty near Ksaira.

The error was serious. Ward's confidence and Anderson's preoccupation with the northern sector had undermined reality. There were close to one hundred enemy tanks at Sidi bou Zid.

While Stack marched his command over a fairly direct road to Kern's Crossroads, Hains and Hightower were briefing Alger, who had yet to lead his battalion in combat. From the top of a hill, they showed him the terrain, pointed out the objectives and routes of approach, and described the appearance and performance of German armor.

Gentleman Jim Alger, whose easygoing air belied his deep sense of purpose, was quietly confident. He was entering battle under ideal conditions. The sun was shining. Visibility was excellent. The enemy was fixed. His troops would do all right.

"Seek the enemy armor and destroy it," Hains said.

Alger was sure he would do just that.

As Stack was readying his forces around ten o'clock on

Monday morning, February 15, a flight of German bombers struck his assault troops. The losses were slight, but the confusion was enormous. It took him two hours to reorganize his units.

The attack started at 12:40 in great precision. Alger's tank battalion was in the lead, his three tank companies moving in parallel columns. On each flank, flaring out toward the rear, was a company of tank destroyers, half-tracks mounting 75-mm. guns. Behind the tank battalion, screened by the tank destroyers on the flanks, came two batteries of self-propelled artillery, side by side. Finally, the infantry, riding in trucks and half-tracks, together with several antiaircraft weapons.

From a height near Kern's Crossroads, Stack had a splendid view of the battlefield. He could see for miles through the clear, dry atmosphere. There was considerable mirage, and the dips and folds of the brown-gray plain undulated like the ocean, the monotonous landscape relieved and marked by occasional patches of dark cactus, by the geometric patterns of orchards and cultivated fields, and by clusters of low white buildings. Through field glasses, Sidi bou Zid, thirteen miles to the southeast, was a tiny spot of dark-hued evergreens and cream-colored houses highlighted against the backdrop furnished by the hazy purple slopes of Djebel Ksaira. To the left, rising majestically from the desert, was Djebel Lessouda, tied to Kern's Crossroads by the straight ribbon of the Sbeitla road.

The most beautiful sight was the formation of Stack's assault elements crossing the plain, the vehicles maintaining proper distances as though on parade, looking for all the world, despite the anachronism, like a print illustrating Jomini's linear tactics.

The careful spacing would soon be disturbed, the purposeful movement arrested.

Several steep-sided wadis creased the desert ahead of the troops. Cutting huge irregular ditches generally north and south across the plain, the dry streambeds forced Alger's tanks to seek the few places where the gullies could be crossed. At the first great wadi, they discovered several paths across, and the rest of the command converged toward them, crawled into the depression and slowly out, fanning into a skirmish line as they proceeded.

As the initial vehicles were crossing, a dozen German dive bombers pounced on the columns. The planes forced the tanks to take the evasive action of ships wheeling and turning in a slow-motion minuet.

When enemy shells came in from the northern flank, half a dozen tanks detached themselves from the main body, lumbered toward the guns, and knocked out four cannons.

While the tanks were crossing the second large wadi, another flight of dive bombers jumped them. The planes were wide of their mark, but the columns slowed.

Leaving a tank company in reserve, Alger pushed his two other companies forward. As the leading elements nosed into the third gully, about 3:15 P.M., German artillery fire came in from Sidi bou Zid.

Stack ordered his own artillery to shell the German guns and instructed his infantry to advance and help clean out the village.

As the artillerymen started to get their howitzers into position, about fifteen panzers on the far side of Sidi bou Zid came out of hiding and rolled toward Alger, who led a company against them.

It took the opposing tanks almost an hour to maneuver into range. Then a duel started as the opponents stabbed each other with shells emitting orange bursts of flame.

Less than ten minutes later, observers on the hill near Kern's Crossroads counted fourteen German tanks crawling from concealment behind Djebel Lessouda and moving westward along the main road to strike Alger's left flank. Alerted to the danger by radio, he called his reserve company up and hurried back himself to direct the action.

The infantrymen were by this time coming forward. As

their vehicles passed through the artillery positions, they found themselves under German planes, which destroyed two half-tracks, killed at least three men, and threw the units into confusion.

From Stack's vantage point, the development of the action was now clear. His forces were about to be trapped.

Ziegler had planned his defensive action with perception. While German planes had delayed and disarranged the American formation, he had prepared an ambush. Sending Stenkhoff's tanks from the south and Gerhardt's from the north to pin down Alger's flanks, he struck hard in the center.

At 4:45, with Ziegler's strength openly arrayed on the plain, Stack informed Ward that he doubted he could reach Djebel Ksaira before sundown.

A few minutes later, he radioed Alger to ask how he was doing.

"Still pretty busy," came Alger's smooth reply.

That was the last communication from his tank. Efforts to re-establish contact were in vain. His radio was silent. They would not know until much later that his tank had been struck and destroyed, his radio operator killed, and the other members of the crew, along with Alger himself, captured.

To those who were watching from the hill, the diorama was now covered by the dust and smoke of distant shells that boomed in muffled grief, while the radios nearby crackled with static and hoarse voices.

By five o'clock, Stack could foresee the ultimate result. He ordered his infantry to hold up — there was no point getting the unprotected riflemen involved in the struggle between the tanks.

Thirty minutes later, as the American tanks were trying desperately to pull back out of the German envelopment, the artillery and infantry came under the threat of encirclement.

At six o'clock, Stack ordered all the troops to disengage and return to Kern's Crossroads.

The infantry emerged relatively unscathed. So did the artillery, which was briefly cut off at dusk but managed to get out after dark.

In contrast, Alger's tank battalion was annihilated. Only four tanks got out, along with several crews who escaped from their disabled and wrecked vehicles and walked across the desert to safety. In its initial action, the battalion lost fifteen officers and 298 enlisted men, all missing, and half a hundred tanks.

For the second successive day, American armor had been driven from the field. Yet, as fires from Alger's burning tanks blazed on the plain during the night, the commanders in the area were slow to realize that another battalion had been knocked out, the second one in as many days. "We might have walloped them," Ward reported to Fredendall, "or they might have walloped us."

The truth soon became obvious. Patrols dispatched along the road toward Lessouda and cross-country toward Sidi bou Zid found no survivors.

In two days, the 1st Armored Division had lost ninety-eight tanks, fifty-seven half-tracks, and twenty-nine artillery pieces, all destroyed or captured.

Satisfied with his triumph, Ziegler withdrew at the end of the afternoon to Sidi bou Zid. He organized strong defensive positions along a north-south line facing the Americans at Kern's Crossroads a dozen miles away.

Behind him, the troops on Lessouda were preparing to break out. Just before darkness of that day, Monday, the 15th, pilots had dropped messages instructing them to try to get back to Kern's Crossroads during the night.

Around 5:45 A.M., just before daybreak on Tuesday, the 16th, a group of 231 Americans came out of the darkness, bringing some German prisoners with them, but leaving their vehicles and equipment on the djebel. Others got out in small groups to the north and south of the crossroads.

There was no word from Waters, and no one knew what had happened to him.

18

WATERS AND three companions — his staff officer, jeep driver, and half-track driver — had spent much of the morning of the first day of battle, Sunday, February 14, in a place of concealment on the south slope of Djebel Lessouda. When he saw the defeat inflicted on Hightower's tanks, he decided he would have to take his men out during the night and get back to Sidi bou Zid. Writing a note to inform the infantry battalion commander, he gave it to his jeep driver and told him to deliver it.

The man returned to Waters an hour later. He had hardly left when he was struck by a bullet. With a gaping hole in his chest, bleeding badly, he apologized for not having succeeded. His regret was deepened by his belief that an American on the hill had shot him by mistake.

Waters made a litter out of his bedding roll and gave the soldier a morphine injection. There was nothing else he could do except to try to make him comfortable.

Late in the afternoon, when the battle subsided, Waters decided to move and disperse his small group, for several Arabs seemed to have noticed his location. Since it seemed best not to disturb the wounded man, Waters left him with the jeep, had the other soldier drive the half-track into another wadi about one hundred yards away, and told his staff officer to find another hiding place nearby so that the capture of one would not necessarily mean the seizure of both.

Shortly afterward, Waters noted German patrols of half a dozen men or so moving around below him. Remembering the radio in his half-track, he sent the driver to take the tubes out and hide them.

Half an hour passed. Then Waters heard footsteps coming up the wadi toward him. Sure it was the driver returning, he rose to motion him to the hiding place. He found himself facing seven German soldiers and two Arabs no more than ten yards away.

Startled by the sight of the American, one of the Germans involuntarily squeezed the trigger of his machine pistol. A burst ripped out, barely missing Waters.

The Germans marched him about half a mile to what appeared to be a mobile command post. Several officers who spoke English were lounging around a captured American half-track and listening to music on the radio. They were elated, and they talked in high spirits about winning the battle, tomorrow the war.

Waters asked about his wounded driver.

He was dead, a German told him. Arabs had stripped him of all his clothing.

Putting Waters into a motorcycle sidecar, with a guard on the back, the Germans drove him through the Faid Pass to a prisoner of war cage, the start of a long journey that would take him through Sfax, Sousse, and Tunis to Italy, then eventually to prisoner of war camps in Poland and in Germany.

As he was going through the Faid Pass, he thought of the young major on Lessouda. Command had now devolved upon him. Was he sufficiently able to get the troops out safely?

*　*　*　*

On Lessouda, Major Robert R. Moore commanded the thirty-four officers and 870 men who made up the 2d Battalion, 168th Infantry. He was somewhat unsure of himself because he had been in command less than two weeks, having taken over when the former battalion commander was wounded at Sened.

Moore and his troops had been on Garet Hadid for several days, until Friday, February 12. Then, while Company E and a platoon of heavy machine guns of Company H remained under Drake, he took the rest of the battalion — twenty-six officers and 620 men — to Lessouda to serve under Waters.

Not knowing Waters, he was rather reluctant to leave Drake. He had confidence in Drake, who was fearless, aggressive, and somewhat awesome. At a conference of unit commanders on Garet Hadid, Drake had said crisply that he wanted no soldier leaving his position under enemy fire; any officer who saw a soldier quit his position was to order him back, and if the soldier disobeyed, he was to be shot at once. He wanted his officers to teach their men to hate the enemy and kill them at every opportunity. "I will notify you," he said, "when I want prisoners taken."

Waters was different, courtly, but efficient in a quiet way, and he was impressive as he assigned defensive sectors to Moore's two rifle companies and suggested where the heavy weapons might be placed. The size of the mountain made it necessary to station small groups at wide intervals, and Waters pointed out the likely avenues of enemy approach and gave his opinion on the best methods of closing them off. He said simply that General Ward expected the positions to be held at all costs.

On Saturday evening, February 13, Waters told him to be ready for an enemy attack that was coming at daybreak. He was to stay in position and hold the hill.

Awakened on the morning of February 14 by howitzers shelling Lessouda, Moore saw tanks moving from the Faid Pass. Were they friend or foe? Was this the expected attack?

He telephoned Waters and got no answer.

Additional tanks, some half-tracks and assault guns, and truckborne infantry came from the east and overran artillery positions on the plain.

What was happening? Why was there no word from Waters?

At 7 A.M., a captain named Dotson reported to Moore. He commanded a reconnaissance group, and he said that the enemy attack had definitely started. His troops had been driven back into the djebel. Could he be of assistance?

Yes, he could. He was to set up his two 75-mm. guns to cover a mine field, put a light machine gun to block a path up the hillside, and place his single light tank to bar another approach.

Two hours later, still uncertain whether all the tanks and infantry and assault guns on the plain around Lessouda were German, Moore withheld his battalion's fire. His instructions were to hold the djebel, and no one was threatening his positions.

Sparks, the Company H commander, phoned to tell him that additional vehicles had come out of the Faid Pass and were heading toward Lessouda. Could he open fire with his mortars?

Not yet, Moore said. Hold fire until the column was positively identified.

Sparks phoned back in a little while. The troops were fifteen hundred yards away, and there could be no doubt. They were enemy.

OK, Moore said.

As he watched, Sparks fired eighty-five rounds with devastating effect. The shells caught infantrymen in open carriers and trucks before they could disperse, damaged at least seven vehicles, and set four ablaze.

In midmorning Apgar reported four small cars and a motorcycle approaching a ravine that led directly to his Company G positions on the top of Lessouda.

Be certain, Moore said, that they were enemy before opening fire.

Fifteen minutes later Apgar had positive identification. They fell easy victim to his company, which destroyed all the vehicles and took eight prisoners — two officers and six non-coms — all wounded. Brought to the battalion aid station, they said they comprised an artillery observation post party. Because no fire had come from Lessouda, they had supposed that the djebel was already in German hands.

Reynolds of Company F discovered enemy troops trying to infiltrate the mountain mass by climbing up the eroded ditches and ravines.

Turn them back, Moore ordered.

He complied.

Where was Waters? What was happening?

In midafternoon Moore began to suspect that Lessouda was isolated and that he was the senior officer on the hill. It was the latter suspicion, he found, that disturbed him. With Waters gone, killed or captured, and the command devolving upon him, what was he to do?

Stifling a momentary surge of panic, he tried to make contact by radio with Djebel Ksaira. Perhaps Drake would tell him what to do. He was unable to get through.

Cut off from the outside world, Moore resolved to do his duty to the best of his ability and act on the assumption that someone was making plans to rescue him.

Upon the approach of nightfall, he alerted Apgar, Reynolds, and Sparks to be ready to repel enemy infiltrators during the hours of darkness. To his surprise, the night passed quietly.

All day long on February 15, enemy artillery shelled Lessouda in a steady barrage.

Around ten o'clock that morning, an American medical aid man came to Moore's tent and said that one of the captured German officers wanted to speak with him. He went to the aid station. The German said that Lessouda was surrounded and would soon be captured. He suggested surrender to avoid useless bloodshed. Without answering, Moore returned to his command post.

A piece of good luck came that afternoon. Dotson made radio contact with CCA and learned that help was on the way. A group of tanks approaching from the northwest was obviously the promised assistance. But German tanks moved out to meet them, and after a two-hour battle the Americans pulled back.

What now?

A plane that flew low over Lessouda at dusk and dropped a message provided the answer: "Tank destroyers and infantry will occupy positions at 2200 [10 P.M.] tonight to cover your withdrawal. You are to withdraw to position . . . [designated] where guides will meet you. Bring everything you can. Signed Ward."

Moore checked his map. The designated location was nine miles away.

Before doing anything, he asked Dotson to verify the communication by radio. Confirmation soon arrived.

After making his plans, Moore called the company commanders together and gave his instructions. The withdrawal would start at 10 P.M. from the southwest edge of Lessouda. The route would be westward and cross-country about a mile north of and paralleling the Sbeitla road. He wanted the men to walk in two single files at least thirty yards apart, with an interval of at least a yard between each man in column. They were to make no effort to sneak through the German positions but to march boldly, though quietly, in an attempt to bluff their way through before the Germans discovered who they were. If they encountered enemy troops, the men were to hold their fire and disperse. They were then to proceed individually and in small groups of twos and threes westward to the rendezvous. All equipment left behind was to be destroyed, the weapons disassembled and vital parts buried, the vehicles disabled. All the prisoners, including litter cases and walking wounded, were to be taken. They were to be told that if they made the slightest outcry, they would be bayoneted. At the first sign of a false move, they were to be killed without pity.

With Moore at the head of the columns, the movement

got under way. Just beyond the edge of the djebel, he saw a German artillery piece. The crew members were in foxholes around the gun, and one of them emerged and came over to him. He said something in German. Moore remained silent. The German soldier looked back at the troops marching behind Moore. After watching for a few moments, he scratched his head and returned to his foxhole.

Moore had walked about a mile when he heard some people talking off to his left in a clump of trees. This, he was sure, was the covering force that Ward had promised to send out. He told Reynolds to keep the men marching while he went over to make contact.

As he walked toward the trees, he saw someone coming toward him on foot. About thirty yards away, this person called out in German.

Moore said nothing and went back to the head of the columns.

The German called again.

Moore made no answer.

For a moment there was a hush, a quiet deepened by the trudging steps of the marching men. Then came the din of machine-gun fire. "Scatter," Moore shouted. "Run like hell."

As the men broke, bullets flew over their heads. Behind them, several automatic weapons on the western slope of Lessouda began to fire. The night erupted into a pandemonium of yells and shots accompanied by the eerie light of flares and tracers.

Moore found himself running as hard as he could. When he was out of breath, he flung himself on the ground.

After a while he rolled over. He noticed that German mortars had joined the machine guns firing on the columns.

Gradually the noise died down. He cautiously got to his feet. Several soldiers joined him. Together they walked across the desert.

Around 5 A.M. of Tuesday, February 16, Moore and the

few men with him reached Kern's Crossroads and passed through the American line into safety.

Checking his people, he discovered that thirty-two members of Company F had reported. Additional soldiers came trickling in. Half an hour later Sparks walked down the road, leading most of his Company H. When the Germans had opened fire, he realized that they were as bewildered as the Americans. He had immediately turned south and away from the confusion. He had reached the Sbeitla road without incident, and then it was an easy march westward to the crossroad.

While trucks transported the men to the rear, Moore waited for others to come out of the desert. The last group, a sizable number, walked in around 10 A.M. It was Apgar with much of his Company G.

Then Moore accepted a ride to a cactus patch near Sbeitla, where his battalion had been placed. His supply officer had a kitchen unit serving hot meals and was trying to get blankets and overcoats for the men who had come back.

A surprisingly large part, nearly half, of the battalion had gotten out, almost three hundred men. For an inexperienced officer who had been somewhat shaky at the start, Moore had not done badly at all. He had learned much from Drake and Waters. But far more important, he had overcome his hesitation, conquered his fears, and proved his mettle.

That evening, trucks carried Moore and his troops to a bivouac area beyond the Kasserine Pass, where they bedded down for the night. On the next day, they went to Thala and bivouacked in a thick forest. The regimental trains and what remained of the Service Company joined. Then all moved to Tebessa and passed into reserve.

On the following morning, Lieutenant Colonel Gerald C. Line, the regimental executive officer, reported in. He had been on Djebel Ksaira. So far as he knew, he told Moore, he was the only one of Drake's headquarters to get out alive.

All the others had been killed or captured. The regimental antitank company was gone. So was the regimental band. The attached units also, cannon company and God alone knew how many engineers, medics, and others.

And his own Company E? Moore asked. How about Company E and the platoon of heavy machine guns he had left on Garet Hadid when he had moved to Lessouda a lifetime ago? Where were they?

They were gone too.

Part IV

SBEITLA

19

As HAD BEEN planned at the Casablanca Conference in January, Alexander arrived in Algiers on February 15. He planned to spend several days becoming acquainted with the conditions in Tunisia before taking command of the ground forces — Montgomery's Eighth Army, which was crossing the southern frontier from Libya, and Anderson's First Army.

After meeting with Eisenhower, Alexander flew to Anderson's headquarters to start an inspection tour of the front. He found all eyes on the disintegrating situation in the south. The second day of combat around Sidi bou Zid contrasted sharply with the quiet elsewhere. If the German attack was more than a diversion, the entire southern flank might be smashed. To forestall that eventuality. would it be wiser to fight on the Western Dorsale. even though this meant a withdrawal, which always disheartened troops?

Anderson believed so, and this he told Eisenhower. The "very exposed southern flank," he said, threatened the whole Allied force. "I feel therefore that it is wise to consider in good time whether we should not voluntarily withdraw to the main ridge of the . . . [Western] Dorsale," starting first in the Pichon and Fondouk areas. An early withdrawal to keep the Allied forces intact was preferable to a costly effort in defense of the line then held. So far as he was concerned, it was "essential that we hold the . . . [Western] Dorsale itself, and I am prepared to fight all out to insure this." But fighting to hold the Western Dorsale would be impossible if the Allies lost heavily while being driven out of their positions.

Could Anderson launch a diversionary attack in the north to lighten the enemy pressure in the south? Eisenhower asked.

No. It would be safer to commit reserves to cover the pullback in the south, and this would leave him without resources for a diversionary effort.

Eisenhower agreed. The losses suffered in two days by the 1st Armored Division in the quicksand at Sidi bou Zid indicated it would be better to withdraw than to lose all — even though an eventual retirement to the Western Dorsale meant abandoning American and French supply bases at Sbeitla and perhaps even the newly constructed airfields at Thelepte.

The point was, Anderson explained, that the Axis forces probably lacked supplies for a sustained offensive. This, together with Montgomery's advance toward the Mareth Line, made it necessary for the enemy to succeed quickly, if at all. Let the Axis expend energy in a short-term offensive. The Allies would roll with the punch and conserve strength for the ultimate knockout blow.

He told Fredendall to extricate the troops from Lessouda and Ksaira, then to hold securely at Sbeitla, Kasserine, and Feriana. To help, he released Robinett's CCB, which was still up north.

At seven o'clock, Monday evening, February 15, Robinett received a message from Fredendall: "Move the big elephants to Sbeitla, move fast, and come shooting." Two and a half hours later, his troops were on the road for Sbeitla, sixty-five miles away.

Just in case the situation continued to deteriorate, Fredendall sent engineers to the village of Kasserine, twenty miles behind Sbeitla, to start building defenses.

* * * *

When Liebenstein learned on the afternoon of Monday, February 15, that the Allies had abandoned Gafsa, he sent his troops into the town, and from there pushed patrols southwest into the desert toward Metlaoui and Tozeur and northwest toward Feriana.

Informed of the easy conquest of Gafsa, Ziegler asked Arnim whether he was still to transfer away part of the 21st Panzer Division. If he did so, he remarked parenthetically, he would probably be unable to advance northwest from Sidi bou Zid toward Fondouk and Pichon.

Arnim, still looking enviously at these passes farther north, told Ziegler to hold on to the 21st Panzer Division. After sweeping the isolated Americans off the djebels behind him, he was to send the 10th Panzer Division against Sbeitla. From there, he could move to the north and easily clear the Allied troops from the western exits of the Fondouk and Pichon passes.

Rommel on that day was bringing to an end his long retreat from El Alamein. His rearguards were pulling back into the Mareth Line. Now he would await Montgomery's approach.

While waiting, he became aware of and puzzled by Ziegler's lack of initiative. He should have followed up his success at Sidi bou Zid immediately and taken Sbeitla. "The Americans had as yet no practical battle experience," he later wrote, "and it was now up to us to instill in them from the outset an inferiority complex of no mean order."

But Ziegler was in no hurry to push his advantage. Filled with a fine feeling of satisfaction, he reorganized his forces, applied pressure against the troops on Ksaira and Garet Hadid, and sent reconnaissance parties toward Kern's Crossroads to discover the American intentions — were they planning to launch another counterattack or withdraw from the field?

And thus, a momentary lull set in. The ambiguous aspects of Operations Fruehlingswind and Morgenlust — the obscure objectives and the lack of an overall commander — would have to be settled. What should be developed out of the initial triumphs? The only person who could make that kind of decision was Kesselring, and he was visiting Hitler in

East Prussia. Until he sent instructions, the field commanders could only wait. Sbeitla remained in Allied hands.

* * * *

In Sbeitla, on a remote, windswept, sun-parched plain, several thousand inhabitants live beside the crumbling ruins of a Roman city. In a field covered with bits of marble stand the remains of three temples, each with characteristic columns, steps, and peristyles; vestigial baths, forum, amphitheater, and arch of triumph. Yellow, almost brown, with the age, neglect, decay, and stains of an old man's teeth, they somehow give the impression of a thriving town that once had class, if not style, and importance, if not grandeur.

The Romans had gone and Patrician Gregory, Byzantine governor, was in command when Arab invaders under Ibn Sa'ad, brother of the Caliph Othman, appeared in A.D. 647. South of Fondouk the armies met in battle. The Moslems attacked, but held their reserves until the end of the day, then struck hard and broke the defenses. Gregory perished, and the remnants of his forces took refuge in the fortified town of Sbeitla. The Arabs assaulted, forced an entrance, massacred most of the people, pillaged and burned the town, and gathered considerable booty. Then they returned to Egypt.

Eighteen years later, the Arabs reappeared, this time to sweep across the North African littoral. The conquest lasted five years, came to a successful conclusion, and achieved permanence in 670 with the foundation of the holy city of Kairouan. There was no resistance on the plain of Sbeitla. The town was in ashes and virtually deserted.

Almost thirteen hundred years later, Germans were at the gates of another Sbeitla, approaching from the east. Whether they too would overrun the town and, if so, whether their hegemony would prove to be lengthy were matters that were soon to be settled.

20

LIKE KESSELRING, his chief of staff in Rome had knowledge neither of the opening date of Arnim's attack nor of its immediate results. He learned quite by accident on Monday evening, February 15, when a staff officer who had just returned from Tunisia by plane made dinner conversation and revealed Arnim's success.

Brought up to date by a telephone call that evening, Kesselring, still in East Prussia, instructed his chief of staff to order Arnim and Rommel — through Comando Supremo — to exploit the triumph westward to Tebessa in the grand maneuver he and Rommel had envisioned, with Rommel in command of the operation.

The chief of staff laid the matter before Comando Supremo on the following day, Tuesday, the 16th. Lacking Kesselring's authority and prestige, he was unable to secure an immediate reaction. He nevertheless sent a message to Arnim, telling him to take Sbeitla. Arnim relayed the word to Ziegler.

Reluctant to attack, Ziegler decided to execute a lesser reconnaissance in force. For he had suddenly recognized the ambiguous place he occupied between the conflicting ambitions of Arnim and Rommel. Figuring that he would eventually have to transfer most of the 21st Panzer Division to Rommel in the south and most of the 10th Panzer Division to Arnim in the north, he saw the forces remaining under his command sharply reduced — unless he could generate enough momentum to warrant a continuation of his own efforts. If the Americans held stubbornly and the panzer divisions were diverted from his control, he would find himself at the head of a small holding force charged with the static mission of containing Sbeitla. Where was the glory in that?

Early in the afternoon of Tuesday, the 16th, he sent a small group of tanks toward Kern's Crossroads.

* * * *

Throughout Tuesday morning, the 16th, a bruised and battered CCA screened the eastern approaches to Sbeitla at Kern's Crossroads. The troops watched warily for a reappearance of hostile forces. Except for small probes that were easily discouraged, the hours passed quietly. Were the Germans recuperating from the battles of the two previous days? Were they disinclined to further aggressive action?

If so, this was fortunate, for Ward was now fully cognizant of the damage his units had suffered. His personnel and materiel losses were enormous, and there was much uncertainty — no one knew where Waters and Alger were or whether Drake could get off the hills and out to safety; no one even knew whether Drake had received the messages instructing him to break out of encirclement.

"Keep an eye on the north," Ward had radioed Drake, "and if necessary get on the band wagon." Surely Drake would understand what Ward meant. And surely — or at least, Ward told Fredendall, he was "reasonably sure" — the message had gotten through.

It was a chastened and somber Fredendall who telephoned Truscott. "The picture this morning," he said frankly, "does not look too good." He doubted that Ward could hold. "It does not look good," he repeated.

And then there was a flash of the old spirit, the indomitable Fredendall who was going to win the war single-handed. Trying to find some semblance of a silver lining, he added, "The worst will be the loss of two battalions of tanks."

He phoned Ward and told him "to get his division straightened out and to hold defensively east of Sbeitla."

Anderson confirmed the order: "Do not counterattack any more, but concentrate your energies on guarding the Feriana, Kasserine, Sbeitla areas."

Ward was pleased to go over on the defense. His foremost concern, he admitted candidly, was to preserve his division "as a fighting force." His chances for doing so improved early that morning when Robinett and his CCB reported for duty after an all-night trip.

The men of CCB had heard rumors of what had taken place around Sidi bou Zid, but the reality surpassed the gossip. It was true that efforts to relieve the isolated units had failed, that the division had been badly hurt, that many men were missing in action, most of them presumably captured, and the loss of Waters and Alger, both widely admired, hit especially hard.

Cheerful and buoyant despite the adversities of the past two days, Ward set up an active defense of Sbeitla. Both CCA and CCB had now been tried by the fire of combat. The division had shaken down. It was time to be steadfast.

Because there was little natural cover and concealment for good defensive positions anywhere for about eight miles behind Kern's Crossroads, Ward selected an extensive belt of olive groves three miles east of town and set up a line of resistance. He put Robinett's CCB south of Sbeitla. He intended to pull McQuillin's CCA back from the crossroads gradually, probably after darkness, to defend north of the town.

During the early afternoon, as CCB was moving to its defensive sector south of Sbeitla, Robinett first heard, then saw air action, gunfire, dust, and the black smoke of burning vehicles. He knew the signs well. A battle was taking place in front of Kern's Crossroads, eleven miles to the east.

* * * *

Shocked by the news that two battalions of tanks, two of artillery, two of infantry, and "no one knew how much more,"

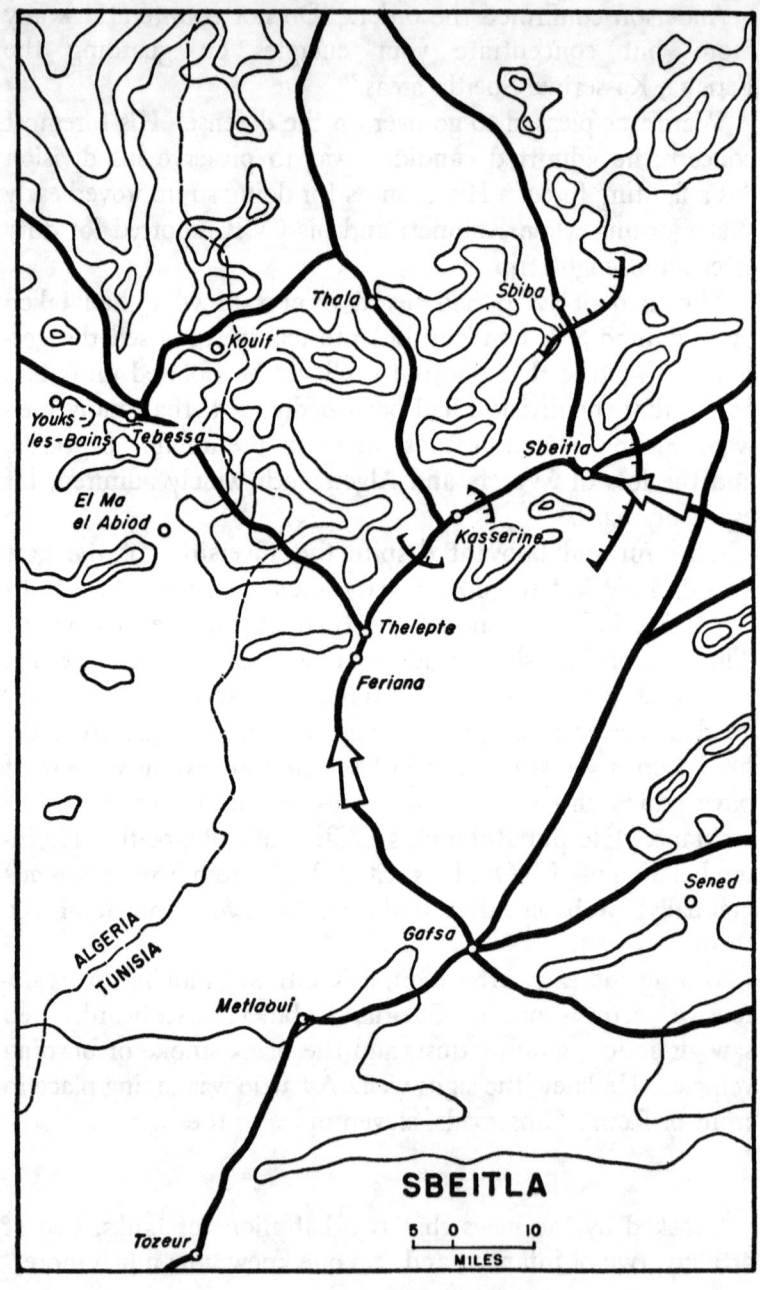

11. Near Sbeitla, an American antitank gun crew manhandles the small and inadequate weapon into firing position. *U.S. Army Photograph*

12. Kasserine Pass, the Allied view. On the northern side of the Kasserine Pass, "the road emerges into a vast triangular basin called the Bled Foussana. Dominated by wooded heights, the basin has sparse vegetation, eroded hills, wadis with sheer sides, rocky draws and gullies, patches of cactus." The road splits into two routes, one to Thala, the other (lower left) toward Tebessa. In the distance, Djebel Semmama is on the left, Djebel Chambi is on the right. *U.S. Army Photograph*

had been overrun and destroyed in the past two days, Eisenhower spurred his logisticians to get equipment flowing to the front. He also suggested that Anderson shift some infantry, antitank guns, and possibly even some tanks to bolster the southern front.

In order to back up the 1st Armored Division, Fredendall specifically asked Anderson to block the Sbiba Gap, twenty miles northwest of Sbeitla. In compliance, Anderson instructed Koeltz to start withdrawing his right flank that evening from the Eastern to the Western Dorsale. The American 34th Division, which was under the French commander's control, was to be moved to Sbiba and tied in with the 1st Armored Division — that is, if Ward could manage to hold Sbeitla.

Koeltz was pessimistic about the possibility. From Welvert, through French channels, had come word of confusion in Fredendall's headquarters. No one seemed to know what to do. Not only was Sbeitla threatened, but more significantly so was Tebessa. If Tebessa was lost, the safety of Constantine came into question. And with that, the security of Algeria became tenuous.

Thus, though Koeltz hated to give up without combat positions conquered and conserved with struggle and pain, he began to plan to pull his troops back slowly from the Eastern Dorsale.

* * * *

Fredendall telephoned Truscott that afternoon to give him the latest news. He was less than altogether coherent.

There was, he said, a "tank battle coming up . . . east of Sbeitla. They are coming in with sixty tanks. . . . Here is the danger: if we are run out of Sbeitla with our armor, that exposes . . . [the southern flank of the French corps and ultimately the British southern flank]. I wanted them [the British] to send something down to block so I could withdraw my armor back on the supply line and also block that pass [Kasserine?] up to the new airfield [at Thelepte]. If we get rocked loose from that place, it is going to expose the . . . [whole central area of Tunisia]."

As for the immediate situation at Sbeitla, he had told Drake to cut his way off Djebel Ksaira and fight his way out of encirclement. He had ordered Ward to stand fast, and maybe he could now, for Robinett's CCB was at Sbeitla, "getting set in behind so if they come through they can take them."

* * * *

The German tanks that crept over the plain east of Sidi bou Zid toward Kern's Crossroads during the afternoon of the 16th were less than aggressive. They were hesitant, and when they were taken under long-range American fire, they slowed perceptibly, took cover in wadis, and worked cautiously forward, interested, apparently, only in verifying the strength and location of the American defenses.

Despite the lack of resolution in the German advance, Ward decided to abandon Kern's Crossroads. He would assume the stronger defenses in the olive groves just east of Sbeitla at once. If he waited until nightfall to move CCA back, the withdrawal might be too late; it would certainly be more confused, for men retiring during darkness often had a tendency to vanish, only to reappear several days later miles behind the front.

He told McQuillin to start sending back his units. Kern was to keep his infantry out of any tank battle that might develop, and he was to move back at his discretion. Crosby was to go forward from Sbeitla with his tank battalion and help cover the withdrawal.

Crosby had been in Sbeitla about a day and a half, having arrived in time to see Hightower come in badly used up on the first day of battle. He had listened on the second day as Hightower had explained to Alger how the German tanks fought. Now, after having kept his men and his vehicles bivouacked and concealed in a large cactus patch, he led them in their initial combat action.

Moving to Kern's northern flank, Crosby was lucky. He caught eight German tanks by surprise and routed them.

At the same time, a provisional company formed by Hightower from a few stray tanks and tank destroyers ventured out on Kern's southern flank. By sudden fire, he too turned back a group of German tanks.

While Crosby and Hightower, along with artillery and tank destroyers, threw shells at the Germans and held them at long range, the units of McQuillin's CCA began to withdraw to the olive groves on the eastern outskirts of Sbeitla. As they came back, they built up defensive positions along a firing line in the angle formed by the converging roads from Lessouda and Fondouk. Upon the approach of night, the artillery, tank destroyers, and tanks, along with Kern's infantry, disengaged and pulled back.

The withdrawal was disciplined and well controlled, with only the normal amount of confusion attending any large-scale movement under enemy fire. Though Kern was out of touch with his companies much of the night, the infantrymen generally took their assigned areas. Summerall's artillery battalion, after firing all day long, leapfrogged its howitzers to the rear in good order and three hours later the pieces were in excellent positions in an orchard. Most of the units found time to replenish their gasoline and ammunition at the supply dumps established among the olive trees.

Casualties were relatively light, even among Crosby's and Hightower's units — in the entire division, seventy-six men killed, wounded, and missing.

* * * *

Anderson went to see Koeltz on the evening of Tuesday, the 16th, taking with him the commander of the 6th Armoured Division, Major General Sir Charles F. Keightley.

The situation at Sbeitla, he said, was going from bad to worse, and it had become necessary to consider what might be done if the Americans abandoned the town. In that case, the enemy might turn northwest and strike toward the Sbiba Gap before Koeltz could get additional units there. For that reason he had already told Keightley to plug the Sbiba Gap with the 26th Armoured Brigade and two battalions of infantry. Where would Koeltz suggest that these forces be placed?

Koeltz pointed out on a map the terrain features he deemed important. Blocking positions a few miles south and east of Sbiba would prevent enemy thrusts from Fondouk as well as from Sbeitla and at the same time allow the 34th Division and a French regiment under General Saint-Didier to withdraw safely from the Eastern Dorsale.

As Keightley's troops moved toward Sbiba from the north, Ryder's 34th Division shifted westward from the Pichon sector. If these forces were to have time to organize a strong defense, Ward's 1st Armored Division would have to hold on to Sbeitla for a while. Since Anderson had specified no time schedule to coordinate the developments at Sbiba and Sbeitla, Ward understood his mission to be an indefinite defense in place. This he was confident he could fulfill.

* * * *

During the late afternoon of Tuesday, the 16th, Ziegler radioed Liebenstein at Gafsa and told him he intended to attack Sbeitla on the following day. An advance from Gafsa to Feriana would help intensify the pressure.

Satisfied that thrusts to Sbeitla and Feriana led inevitably westward toward Tebessa despite Arnim's continuing interest in Fondouk and Pichon, Rommel instructed Liebenstein to advance to Feriana but to try to avoid a costly battle.

Continuing toward Feriana and Sbeitla went beyond the

operations authorized by Comando Supremo, which had in mind little more than keeping the Americans off Rommel's back at the Mareth Line. But events were generating a momentum of their own, and that evening, after a long debate on the information presented by Kesselring's chief of staff, the Italian High Command finally decided to extend the offensive.

Around 11 P.M., Arnim received formal instructions to exploit his success toward Sbeitla. Rommel's mission remained unchanged: he was simply to secure Gafsa, which he already had accomplished. He would later justify his movement to Feriana on the basis of adding to and insuring the security of Gafsa.

Meanwhile, Ziegler had learned that the Americans had abandoned Kern's Crossroads. Having no desire to risk a night attack against what he estimated to be strong defenses in the olive groves just east of Sbeitla, he wondered whether he needed to give battle at all to force the Americans out of the town. Discreet pressure might be enough. He instructed his tank commander to stay on the heels of the American rearguards pulling back from the crossroads — but to do so carefully, most carefully.

* * * *

By 10 P.M., Tuesday, February 16, the 1st Armored Division had assumed excellent defensive positions among the olive groves. All the troops were accounted for and in place despite a sporadic shelling that came from German guns. CCA had successfully pulled back to protect Sbeitla on the north. CCB had moved into positions south of the town. Though reduced in numbers, the division was finally, for the first time since the opening of the North African campaign, operating as a single unit. The defenses were good, the troops seasoned. Only aimless and desultory machine-gun and high-velocity fire came from the abandoned area of Kern's

Crossroads, now occupied by Germans. Only a few enemy tanks seemed to be pushing cautiously down the road toward Sbeitla. There was every reason to believe that Ward would hold indefinitely.

At ten-thirty that night, Truscott telephoned Fredendall for news. The operations staff officer answered the phone. Everything was quiet, he reported cheerfully. Everything was in good order. The tank battle that had earlier been noted had petered out. The Germans had only been reconnoitering and had now withdrawn out of sight. Everything was under control. Everything looked good. Everything was dandy.

That was just about the time that everything went to pieces.

21

IN THE olive groves, where gnarled and misshapen trees assumed grotesque and frightening forms, the Americans were jumpy on that cold and frosty night of Tuesday, February 16. Even the patches of moving overcast seemed menacing, and the pale moon that showed occasionally between the scudding clouds appeared wan and sickly.

The clank of tank treads and the sound of motors mingled with muttered warnings and hoarse commands as troops refueled their vehicles at the supply dumps. Taking their positions, the men waited as the winking lights and muffled booms of shooting in the distance moved toward them. With increasing frequency, shells began to fall nearby. Then came the clatter of machine guns and the piercing screech of bullets. Flares lighted up the plain. Machine-gun tracers flashed by.

German tanks approached in three columns, preceded by lighter vehicles of reconnaissance units. One group on the Lessouda road, picking up the dim outlines of a few American trucks, opened fire and dispersed an improvised mine-laying detail.

Some of the German machine-gun fire carried into the olive groves and came close to the command post of McQuillin's CCA. This, together with the shells that were landing nearby, prompted the commander to shift his headquarters to the other side and west of Sbeitla, near the Roman ruins.

His deputy, Hains, with reduced communications facilities and in an increasing hail of artillery shells and machine-gun and rifle bullets, remained in the old command post in order to maintain control during the move.

As the main headquarters party began to leave, other troops, misinterpreting the movement as flight, followed suit.

Crosby, who had completed a skillful withdrawal from Kern's Crossroads and who was coming to the CCA headquarters for further instructions, was surprised to see a growing stream of vehicles hurriedly driving to the rear. He found Hains somewhat distraught, not because of the incoming fire but because of his feeling that things were falling apart. He had no specific instructions for Crosby — only that he do the best he could and try to hold at least until morning.

As Crosby departed to rejoin his troops, he discovered that the road leading into Sbeitla was jammed with vehicles. When he asked several drivers where they were going and why, he received a variety of excuses, many of them incoherent. Several days of uncertainty and defeat, he reflected, had suddenly come to a head. The combat command was collapsing.

Though some units of CCA stood fast, notably Crosby's and Hightower's tankers, others fled.

The panic, though unpardonable, was understandable. Night fighting was a new and terrifying experience for most of the men. The solidity of the defensive line was more apparent on a map than on the ground. Because of the darkness, the troops were not well placed. Because of the haste of the withdrawal, they were not well dug in. The harrowing events of three days of defeat had exhausted many soldiers, morally and physically. Uncertain and nervous, fatigued and confused, hemmed in by widespread firing that seemed to be all around them, believing that the Germans were already in Sbeitla, demoralized by the piecemeal commitment and intermingling of small units, no longer possessing a firm sense of belonging to a strong and self-contained organization, and numbed by a pervading attitude of weariness and bewilderment, many men lost their confidence and self-discipline.

As vehicles in increasing numbers moved out of the olive groves, a dense mass of churning traffic, bumper to bumper and hub to hub, choked the road.

"We just lost our heads," a soldier later admitted sheepishly.

When engineers demolished an ammunition dump, a railroad bridge, and part of an aqueduct, the explosions intensified the feelings of fear and insecurity among those who were quick to attribute the destruction to the enemy. Crosby himself, who recognized that demolition portended withdrawal, had a moment of doubt; he had no inkling that anyone was thinking of abandoning Sbeitla. Robinett was disturbed, and he wondered whether the demolitions were authorized, for they were, he later said, "practically an invitation for the enemy to enter."

As leadership and command broke down in CCA, the conviction spread that the division was too poorly deployed and established to withstand the further punishment of continuing German attack.

"I guess we didn't think we could hold."

While McQuillin was moving his command post, he temporarily lost communication with the division headquarters. When someone at division wondered out loud whether CCA had been overrun, a rumor was started. Since Hains lacked the means to keep in touch with all the subordinate units, he lost control. As speculation of disaster ran riot, the situation got entirely out of hand.

Ward had had very little accurate information about what was happening until around midnight, when several officers who had witnessed the mass panic told him of the breakdown. Piecing together fragmentary bits of evidence and concluding that CCA must be under attack by a large armored force, Ward suggested that the French start moving at once toward Kasserine. Telephoning Fredendall, he informed him of approaching disaster. The Germans were at the edge of Sbeitla, and a spearhead had already pierced the covering line along the olive groves.

Fredendall telephoned Truscott to tell him that the situation was "extremely grave." Ward was "uncertain of ability to hold." If the Americans were kicked out of Sbeitla, Feriana and Thelepte became exposed, as did the whole central area of Tunisia. The situation, he repeated, was bad, even though, he admitted, Ward "was doing best he could."

Truscott had hardly finished talking when he received a report from an officer he had earlier sent to Sbeitla with a high-powered radio to keep him directly informed of developments. Tanks, he learned, were battling in the moonlight all around Ward's command post. Ward himself was determined to fight it out, for even if he wanted to he was unable to withdraw.

Having no way of knowing that the news was exaggerated, Truscott believed that the 1st Armored Division was about to be engulfed.

Ziegler, unaware of what was taking place, thought that the Americans were evacuating Sbeitla, but, curiously enough, his leading elements were receiving strong resistance. He decided to wait until daylight to enter the town.

Persuaded at last that the attack in the south was the main enemy thrust, Anderson at 1:30 on the morning of Wednesday, February 17, authorized a withdrawal from Sbeitla. But he wished Ward to hold all day Wednesday in order to give Koeltz time to get set at Sbiba. Fredendall thought it would be impossible to remain that long, and he favored letting Ward get out while he could.

A "big argument," Fredendall later said, ensued. The difference was resolved by compromise. The Americans would try to stay until 11 A.M., longer if they could.

"Everything is going badly at Sbeitla," Anderson told Koeltz. "The II Corps cannot continue the battle with its tanks because it no longer has any."

At that moment, word came that German troops had just entered the town. The information was incorrect, but it gave weight to the wisdom of withdrawing to the Western Dorsale. The Allies would thus preserve their offensive power and be able to thrust forward later in cooperation with Montgomery.

Learning also that German troops were advancing from Gafsa toward Feriana, Anderson gave permission to pull back to Kasserine and Tebessa.

Fredendall's defensive walls were crumbling, but at dawn of Wednesday, February 17, he was trying to shore them up. He issued a series of orders. First, Ward and his 1st Armored Division were to leave Sbeitla only when forced to do so, then retire through the Kasserine Pass toward Thala. Second, Colonel Anderson T. W. Moore and his 19th Engineers were to man a line at the eroded bed of the Hatab River just east of the village of Kasserine on the Sbeitla road, cover the retirement of Ward's 1st Armored Division through the Kasserine Pass, then pull back into the pass and organize it for defense. Third, Stark was to defend Feriana as long as he could, then pull back toward Tebessa. Fourth, the Thelepte fields were to be abandoned, the planes flown to rear bases.

In explaining these measures to Truscott, Fredendall was less than optimistic. "Ward," he said, "fears we may have lost the 1st Armored Division." He added a final observation: the trouble was that Anderson had failed to accept the gravity of his earlier reports.

At Sbeitla, despite the confusion that continued throughout most of the night, CCB remained solidly in line south of the town and discouraged German advances, while enough of CCA remained in place to prevent an incursion into the northern part. By the morning of Wednesday, the 17th, officers posted along the roads had stopped the fleeing troops and had sent many back to their positions. Artillery continued their interdictory and harassing fires and helped keep the Germans at arm's length. Though the road leading westward to Kasserine was clogged with the vehicular traffic of American supply and support units, and French troops marching on foot and on horseback, some soldiers driving mule teams, Sbeitla remained in American hands. The expected German attack had failed to materialize.

Ziegler had again postponed his attack, this time until noon. For he had a more immediate task. The Americans stranded on Djebel Ksaira and Garet Hadid had made a break for freedom.

As Fredendall informed Truscott that morning, "We are going to have to write Drake and his battalion off. I am going to get a plane over him and tell him to give in. There is no out. He is completely surrounded. He had two days' ammunition and two days' rations. He has been out for twenty-four hours. There is no use prolonging the agony. We have got to write him off."

Write him off they did, Drake and his sixteen hundred men. Only a pitifully small number managed to escape.

22

THE AGONY was nowhere apparent on the morning of Sunday, February 14, when the members of the 168th Infantry heard the distant sound of firing to the north around Lessouda. Lieutenant Colonel Gerald C. Line, Drake's executive officer, who handled the details at the regimental command post while Drake operated from an observation post several hundred yards away, received a telephone call from McQuillin around 9:30 A.M., asking that Drake prepare a plan for withdrawing the troops from Ksaira. Though only Lessouda was under attack and no immediate action was required at Ksaira, it was better to be on the safe side.

Drake consulted with Line and other members of his staff, then called the 3d Battalion commander, Lieutenant Colonel John H. Van Vliet, back from Ksaira for a conference. During the meeting, German tanks appeared in the south. Coming out of the Maizila Pass, they headed up the road from Maknassy toward Ksaira. A mass withdrawal of Van Vliet's troops during daylight, Drake decided, was already impossible.

About an hour later, somewhere around noontime, Line was talking on the telephone with McQuillin when the conversation was interrupted. "No more over the phone," a voice broke in. "We are leaving." The receiver went dead.

Drake then moved his miscellaneous troops up on Garet Hadid while Van Vliet's battalion remained on Ksaira. The positions were excellent for defense. Engineers had wired the most likely approaches with entanglements and attached trip wires to mines, and the infantry had added tin cans half filled with rocks to give warning of enemy approach.

As darkness fell, enemy activity slackened. The night was quiet.

Around 7:30 on Monday morning, February 15, the Germans put pressure on the hills with artillery shelling and infantry assault. About two hundred Germans penetrated into the positions held by engineers, who expelled them with hand grenades. The thirty-odd members of the regimental band, who usually doubled as litter bearers, made beautiful music on rifles accompanied by machine guns.

All day long the Germans tried to storm the hills. And when darkness drew near, the enemy activity again fell off.

The telephone connecting the two hills went out around six o'clock in the evening, but Van Vliet reported by radio that about three hundred Germans were occupying the lower slopes of Ksaira. He was keeping them there, he said, with heavy doses of mortar fire.

Later that evening Drake lost radio contact with CCA. Now there was no way of telling what higher headquarters were planning. Would they rescue the troops isolated on the hills?

Once more the night was calm. And again, about seven o'clock on Tuesday morning, the 16th, the Germans attacked. Drake's troops fought in desperation and with declining hope. What would they do when their ammunition ran out?

At 3 P.M., word by radio was miraculously received from McQuillin's CCA: "Fight your way out. Time and place yours. Air cover will be provided. Instructions will be dropped by plane this afternoon."

Drake displayed his cerise silk panels to show the pilots where to drop the message. But a flight of four planes coming over around 4:30 passed over and dropped a note on Ksaira. Van Vliet relayed the communication. Drake was to take his troops off the hills and try to get them to safety. That was all. Not even a definite location for meeting friendly forces.

In what would be his last message, Drake acknowledged the permission finally granted. He showed no bitterness, only unbroken spirit. "Besieged," he radioed, "good strength, good morale." He mentioned neither the hunger and thirst of his men nor the fact that they were crowded into a small area on each hill.

Calling his unit commanders together at 6:30, Drake gave his instructions. The withdrawal would start at 10 P.M., with all units leaving their positions simultaneously. The route of march was to be around the northeastern nose of Garet Hadid, back along the foothills to the southwest for about five miles, then northwest for another five miles to a small hill in the desert. There the troops were to stop and take cover. They were to rest during the day for the final breakout, five miles farther to Kern's Crossroads, to be made on the following night.

He had no idea that CCA had abandoned the crossroads and had pulled back eight miles to the olive groves just east of Sbeitla.

Drake wanted the men to leave their helmets and wear overseas caps, which resembled those of the Afrika Korps. They were to carry out all the light machine guns and small 60-mm. mortars. They were to destroy all the equipment they could not take, but without lighting fires. Motor vehicle parts were to be buried, radios smashed by hammer and wrench. One medic was to remain with the wounded at the aid station on each hill.

His instructions delivered, Drake radioed Van Vliet and passed the word.

Ten minutes before the appointed hour, everything was in readiness and the withdrawal started off Garet Hadid. All units were accounted for except the attached Cannon Company of the 39th Infantry. The absence of these men was inexplicable, their whereabouts unknown. Where were they? Line asked. The regimental commander had too many other matters on his mind to be much concerned. They had probably departed ahead of schedule, he told Line, and they were very likely in front of the column.

Almost at once Drake discovered he was leading his men through a German tank park and bivouac area. A panzer came toward him, and the tank commander shouted in German. Drake ignored him. The tanker hesitated, then turned aside and rumbled away.

While crossing an open stretch of ground, the men were challenged by occupants of a German scout car. An American tossed a grenade into the car and set it on fire. Since there was some firing and a little confusion in the area, the Germans paid no attention to the burning vehicle.

The first part of the march took place over very rough ground. Later the land turned into cultivated fields. The men kept up a relatively rapid pace, making very few halts. In the darkness, most who were carrying the machine guns and mortars threw them away.

At daylight of the 17th, Wednesday, the column was about five miles from the small hill that was the immediate objective. Drake divided the troops into two files, placed them about fifty yards apart, and continued the march.

It was not long before the Germans detected the movement of this large group of men walking across the plain. Trucks carrying infantrymen came up on the left flank of the marching body, and about one thousand yards away the vehicles halted and the soldiers took firing positions.

Three Allied planes came into sight and brought hope as they passed overhead. One pilot fired into the line of German trucks. Then all three aircraft flew away. Was this the air cover that had been promised?

When the German soldiers opened fire with machine guns, rifles, and mortars, the Americans scattered. There was little cover in the large open fields, and the cohesion of command and discipline fast disintegrated.

Retaining command over several hundred men, Drake formed a perimeter. It was a wagon-train defense, with Drake in the center directing a desultory firing against the Germans, who soon brought up several tanks, all of them appearing to Drake as "huge monsters, with a yellow Tiger painted on their sides."

A German scout car bearing a white flag came dashing into the perimeter. Drake ordered his men to wave it out of the circle, but the vehicle continued, the first of several that penetrated the line. Tanks soon followed, cutting the Americans into small groups.

One tank came directly toward Drake. A German officer standing in the open turret pointed a rifle and called, "Colonel, you surrender."

"You go to hell," Drake answered. He turned his back to the tank and folded his arms across his chest, awaiting the impact of a bullet or the tank itself.

The tank swerved at the last moment and brushed past Drake's elbow.

All firing had now stopped, and the Germans were herding Americans into columns. Drake walked away, visiting the dead and wounded who lay on the field. Two German soldiers carrying rifles followed him.

Finally, a German major came forward and, in excellent English, asked Drake to do him the honor of getting into his scout car. He said he had once practiced law in Chicago.

Before getting into the car, Drake asked him to allow the American medics to care for the wounded.

The German officer was agreeable. He needed his own medical troops to look after the considerable casualties inflicted on his own force.

The tank officer who had almost run over Drake came up, saluted, and asked something in German. The English-speaking major translated. Would Drake do him the honor of shaking hands? He admired courage.

Drake shook hands stiffly.

The major took Drake in his car to a headquarters where a general came forward to see him, drew himself to attention, saluted, and said, "I want to compliment your command for the splendid fight they put up. It was a hopeless thing from the start, but they fought like real soldiers."

To Drake's question, the general officer also promised to see that all the American wounded were cared for.

Drake later learned that all the American medics had been marched off the field, and the dead and wounded left to Arabs who proceeded to strip them of their clothing, beating insensible the wounded men who protested.

The prisoners taken were searched by their captors, often at the point of rifle or bayonet. Watches, rings, pocketbooks, pens, as well as valuables and keepsakes, were snatched.

With three armored cars at their heels and several along their flanks, the Americans were marched all day through the desert, past Lessouda and through the Faid Pass. The thirst of the men was virtually unbearable, and Drake appealed to the German officer in charge who said he had only enough water for his own troops. Darkness came as they walked, and their clothes, soaked with sweat, turned clammy. At midnight, the column of prisoners was halted, and the men were allowed to rest in a field. The temperature had fallen drastically, and the men almost froze. Too cold to sleep, tired, hungry, and disconsolate, they huddled together for warmth.

At dawn, trucks came, picked up the men, and transported them to Sfax, where they received their first food in five days — black bread and water. Trains took them to Sousse, then to Tunis; planes or ships transported them to Italy. Two weeks later, trains carried them to prisoner of war camps in Germany and Poland.

* * * *

Near Sidi bou Zid, Drake's executive officer, Line, had somehow found a hiding place. Late in the afternoon he made his way across the desert, a solitary figure moving cautiously from the concealment of a wadi to the shadow of a cactus plant. Reaching high ground after dark, he struck out rapidly across a range of hills. He had little idea of where he was or where he would end up. He came to a road, and soon afterward a vehicle came along. It was an American truck, and the driver picked him up and took him to Tebessa.

Line reported to the II Corps Personnel Officer by phone that night and in person the following afternoon. Sent to Moore's 2d Battalion of the 168th, Line discovered that practically nothing remained of the regiment.

* * * *

First Lieutenant Harry P. Hoffman commanded Company K in Van Vliet's battalion, and his most pressing concern on Ksaira had been food for his men. The last hot meal had been served on Wednesday, the 10th, and water was rationed to one canteen per man per day. The final delivery of rations and water arrived on Saturday night, the 13th, just before the German attack.

By the end of Sunday, the 14th, when the enemy had forced the battalion to consolidate positions on the upper part of the hill, the lack of sustenance was a major problem. Fortunately, Hoffman found a spring on the djebel. Water was available, if not plentiful.

The Germans shelled Ksaira heavily throughout Monday, the 15th. They pulled up vehicles in the flat between Ksaira and Garet Hadid, unlimbered their guns, and shelled the Americans at will. The battalion had no artillery with which to reply, and the infantry weapons lacked the range to reach the German guns.

The men learned that they were surrounded, but their morale continued to be good. They were sure they would be rescued. It was their hunger rather than their isolation that worried them.

Almost constant enemy shelling on Tuesday, the 16th,

the absence of rescue parties, and the lack of food began to weaken the men physically and morally. That evening, Van Vliet called a meeting of company commanders and announced the breakout. The men were to take only enough vehicles to carry the wounded, bury the equipment they had to leave, puncture tires with bayonets, and put engines out of commission with bullets.

The evacuation of Ksaira began on a relatively clear night. A full moon broke through the clouds from time to time, giving enough light to see the floor of the plain. Moving onto the flats, the Americans encountered a German outpost, which they overwhelmed and silenced. The march became very fast. Then they came upon very rough ground cut by great dry watercourses, and the men, weakened by short rations, began to close up and lose cohesion. Troops began to discard equipment, to straggle behind, to make noise, to offer a thousand francs for a drink of water. By daybreak on Wednesday, the 17th, the column was broken into fragments. The companies were intermixed, the men strung out over a large area. Fires from small arms, cannons, and mortars started to fall among them.

Hoffman went back to look for a group of stragglers, found himself headed eastward toward Faid, and became separated. Taking cover, he awaited darkness. Then he worked his way westward, using his compass to check his bearings. Two soldiers who had been on Lessouda joined him. They moved into the mountains, making their way to the west. The hunger pains disappeared.

At daybreak of Thursday, the 18th, Hoffman and his two companions were on a hill overlooking Sbeitla. Seeing enemy tanks going into the town, they continued westward toward Kasserine, stopping every half hour to check the compass. During the day ten American soldiers from a variety of units came out of the hills and became part of the group. They traveled together, reaching the outskirts of Kasserine at the end of the day. German vehicles were there too. The men bypassed the town and turned north. Weak and footsore, they continued walking all day on Friday, the 19th, keeping to the hills and under cover as much as possible.

That night they met an Arab who spoke German. One of the soldiers who spoke the language made a deal. For fifteen hundred francs, the Arab guided them around a mountain that he said was occupied by German troops.

On the morning of Saturday, the 20th, they reached a road. Exhausted, they stopped, waiting for a vehicle to come along, any vehicle. The first one was an American half-track, which halted. Hoffman's party pulled themselves painfully aboard. Taken to a medical installation, they had something to eat. From there, Hoffman got a ride to Tebessa, where he rejoined the remnants of the 168th Infantry.

Not much was left. Of the forty officers in the 3d Battalion at the start of the battle, he was the only one who was neither killed nor captured.

The strength of the 168th Infantry — the regimental headquarters and the three battalions — on February 10 had totaled 189 officers and 3,728 men. Two weeks later, though one battalion had not been involved in the operations and was virtually intact, there were only 50 officers and less than 1,000 soldiers who remained. It would take 79 officers and almost 2,100 men to replace the losses.

23

ON THE MORNING of Wednesday, February 17, while Drake's men were being swept off the Sbeitla plain, Liebenstein's Italo-German elements advanced up the road from Gafsa and entered Feriana. There Liebenstein was wounded by a mine, and he turned over his command to General Karl Buelowius.

A few miles away, at Thelepte, American airmen had been evacuating both airfields throughout the preceding night. Most of the thirty-five hundred officers and men at the air bases moved out by truck, taking their equipment and supplies, while pilots flew out the operational planes. All headed for the airfields at Tebessa and Youks-les-Bains. What they were unable to take with them they destroyed by burning — approximately sixty thousand gallons of gasoline, thirty-four disabled aircraft, and a variety of shops and facilities.

Flames from the burning gasoline, explosions set off by demolition teams, and roads crowded with vehicles marked a wholesale withdrawal that had the elements of haste and near-panic.

"Their command appeared to be getting jittery," Rommel later wrote, "and they were showing the lack of decision of men commanding for the first time in a difficult situation."

Informed by Arabs that Allied troops were already setting fire to depots and installations as far away as Tebessa, Buelowius pushed his troops boldly into Thelepte around noon. He found and salvaged twenty tons of aviation gas and thirty tons of lubricants, together with large piles of useful ammunition and other supplies.

At Sbeitla, the men of Ward's 1st Armored Division were also blowing up ammunition dumps and destroying supplies that morning as they prepared to abandon the town.

The smoke rising from Thelepte and Sbeitla and the crowds of Allied soldiers clogging the roads brought unrest to Tebessa. "The French railroad people in Tebessa," a staff officer reported, "are packing up and evacuating — apparently on orders from their higher headquarters. I wonder if something could be done to cancel this and make them stay here. They are sort of panicking the population."

"There is some confusion," Fredendall admitted, "but we are getting along pretty well."

His statement was somewhat misleading. Though disorder at Tebessa calmed during the afternoon, Fredendall moved his corps headquarters out of the nearby canyon to a safer location. During the shift he was out of touch with his superiors, who needed information, and his subordinates, who needed direction.

Not until 6 P.M., when his headquarters was re-established fifteen miles northeast of Tebessa at the mining hamlet of Kouif, did he telephone Truscott to find out what had been happening.

* * * *

At Sbeitla, Ward's 1st Armored Division had awaited the Germans with McQuillin's CCA on the north and Robinett's CCB on the south. Pledged to hold the town until at least 11 A.M., Ward instructed McQuillin to be ready to withdraw northwest to Sbiba, there to facilitate the arrival of the 34th Division that Koeltz was shifting from the Eastern Dorsale. Robinett was to go westward to Kasserine, move through the pass, then swing around to guard Tebessa against incursion from the south.

The entire southern front was swinging back, pivoting on the left. At the completion of the maneuver, the right wing would have fallen back from Gafsa to Tebessa, and the Allied units would no longer be facing eastward but defending against the south, along a line from Tebessa eastward through Kasserine to Sbiba.

Ziegler, occupied with rounding up Drake's troops, let the morning pass. Early in the afternoon, unaware of how thinly stretched CCA was on the northern side of the town, he made his main effort in the south, where the approaches were better. There, Robinett's CCB had established a solid line of defense.

German tanks came over the rough plain on a broad front, slowed first by dry stream beds across the desert, then by shells from American artillery, but they advanced doggedly.

The first break came when a battalion of tank destroyers screening Robinett's northern flank, after firing for half an hour, streaked back to a previously designated rally point. Finding that place under enemy fire, the men panicked and drove their half-tracks helter-skelter into Sbeitla.

The town was in turmoil. Vehicles roared into the main street only to encounter a traffic jam. Enemy planes came over, dropped bombs, and increased the confusion. Drivers lost control of vehicles, smashed fenders, ran into ditches, and many abandoned their trucks and jeeps in the hope of getting out faster on foot.

In this eccentric flow of machines streaming to the rear, most of the tank destroyer men allowed themselves to be swept along toward Kasserine.

McQuillin's CCA pulled back toward Sbiba, the troops periodically harassed by dive bombers but untroubled by pursuit from ground forces. That evening they dug hasty defenses to block the road just below Sbiba. This gave the units coming into the village from the north and east enough time to establish firm positions.

Meanwhile, CCB battled the Germans. Lieutenant Colonel Henry E. Gardiner's tank battalion fought off one attack, but when another assault threatened to outflank the defenses, the Americans began to withdraw.

Around 5 P.M., February 17, German troops entered Sbeitla. They found little booty. The Americans had removed or destroyed most of their supplies and installations. They had blown up bridges, water mains, and part of the aqueduct running to Sfax. They had mined the roads. They had left the town in shambles. They had also lost, in four days of fighting, more than 2,500 men, 100 tanks, 280 vehicles, and 25 guns.

With Gafsa, Feriana, Thelepte, and Sbeitla now in German hands, Operations Fruehlingswind and Morgenlust had exceeded all expectations. Instead of pressing the advantage, Arnim dissolved Ziegler's command and dissipated his private ambitions. Leaving the 21st Panzer Division at Sbeitla, he sent a group of tanks toward Sbiba and the rest of the 10th Panzer Division to an assembly area behind the Pichon and Fondouk passes, which still interested him. Since Buelowius, by holding Feriana and Thelepte, threatened the passes of Kasserine, Dernaia, and El Ma el Abiod, which gave access to Tebessa, Arnim figured he had more than fulfilled his obligations in the south.

CCB, having successfully disengaged, withdrew from Sbeitla with the loss of sixteen men, nine tanks, and two halftracks. The troops reached Kasserine village shortly after darkness of February 17. At a gasoline dump just off the highway, while maintaining blackout conditions because the Germans might be following closely, they gassed up and piled five-gallon containers of fuel on their vehicles. Ward was there, and he complimented them on their orderly retirement.

Moving through the Kasserine Pass, CCB bivouacked along the road going north to Thala. There the men discovered that Gardiner was missing.

* * * *

Gardiner's 2d Battalion of the 13th Armored Regiment was composed of a headquarters company with three tanks; three tank companies, each with seventeen tanks — giving him a maximum strength of fifty-four tanks, if all were in operating condition; a platoon each of 81-mm. mortars and 75-mm. howitzers mounted on half-tracks; and a reconnaissance platoon of two half-tracks and four jeeps.

After making the invasion of North Africa at Oran, Gardiner's battalion had rushed into Tunisia and fought with the First Army. Early in January, Gardiner, along with the rest of CCB, moved to Tebessa, then to Sbeitla. Except for the native huts, the Arabs, and the camels, the terrain seemed to him much like the area between Las Vegas, Nevada, and Phoenix, Arizona, with barren mountain masses rising from a flat and semi-arid country sparsely covered with scrub sage. Occasional olive orchards and patches of prickly pear cactus growing to a height of ten feet provided fair cover for a tank or infantry battalion.

After a ten-day stay at Sbeitla, CCB rushed to Pichon and fought in a week-long engagement. Then the command marched 133 miles back to Tebessa. Three days later CCB turned around and rolled north again.

At midnight of Monday, February 15, CCB took to the road for Sbeitla. Well before daylight on Tuesday, the 16th, a guide posted on the road waved Gardiner's battalion into an assembly area. Summoned that afternoon with the other unit commanders to the CCB command post, he listened as Robinett issued the orders. A general withdrawal was taking place, and the 1st Armored Division was covering Sbeitla, with CCB defending south of the town. Gardiner was to defend a seven-mile front with some tank destroyers on his left and an infantry battalion on his right. An artillery battalion would give support.

Thoroughly familiar with Sbeitla and its environs, Gardiner quickly led his troops to the assigned sector. As he passed through the town at the head of his command, he noticed that men defending supply dumps with antiaircraft guns looked rather relieved to see the tanks.

Gardiner sent his reconnaissance platoon well out to the front and placed his three tank companies along a wadi to form the backbone of the defense.

During the night a high-pitched staccato voice jabbering in German kept cutting in on his radio net. This was unnerving enough, but worse was the arrival of about fifty replacement troops, green soldiers who were brought up in several trucks, "dumped on us and the trucks that brought them up left before we could refuse them." It was a rotten time, just before a battle, to get untried replacements. If they arrived while a unit was in bivouac, they could be fitted into the command where they were most needed and could best be used. Now there was nothing to do but try to find a vacancy for each man, whether qualified or not.

"Just in case there was any possible doubt in the enemy's mind as to how hard pressed we were, how hopeless our higher command regarded the situation, and how little confidence it reposed in our ability to perform our assigned mission," Gardiner wrote later, "the ammunition dumps were blown up in Sbeitla, with a wonderful show of pyrotechnics. The display was completely unappreciated so far as we were concerned."

Shortly before dawn on Wednesday, the 17th, Robinett told him that the division had moved its service elements out during the night and that other units were leaving. The mission of CCB remained unchanged, except that now Sbeitla was to be held until at least eleven o'clock in the morning. Robinett would give the order to withdraw.

Gardiner drew up a scheme of withdrawal. There would be no difficulty pulling out, and the troops could avoid the narrow streets of Sbeitla, which might be under fire.

The morning dragged. Nothing happened. Eleven o'clock came and passed.

At noon, Gardiner counted thirty-five German tanks coming over a rise almost directly in front of his battalion positions and about three miles away. Other tanks followed. Shells came in.

The reconnaissance troops out front soon found the situation too hot and came streaming back. Gardiner sent his mortar and assault gun platoons farther to the rear. He told the artillery to start back. He warned his tankers to hold their fire until he gave the word. They were well placed, in partial defilade in several small wadis running at right angles to the enemy approach.

Gardiner opened fire with a concentrated volley that stopped the German tanks momentarily. They came on doggedly, locating individual American positions and working up to them.

Beginning to take losses, Gardiner advised Robinett by radio that he would be in serious trouble unless he could withdraw. Instructed to hold until the infantry on his right managed to get out, he was happy to receive word soon afterward that the infantry was away all right and he could retire as he wished.

The battalion began to move back according to his plan. It was a simple leapfrog maneuver, with one company displacing while the two others increased their rate of fire to cover the movement. Gardiner's right-wing company was well on its way to a designated position astride a large wadi, when he ordered the second company to move. He started back himself at the same time.

As his command tank entered the large wadi, he saw a panzer already in the dry stream bed. The German was coming around a bend about three hundred yards away and was only partially visible. Gardiner's gunner let loose a hasty shot. Without waiting to see the effect of the round, Gardiner continued across the wadi.

Hope that he had put the enemy tank out of commission soon vanished. A shell hit and broke the right track on Gardiner's tank, which came to a jarring halt.

Another shell completed the destruction. Penetrating the armor and killing the driver, the second round set the tank on fire.

Gardiner and the surviving members of the crew jumped out. They were under machine-gun fire from the moment they hit the ground, but the burning tank gave them protection. They crawled and scrambled around a bend in the wadi.

Getting to their feet, they ran. Americans from other knocked-out tanks were running too. Like a herd of frightened animals, they stampeded up the dry watercourses, stumbling over boulders, tripping over rocks, sliding in the loose shale in a nightmare of tearing gasps of breath and blind panic.

Two German tanks came around a bend and opened fire with their machine guns. With screaming slugs spewing toward them, the Americans scattered into adjoining ditches.

Gardiner flung himself under a small bush. For more than an hour he lay there motionless. American artillery was pounding the German tanks, and he found himself wondering whether he would be killed by an American shell, crushed by the next German tank that came along, finished off with a spray of machine-gun fire, or dispatched by a hand grenade tossed blithely in his direction.

Nothing happened. The sounds of battle gradually diminished. When dusk arrived, Gardiner took off across the desert.

Enemy troops kept shooting flares into the sky, apparently to mark their progress, and Gardiner used them as guidance to keep out of their way.

He headed toward Kasserine. Knowing the road well from previous trips, Gardiner looked for a large wadi — the Hatab River — a few miles east of the Kasserine village, remembering that the eroded stream bed had required continual engineering work to make it passable. This, it seemed to him, would be a logical place for American troops to establish a roadblock.

As he trudged through the desert, keeping the main road

within sight, he found the night quiet except for the distant barking of Arab dogs and an occasional explosion.

He reached the large wadi east of Kasserine before daylight on the 18th. Fearing he might be fired on by American troops, he waited, lying in a ditch, for dawn.

When it was light enough for him to be seen and identified, he approached cautiously. The wadi was undefended. An effort had been made to block the giant fissure. But the engineering job had been obviously hasty, and the result was poor. The troops, he figured, had been concerned more with getting back than with denying the enemy a crossing.

If no troops defended the wadi, was he then still behind the enemy lines? Had the Germans already taken Kasserine?

He set off along the bank of the wadi, the Hatab River, which bypassed the village and led to the Kasserine Pass. Two French colonial soldiers emerged from the brush and joined him. They met an Arab family, who invited them into their tent and who fed them until a little boy same rushing in shouting excitedly, "*Allemands, Allemands,*" and Gardiner and the two French soldiers dashed out and scurried away.

As the three men approached the Kasserine Pass, a jeep came cautiously out of the defile. The men took cover until they could establish the identity of the vehicle and its occupants. They were Americans who were looking for survivors, and they took Gardiner and the soldiers into the pass.

Gardiner observed a few men and several 37-mm. guns set up to cover the road entering the pass. They were engineer troops, he was told, who were organizing a defense.

In one of the command posts behind the defile, Gardiner discovered that his battalion had come through the pass the previous night and had gone to the Tebessa area. Hitching a ride, he rejoined his command. He was pleased to learn that the battalion had made an orderly withdrawal from Sbeitla.

It could have been worse, he reflected. But then, he thought, the worst was probably still to come.

Part V

KASSERINE

24

IF THE LOSS of Sbeitla and Feriana had been the work of bumbling Allied commanders who were only amateurs, the next phase of operations would show how much better the Axis professionals and veterans could be at the business of bungling.

Since the seizure of Sbeitla and Feriana had upset the Allied dispositions far more than the plans for Fruehlingswind and Morgenlust had anticipated, Rommel was all for exploiting the success. He wished to intensify not only the disorder and excitement created in the Allied camp but also the momentum and enthusiasm generated among the Axis troops. What he had in mind was an immediate and converging thrust on Tebessa by all the forces that had brought Fruehlingswind and Morgenlust to a triumphant conclusion and were now concentrated and poised for further action. By pushing with all their strength to Tebessa, they could destroy a vital Allied nerve center that controlled airfields, communications, supply bases, and transportation. Just across the border in Algeria, Tebessa also had symbolic value. But even more important, once Tebessa was gained, the way was open for a strike deep into the rear of the Allied forces in Tunisia, as far as Bone, even beyond.

There were difficulties and dangers, of course: a long and vulnerable flank, for example, and easily threatened supply bases.

But he dismissed the thought. Commanders who had fought in theory alone, he reasoned, would tend, as a rule, to react directly to a threat rather than to seek the root of the trouble. Beginners generally lacked the nerve to take imagina-

H

tive decisions. Given the inexperience of the Allied command, the conditions were ripe for expanding a rousing tactical success into a resounding strategic victory.

And instead of understanding the glowing vision that stretched ahead, instead of being aware of it, Arnim was halting the 21st Panzer Division at Sbeitla and sending the 10th Panzer Division to Fondouk and Pichon. The triumphant forces were being dispersed, their momentum was being dissipated.

Telephoning Arnim on Wednesday evening, February 17, Rommel asked whether he intended to strike toward Tebessa. His own forces, the Afrika Korps Detachment and the Centauro Division, he candidly said, were too weak for that kind of attack. An operation against Tebessa was of such scope and significance, he continued, that it could succeed, he believed, only if two preconditions were met: first, the use of the main body of Arnim's mobile forces in the south — his two panzer divisions; and second, the support of a holding attack along the northern front in order to tie down the bulk of the Allied forces.

Arnim was unimpressed. The low levels of his supplies, he said flatly, prohibited a strong exploitation.

Rommel gained the distasteful impression that Arnim was keeping the panzer divisions for a private show of his own.

Since both were army commanders, neither enjoying primacy over the other, and since authoritative coordination from a higher headquarters was lacking, there was no possibility of getting both to execute a strong push into the Western Dorsale. Fruehlingswind and Morgenlust had produced a glorious potential that was coming to a premature and mediocre end.

Disappointed, Rommel started the Centauro Division back to Gafsa on the first leg of its eventual return to bolster the Mareth Line against the approaching British forces under Montgomery.

The weather was rainy and dismal on Thursday, February 18. Yet enough German aircraft were able to fly reconnaissance missions to discover that no Allied troops were concentrated anywhere along the Tunisian front for a counterattack.

The situation was terribly tempting for a lightning thrust to Tebessa.

During the day, the bulk of the 10th Panzer Division assembled behind Pichon; the Centauro Division moved back from Feriana to Gafsa; Group Gerhardt probed from Sbeitla toward Sbiba; Buelowius's Afrika Korps Detachment sent one small force into the passes south of Tebessa and another into the undefended village of Kasserine, where the troops captured about sixty French soldiers trudging back from Sbeitla and welcomed a reconnaissance group coming from the 21st Panzer Division.

Rommel continued to ponder his problem. A fleeting opportunity existed, he was convinced, to accomplish the operation he had envisioned and championed as the reason for bringing his Italo-German army swiftly across Libya into southern Tunisia.

He tried Arnim again on the telephone, but Arnim was unyielding against his blandishments.

At 2:30 that afternoon, Rommel sent Kesselring a message for Comando Supremo: "On the basis of the enemy situation as of today, I propose an immediate enveloping thrust from the southwest on Tebessa and the area to the north of it, provided Fifth Panzer Army's supply situation is adequate. This offensive must be executed with strong forces. I therefore request that 10th Panzer and 21st Panzer Divisions be assigned to me and moved immediately to the assembly area Thelepte–Feriana."

Rommel's concept was clear. He would make a wide sweep around the Allied flank through Tebessa toward the ultimate objective of Bone. This would encircle the Allied reserves being fed into a lengthening line of communications, disrupt those supply lines, and eventually force the Allied troops to pull out of Tunisia altogether.

He figured he had a fifty-fifty chance of approval. The loss of Libya had badly hurt the Duce, who desperately needed a victory to sustain his internal political position. An offensive through Tebessa to Bone would capture the public imagination. And the expulsion of the Allied forces from Tunisia would compensate for the retreat across Libya.

Kesselring had just returned to Rome after his visit with Hitler, and he found Rommel's proposal cogent and persuasive. At 4:30 he sent a radio message to both Arnim and Rommel: "I consider it essential to continue the attack toward Tebessa and northward by concentrating all available forces on the left wing and exploiting our recent successes with a blow that can still have vast consequences for the enemy. This is for your preliminary information. I shall speak in this manner to the Duce and . . . [Comando Supremo] today."

Rommel waited impatiently for a decision.

The Italians were in no hurry.

At 10:30 that night Rommel could no longer restrain himself. He sent an urgent message to Kesselring. A decision was needed quickly, he said; otherwise, as time was lost, the possibility of success was jeopardized. Could the 21st Panzer Division be rushed to Thelepte and the 10th to Kasserine in order to make possible an offensive to be opened toward Tebessa on the following evening?

Comando Supremo had already reached a decision. Word dispatched from Rome at 9:15 reached Tunisia around midnight.

The message was far from clear, and its ambiguous and ambivalent nature made it possible for the principal commanders to interpret at least parts of it as they wished.

Recognizing that "a unique opportunity is now offered to force a decisive success in Tunisia," and convinced that the Mareth positions would be safe from attack for another week or longer, Comando Supremo authorized a deep thrust to the north. To this end, though Rommel had been supposed to hand over command of his Italo-German army to Messe and return to Germany, he was now permitted to stay, his departure deferred to enable him to command, as the phrase was euphoniously stated, "certain operations" before retiring from the field.

While retaining command of the troops manning the Mareth Line, Rommel was to concentrate between Sbeitla and Tebessa all the available mobile elements of his own Italo-German Panzerarmee as well as the 10th and 21st Panzer Divisions formerly assigned to Arnim and now placed under his control. With these forces, he was to strike toward the initial objective of Le Kef, seventy miles north of Kasserine. This would result in a thrust through the French-held sector and bring pressure against the rear of the British troops in the north.

To assist, Arnim was to execute a holding attack along a wide front in the north to tie down and harass the Allied troops; organize a parachute drop on Le Kef in order to destroy the bridges there and prevent the Allied forces from escaping; and, in case Rommel got beyond Le Kef and threatened to reach the northern coast, prepare an amphibious landing on the north shore of Tunisia a few miles from the Algerian frontier.

Both commanders, Comando Supremo promised, would receive stepped-up shipments, by air and by sea, of troops, materiel, and supplies.

Despite Comando Supremo's authorization to attack, the directive displeased and disappointed Rommel. It was, he believed, "an appalling and unbelievable piece of shortsightedness." Selecting Le Kef as the initial objective, in effect, rejected Rommel's proposal for a wide circling movement through and beyond Tebessa into the deep Allied rear. Instead of seeing Tebessa as the first objective of a grand enveloping sweep toward Bone, Comando Supremo regarded Tebessa as the western anchor of a smaller drive to Le Kef. Whereas Rommel envisaged a deep envelopment, Comando Supremo more cautiously saw the possibility of a shallow maneuver, an error, Rommel believed, for the main Axis forces would go directly against incoming Allied reserves and be unable to seize and destroy Tebessa, the principal American base. While he sought a strategic success, Comando Supremo pursued the lesser satisfaction of a tactical triumph. What the Italian command overlooked, in Rommel's opinion, was the essential condition for victory: a thrust far enough behind the Allied front to intercept the Allied reserves and prevent them from rushing into the passes of the Western Dorsale, where they could block the Axis advance.

But there was no time for argument. Otherwise, there would be no operation at all.

Rommel was anxious to start for another reason. The assignment of the two panzer divisions to his control meant a reorganization of the command in Tunisia. He wanted to give Comando Supremo, which was, he knew, far from being entirely well disposed toward him, no time for a change of mind or heart.

At his urgent request for a formal notice of the alteration in the command structure, Comando Supremo established, effective Friday, February 19, a new headquarters called Group Rommel. He was to relinquish at last to Messe the direct command of the Italo-German Panzerarmee, which was renamed the First Italian Army, which was to have immediate responsibility for defending the Mareth positions, and which was to remain under his operational control. He was to take charge of the 10th and 21st Panzer Divisions, which, together with the Afrika Korps Detachment and the Centauro Division, were to perform the "certain operations" authorized. He was to have no authority over Arnim.

Taking Comando Supremo's operational directive literally,

Rommel prepared to strike toward Le Kef rather than Tebessa. There were two routes to Le Kef, through the Sbiba defile and through the Kasserine Pass. Initially, he would attack through both. When he determined which was less firmly held, he would make his main effort through that opening in the Western Dorsale and pour troops through that gap.

He planned to start his attack on Friday morning, February 19, as directed. The 21st Panzer Division, striking from Sbeitla, was to try the Sbiba Gap and if possible get fifty miles beyond to the north and only twenty-five miles short of Le Kef. The composite units of the Afrika Korps were to strike into and through the Kasserine Pass, clearing it if possible in one swift push. The 10th Panzer Division was to return from the Pichon area to Sbeitla, there to prepare for commitment northwest through Sbiba or westward through Kasserine, depending on where the break came.

To give his twin thrusts breadth and to stretch the defenses, Rommel called back from Gafsa the mobile elements of the Centauro Division and directed a strike toward Tebessa through the difficult ground of the Dernaia Pass. Anticipating that the terrain would inhibit a swift advance through this defile, he instructed Buelowius to assist by sending some troops, after getting through the Kasserine Pass, westward to take the Dernaia defenders in the back. Buelowius was also to protect the extreme left flank by probing the opening at El Ma el Abiod, almost due south of Tebessa.

Rommel planned to open his command post near Feriana around noon of Friday, February 19. After progress of the initial attacks demonstrated the softer defenses and the more promising area for a slam-bang exploitation, he would commit the 10th Panzer Division and move his own headquarters close to the main arena.

As Rommel was getting his attack under way on Friday morning, Kesselring flew to Tunisia to guarantee the prompt execution of the directive that he had pried out of Comando

Supremo after considerable exertion. He wanted to make sure that Arnim gave the support needed to make the offensive succeed. Displeased by his failure to report the start of Fruehlingswind, equally dissatisfied by the vague and meager informational reports on the progress of that operation, and uncomfortable because he could not tell from his messages exactly where the 10th Panzer Division was located, Kesselring suspected that Arnim might try to subvert Rommel's attack.

Arnim, he discovered, had an interesting suggestion. Expecting Rommel to make his main effort against Tebessa and seeing no need for a holding attack in the north and center, he recommended instead a concentric attack of his own, generally westward, to Le Kef. He could, he said, tear into the Allied vitals. He would have the 21st Panzer Division strike northwestward from Sbeitla through Sbiba and the 10th Panzer Division westward from Pichon. The dual thrust would engage the main Allied forces and have the additional advantage over Rommel's advance to Tebessa of being closer to the major Axis supply installations in the north and thus more easily supported and sustained. It would, furthermore, permit all the Axis forces to participate in offensive action rather than simply the mobile elements. It would, he was certain, "ensure the complete liberation of Tunisia," whereas Rommel's plan, he felt, would merely force the Allies to fall back toward their principal centers of supply, exactly as the British had done much earlier when they had been pushed back into Egypt.

The argument made sense, but Kesselring rejected the concept. The attack Arnim proposed would plunge directly into the strongest Allied defenses. And it was somewhat late to be tampering with Rommel's arrangements.

Kesselring also had the feeling that Arnim's motivation was less than altruistic. He probably feared that a full-scale attack on Tebessa would draw the bulk of the Axis forces in Tunisia away from his control and into Rommel's.

In addition, Kesselring himself, like Rommel, favored a major stroke against Tebessa and a subsequent wide sweep around the main Allied forces. He believed that the directive issued by Comando Supremo was flexible enough to permit Rommel to make an all-out attack wherever he wished, and he knew that Rommel preferred Tebessa. What he expected Rommel to do was to make his major thrust against Tebessa while launching a nominal and minor show against Le Kef to satisfy Comando Supremo.

Not until Rommel's attack was under way did Kesselring learn that the wording of the directive had failed to make this intention clear.

25

Rommel's long wait on Thursday, the 18th, for authority to continue the attack gave the Allied forces an important day of respite, a lull that was used to good advantage on all echelons. The II Corps was in a state of shock, for a catastrophe had been averted by a small margin, and danger still threatened to deepen the crisis. Badly mauled units were dispersed and intermixed. Many commanders lacked specific missions, and some felt their troops slipping out of control. Everyone was extremely fatigued. The relaxation of the German pressure gave time to restore some kind of personal order that spread cohesion among the men.

"We are a little thin," Fredendall said, "but if they [the Germans] will just reconnoiter for a while, we'll be all set. The longer they let us alone, the better we'll be set."

He wanted, above all, more strength, an infantry battalion "worse than hell," for he was holding "a lot of mountain passes against armor" without a "damn bit of reserve."

Eisenhower had been trying to get men and materiel dispatched from rear areas to replace the combat losses. There was no point in sending the 2d Armored Division, stationed in French Morocco, for the long wearing journey would take too long to have immediate effect. But other units, artillery and tank destroyers, started moving into Tunisia from Algiers, Oran, and even from as far distant as Casablanca. The 9th U.S. Infantry Division would follow from Oran as quickly as transportation could be found. And logisticians were scheduling shipments totaling almost one hundred tanks from dispersed locations in Algeria. Whether the reinforcements would get to the battlefield in time to be of use against Rommel seemed doubtful, but knowledge alone that help was on the way raised morale among the battered troops.

Brand-new American tanks had recently arrived to re-equip the British 6th Armoured Division, which was to turn over its Valentines to the French. A total of 241 Shermans had reached North Africa late in January, and fifty-four diesel-powered tanks came during the second week of February. But instead of getting acquainted with the workings and performance of the Shermans, the tankers of the British division were moving into Sbiba with their old equipment.

Fredendall wanted some of the new machines, at least 120 M-4's, and particularly the fifty-four diesels, to make up the losses in the 1st Armored Division, which, he said, still had a "very fine spirit." He thought it only fair to give the American tankers the new tanks, for he said he sensed a definite feeling of resentment because the British were receiving modern American equipment while the Americans struggled along with obsolute weapons that gave them an overpowering inferiority complex against the Germans.

Most of the Shermans remained in the rear. Eisenhower was unwilling to risk their loss if the Allied front continued to fall back. He had no desire to see the new tanks arrived in the forward area in time to be overrun. Though he decided to hold them until the situation became stabilized, he relented to the extent of permitting the release of about sixty, half to the British, half to the Americans.

Alexander, who had toured the British zone in the north on February 16 and the French sector in the center on the 17th, came to the II Corps headquarters on the 18th and found conditions far worse than he had imagined. A visit to the Kasserine area horrified him. Confusion among the retreating units, uncertainty among commanders, and the lack of a coordinated plan of defense convinced him that drastic measures were necessary to restore stability.

It seemed clear to him that Rommel had originally intended to do little more than slap the II Corps in order to secure his rear and flank at the Mareth Line before meeting Montgomery's Eighth Army. But the consequences of the slap had given Rommel bigger ideas. A proponent of exploiting success to the limit of rashness, Rommel no doubt saw the glittering prospect of a great tactical victory. If he could break through the Western Dorsale at Kasserine or Sbiba, he would find few natural obstacles opposing his advance to the north. A short step beyond the Dorsale would take him into the rear of the French XIX Corps, and another step to Le Kef would get him behind the British. The entire Allied front in Tunisia would be disrupted, and a large-scale withdrawal would be necessary to avoid disaster.

Deciding to take command in Tunisia a day ahead of schedule, on the 19th instead of the 20th, Alexander would issue simple and direct instructions: there could be no withdrawal beyond the Western Dorsale; the front would have to be made stable on the positions then being organized for defense.

* * * *

The area about to erupt in the fury of combat is contained by what might be called a circumferential highway. Picture roads on a map forming a rough and rather lopsided circle. Start at the bottom, at Feriana, and move clockwise. Go northwestward for forty miles through the Dernaia Pass to Tebessa. (Outside the circle, south of the road, fifteen miles almost due south of Tebessa, is the pass of El Ma el Abiod; inside the circle, several miles north of the road, is the Bou Chebka Pass.) At Tebessa, turn right, to the northeast, and follow a narrow mountain route for thirty-five miles through the mining hamlet of Kouif and the ancient Roman military post of Haidra to the hillside village of Thala. This is the top of the circle, almost due north of and forty-five miles from Feriana. From Thala, go to the east, along a trail, twenty-two miles to Sbiba. Then southeast for twenty miles to Sbeitla. Bend to the southwest and move almost twenty miles to Kasserine. Continue another twenty miles to complete the circle at Feriana.

Between Tebessa in the west and Sbiba in the east, a distance of fifty-five air miles, Allied troops awaited the inevitable resumption of the German attack.

At Sbiba, the defenses were relatively strong. McQuillin's CCA had covered the arrival of Keightley's 6th Armoured Division and Ryder's 34th Division, and by the 18th, both divisions had established good defenses that CCA passed through in order to make a long detour to the west and south toward Tebessa.

In front of the defenses established by Keightley and Ryder were impressive mine fields; behind them were British and American artillery. The 16/5 Lancers were in immediate reserve, and the French Light Armored Brigade under Saint-Didier and a small unit called Detachment Guinet guarded against enemy infiltration north of Sbiba.

So confident were the Allied commanders of their ability to repulse an attack that Anderson sent the 26th Armoured Brigade, part of Keightley's division, westward from Sbiba to Thala during the evening of February 18. At Thala, the commander, Brigadier Charles A. L. Dunphie, was to be ready to lend a hand either at Sbiba or at Kasserine, depending on where he was needed.

In the Tebessa area, covering the passes of Dernaia, Bou Chebka, and El Ma el Abiod, were the remnants of Welvert's "Constantine" Division, some units still making their way back from Sbeitla and Feriana on the 18th. Though Welvert lacked precise information on what was happening and exact instructions on what he was to do, he improvised a defense as best he could. Two American battalions, one Ranger and one infantry, plus British troops of the Derbyshire Yeomanry, bolstered the positions his French soldiers set up.

Robinett's CCB marched all day long on the 18th over sodden roads in radio silence, the troops intermingled with other American units and with French groups. Horse-drawn wagons, tired horses, and lame foot soldiers, together with tanks, trucks, and jeeps, moved toward the Tebessa area, while everywhere Arabs stood along the shoulders of the routes bartering chickens and eggs for chewing gum, candy, cigarettes, and clothing. That evening, CCB strengthened Welvert's defenses. CCA would arrive on the 19th.

As soon as CCB settled into the Tebessa area, Fredendall gave Ward the job of coordinating with Welvert the defenses of Dernaia, Bou Chebka, and El Ma el Abiod. He was also to be ready to furnish artillery fires for the troops occupying the Kasserine Pass. For there, the defenses were positively flimsy.

* * * *

To enter the Kasserine Pass from the south, take the blacktopped road out of the village of Kasserine, and head for the midnight-blue mountain range of the Western Dorsale. Cross a flat, grassy prairie for about five miles beyond the village, ascending so gently that the rise to two thousand feet is almost imperceptible.

Suddenly, a small opening appears between two looming hill masses lifting their crests four thousand feet above the floor of the Sbeitla plain. On the left is Djebel Chambi. The one on the right is Semmama. The road runs between them for little more than a mile, and this is the Kasserine Pass. A narrow-gauge railroad goes alongside the highway. So does the Hatab River.

At its most constricted point, the pass is hardly eight hundred yards across, a ravine full of rocks.

On the other side of the Western Dorsale, the road emerges into a vast triangular basin called the Bled Foussana. Dominated by wooded heights everywhere, the basin covers deposits of lead, zinc, and phosphate, all of which are mined. The vegetation is sparse, except along the banks of the Hatab, which bisects the basin. Near the water are cultivated farms and groves, scattered houses; elsewhere, eroded hills, wadis

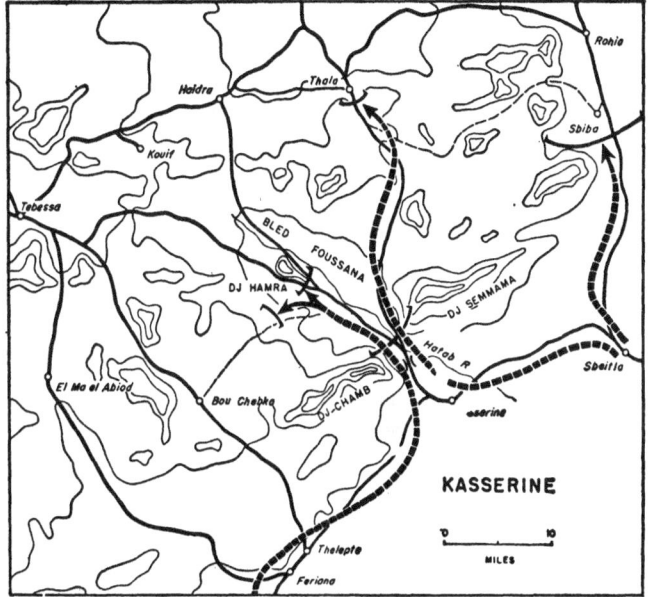

with sheer sides, rocky draws and gullies, patches of cactus.

Soon after the road emerges from the pass and enters the basin, it splits into two routes. The left fork is a dirt road that goes westward for about fifteen miles to a large hill named Djebel Hamra. There the unpaved road gives out. Two trails pick up the track: one goes around the left side of Hamra to Tebessa, twenty miles away; the other around the right side for fifteen miles to Haidra.

At the entrance into the basin, the right fork of the road continues black-topped and goes north. After crossing the Hatab River, it runs for twenty-five miles up a gentle slope and across three small lateral ridges to Thala.

In February, 1943, the ground in the pass and in the Foussana Basin was wet and spongy from heavy rainfall. Wintry clouds, a clammy mist, and bitter cold would add their discomforts to the proximity of death.

* * * *

The first defensive preparations at Kasserine had been carried out on Tuesday, February 16. Moore's engineers laid close to three thousand mines along both sides of the road between the village of Kasserine and the pass. On the 17th, they manned a defensive line east of the village, at the giant fissure washed through the plain by the Hatab River, and covered the withdrawal of the troops from Sbeitla. Early on the 18th, they moved back through the pass and prepared to defend, together with an infantry battalion under Moore's command.

Just inside the Foussana Basin, Moore placed the infantry astride the Thala road. He put his engineers on the western road. His main line of resistance extended almost three miles across the Bled Foussana and was held by about two thousand men who covered the exit from the pass. His idea in defending behind the pass was to canalize the approaching enemy forces, constrict their passage through the Dorsale, and smash them as they were bunched together in the narrows.

Moore's defenses consisted of a triple belt of mines across the roads, the small-arms and automatic weapons fire of his foot soldiers, and the artillery support of two batteries of American 105-mm. howitzers, plus one battery of horse-drawn French 75's. He had patrols covering the high hills on the flanks of the pass to check infiltration. A battalion of tank destroyers in the rear would give general supporting fires and throw back any enemy soldiers who slipped past the patrols.

Employing engineers as infantry is practical in theory, for they are supposedly capable of performing as infantrymen. Yet their training, organization, and equipment are not comparable. Moore's unit consisted of 53 officers, 2 warrant officers, and 1,350 enlisted men, who had 12 motorcycles for message-bearers, and 130 other vehicles; 122 of these were purely for engineer work — 54 dump trucks, 33 cargo trucks, 6 bulldozers, 12 trailers, 11 wreckers, and 6 air compressors;

the other 6 vehicles were jeeps. From the equipment alone, the combat capability was decidedly inferior. Furthermore, only one officer, a captain, had been under fire. Everyone else had yet to experience combat firsthand.

When enemy reconnaissance units gently probed the Kasserine Pass Thursday afternoon, the 18th, and wounded one man slightly, many engineers left their positions and fled to the rear. Some were rounded up and returned to their posts. Others vanished from sight. The reason, Moore later admitted candidly, was fear. Poorly controlled by their officers and non-coms, they were frightened by the enemy fire and by rumors of disaster that had no basis in fact. Discipline began to erode.

The appearance of Germans in front of the pass convinced Fredendall that an attack was imminent. Deciding that he needed an experienced combat officer in charge, he telephoned Stark, commander of the 26th Infantry, who had fought under McQuillin at Faid and Sidi bou Zid and who was then at El Ma el Abiod. "I want you to go to Kasserine right away," Fredendall said, "and pull a Stonewall Jackson. Take over up there."

Stark was flabbergasted. "You mean tonight, General?"

"Yes, immediately. Stop in my C [ommand] P [ost] on the way up."

Stark, together with his staff, set out on that dark night for Kouif, where he conferred, then went on to the pass. He reached his destination around 7:30 A.M., Friday, February 19.

He took control at once, exercising direct command of the infantry along the Thala road and indirect command through Moore of the engineers on the other side of the Hatab River.

Just as Stark was taking over at the Kasserine Pass, the Germans started their attack. The first obstacles they encountered were mine fields.

26

To HELP defend Kasserine, Fredendall had requested that all the mines available in North Africa be supplied to him. About twenty thousand were located in depots near Casablanca and Oran, placed aboard aircraft, and flown in fifty-two planeloads to Youks-les-Bains, the most forward airfield. From there they were trucked to the pass.

A land mine, according to a War Department Field Manual, is an encased charge of explosive fitted with one or more detonating devices designed to be activated by vehicles or personnel. There are two common types: antitank and antipersonnel.

Antitank mines, each with a normal charge of six to twelve pounds, are used to immobilize tracked and wheeled vehicles. Since heavy pressure is necessary to detonate them, they generally pose no danger to personnel passing over them, though the impact of a running man may set one off.

Antipersonnel mines produce casualties to personnel on foot and are ineffective against armored vehicles. Used to protect other mines or obstacles, to enhance local security, or to harass and delay enemy troops, they have an explosive charge anywhere from one-quarter of a pound to four pounds.

The fuse of a mine, the device that produces the flame or concussion to set off the charge, operates by the application or release of pressure, by the pull on a trip wire, the removal of tension, or a delayed-action mechanism.

A booby trap is a device so connected to an explosive charge that the slightest disturbance detonates the charge. It is probably so called because it is designed to ensnare careless boobs. Directed against personnel principally to delay and demoralize by killing and maiming in the most unexpected manner, it is effective in direct ratio to the ingenuity of its installation. Since it relies for its success entirely on surprise, the charge and the operating mechanism are always concealed, attached to a harmless article, or made to resemble a common object.

Mines and standard booby traps are fitted with one or more safety devices, usually a pin. To disarm one, a man locates the hole from which the pin has been withdrawn. Then he inserts a nail or piece of wire, which, normally, makes the mechanism safe. Some booby traps are not standard. Some mines are booby-trapped.

A mine belt is a strip of ground in which mines have been laid in a standard pattern. Normally, there are 1½ mines per yard. In a hasty mine belt, the mines are laid in shallow holes dug in a regular pattern determined by pacing off the required distances. In a deliberate mine belt, the mines are placed in holes of greater depth, and the pattern is established by accurate measurements.

A mine field consists of several mine belts, which are designed to break up and canalize an enemy's attack formation and restrict his movements to areas covered by defensive fires, particularly those of antitank and automatic weapons. To prevent the enemy from removing mines, there must be maximum coverage of a mine field by small arms and antitank fires.

Selecting the site for a mine field is of vital importance, for once laid the mine field fixes the location of supporting weapons and determines to a large extent the course of future operations. Close cooperation among all troop components to site, lay, and protect mine fields is essential. The ground must be thoroughly reconnoitered. All mine fields must be clearly marked, accurately recorded, and promptly reported to prevent friendly troops from falling victim to the installation. Unless covered by fire, a mine field usually fails to delay the enemy enough to warrant the labor and materials expended on its emplacement.

Installing each section of a hasty mine belt is normally the work of a platoon. An officer is in charge. One non-commissioned officer and two men form the siting party. One non-com and twelve men place the mines. One non-com and eighteen men bury them. One non-com and four men mark them. One non-com and two men record their locations. Total personnel required: one officer, five non-coms, thirty-eight men.

A 2½-ton truck can transport 370 unboxed or 500 boxed antitank mines. Using carrying handles, one man can carry four mines, two in each hand, a total weight of approximately forty pounds.

Accidents sometimes happen. Near Gafsa, the unexpected explosion of a mine while a field was being laid killed one man and wounded three. Near Sidi bou Zid, when a jeep ran over and activated a mine, the driver was injured, the lieutenant had both feet broken, a French soldier hitching a ride on the hood had his leg blown off and died from shock and loss of blood.

* * * *

Around 7:30 on the rainy night of Thursday, February 18, First Lieutenant Edwin C. Dryden of the 19th Engineers was summoned to the regimental headquarters. He learned that the battalion of infantry on the Thala road wanted a hasty mine field for additional security. With the help of two sergeants, both good men, he was to get the mines in before daybreak. The infantry would furnish the transportation and the men for the work, and would show him where the mines were to be put.

A truck from the infantry battalion arrived shortly before midnight, and several engineer soldiers placed a load of mines aboard. Dryden and the two sergeants climbed into the truck, and the driver headed back to the infantry.

The night was dark. The route to the infantry positions was roundabout and over very poor roads made slick by the rain. Using blackout lights, the driver crawled cautiously in low gear most of the way.

It was about 1:30 in the morning when the driver stopped. There, he pointed, in a clump of cactus was the headquarters of an infantry company. There Dryden would find the mine-laying detail.

He found only the company executive officer, who knew nothing about the request for mines. He advised Dryden to go toward Kasserine for two or three miles. Somewhere along the road, he would undoubtedly find someone who was waiting for him.

As Dryden turned to go, the executive officer had a further thought. Watch out for the Jerries, he added.

Getting back into the cab of the truck, Dryden told the driver to continue. Take it easy, he warned.

Slowly, the truck traveled a mile or two. Dryden saw no one.

Except for the motor of the truck and the rainfall, the night was quiet, the abnormal quiet of someone holding his breath. Occasionally, the sharp clacking stutter of a machine gun sounded in the distance.

Turn around, he told the driver, and go back to the company.

Backing the truck, cutting the wheels hard, going forward, backing once more was an interminable process finally completed.

They were soon back at the company. The executive officer still had no information about a mine field.

Where was the company commander? Dryden asked.

Asleep.

Dryden insisted that he be awakened.

Reluctantly, the executive officer roused the company commander.

Dryden told him that he wanted to be shown the position selected for the mine field. He needed a platoon of forty men with picks and shovels.

The company commander could spare only twenty men at most. He assured Dryden he would send them with an officer, who would point out where the road was to be blocked by mines.

Dryden returned to the truck and waited.

Around 3:30, an infantry lieutenant showed up with about twelve men. He was apologetic. Three of his party, he told Dryden, had vanished into the night when patrols from their own company had fired into the group.

But he was ready to go. What did Dryden want him to do? Didn't he know?

No, the lieutenant said. He had been awakened and ordered to take a detail of men to this point and meet an engineer officer. That was all he knew. He had no other instructions.

Dryden presented the problem.

The lieutenant wasn't much help. He didn't have the slightest idea where a mine field could be effectively established and covered by fire.

There was no time for discussion. Or for reconnaissance. Daybreak was fast approaching.

Though Dryden had never seen the ground in daylight, he arbitrarily chose a level space of about one hundred yards between an embankment on one side of the road and a steep hill on the other.

Quickly, he and his assistants instructed the men of the detail how to lay and arm mines. Then they put the men to work.

The mines were wet and slippery. The infantrymen were clumsy. Many had never seen a mine before. Their short-handled entrenching tools were of little value for digging in the rocky soil just below the soggy surface of the ground.

Seeing no possibility of getting the job done right, and certainly not before daylight, Dryden had the men lay a very hasty field. An exceedingly hasty mine field. They left most of the mines unburied. Strewn across the ground, the mines were worse than useless. Except maybe to make the Germans stop for five or ten minutes.

As dawn edged the horizon, Dryden released the men. Together with the sergeants, he returned to the engineer headquarters, getting back around 7 A.M., February 19, twelve hours after he had received word of his mission.

The rain had stopped, but the sky was covered with clouds, and a cold wind blew through the Kasserine Pass.

He felt somewhat uncomfortable. He didn't know that the German attack would start in thirty minutes, but he wished his mine field had not been quite so hasty.

27

The sky was cloudy on the morning of Friday, February 19, the ground soggy. The stream beds, normally dry and empty, were filled to overflowing, and the water rushed and roared through the channels in great excitement.

The Hatab River was unfordable for most of its course through the Foussana Basin, and physical contact between Moore's engineers along the Tebessa road and Stark's infantry along the Thala road was difficult. Rain had filled the bowl of Bled Foussana with mud, and even tracked vehicles would have difficulty moving off the roads.

Rommel's attack jumped off as Buelowius sent a battalion of infantry through the narrows. In the hope of slipping through and overwhelming the defenders by surprise, he withheld an artillery preparation.

The appearance of the Germans triggered an immediate reaction on the Allied side. Artillery and small-arms fire sent the attackers scrambling up the sides of the heights flanking the pass in search of cover.

While Stark was surveying his situation and concluding that he probably lacked enough forces to hold the pass, Buelowius committed more troops. About forty trucks brought panzer grenadiers to the pass, 88-mm. cannons opened up, and some German soldiers entered the basin while a sizable group climbed the shoulder of Djebel Semmama.

As Buelowius was deciding to commit still another battalion to the attack, Stark was telling Fredendall that a strong attack might be under way, it was hard to tell. Shells were falling near his command post tent, but this didn't seem very serious.

Early in the afternoon, when a handful of French soldiers who had been driven off the heights overlooking the pass informed Stark that Germans were scaling the slopes of Chambi and Semmama, he no longer doubted that he was under attack.

Some British mortars and reconnaissance troops arrived to reinforce him that afternoon, along with a battalion of the 39th Infantry, a regiment of the 9th U.S. Division.

Moore immediately asked for a rifle company of the 39th Infantry. "Wire out," he radioed — meaning his telephone wires had been cut by artillery shells or enemy action. "Four [engineer] companies committed" — meaning he had no reserves. "Can I take [a] line company [of the] 39th and place on right flank[?]" And somewhat plaintively, "[It] will take orders from you to get them to move" — meaning that infantrymen disliked receiving orders from engineers; they would respond better to instructions from Stark, an infantry officer.

Stark gave him two companies, one for each flank. But the riflemen lacked knowledge of the area and were wary of the enemy fires. It took them all afternoon to get into position.

On the other side of the pass, Rommel had motored from Feriana to the village of Kasserine, where Buelowius had his command post. On the road, he had passed knocked-out American vehicles, their drivers dead at the wheel; he had seen small groups of American prisoners being marched to enclosures in the rear; he had become aware of the rubbish of warfare — scraps of metal, blown-off fenders, the cab of a truck, a dead horse, tattered clothing, burned tires.

Announcing his intention to make his main effort through the Sbiba Gap, he wanted the Kasserine Pass in order to prevent the Allies from attacking the flank of the major forces to be committed through Sbiba. When Buelowius gained control of the narrows, he was to launch a feint toward Tebessa to keep the Allied troops off balance and disguise the direction of the principal thrust.

Buelowius assured him he would have the pass before the end of the day.

* * * *

That morning, on the plateau of Bou Chebka about twenty miles west of Kasserine, Robinett had visited Ward, who seemed to lack "his usual good cheer." Part of his depression came from fatigue, but more came from his grief over the losses his division had suffered. He offered one observation. The orderly manner in which the troops had pulled out of Sbeitla pleased him. "The division made a good withdrawal," he said with a tight, wry smile.

About the same time, Anderson was asking Koeltz for a favor. Since Fredendall had no infantry reserves, could Koeltz cede the 16th Infantry at once and the rest of Allen's 1st Division later?

Koeltz understood the need. That evening, the 16th Infantry would start marching toward the Bou Chebka Pass.

* * * *

At the Kasserine Pass, Buelowius launched a powerful attack around 3:30 in the afternoon of Friday, the 19th. German infantrymen and tankers who struck to the north beyond the fork in the road were stopped cold by a mine field, machine-gun bullets, antitank fires, and artillery shells; those who thrust westward were halted by furious fires from engineers who were standing fast despite their nervousness. At least five German tanks were knocked out, and others became bogged down in the mud.

At Thala, the noise of the German attack disquieted Dunphie, who commanded the 26th Armoured Brigade. Going forward to see what was happening, he found Stark confident, even optimistic, though his headquarters was under occasional enemy rifle fire. He had the impression that Stark was whistling to keep up his courage.

Stark said he was going out to look around. Would Dunphie care to join him?

The two commanders started to walk toward the front, but they had to return quickly, for several soldiers fired at them from a ditch. Whether the bullets came from enemy infiltrators or from friendly troops with itchy trigger fingers was beside the point. Dunphie judged Stark's communications tenuous, his control about to collapse. A coordinated defense appeared impossible. The Germans, in Dunphie's opinion, were about to break through the pass.

While Stark calmly ordered out a patrol to check on the source of the nearby firing, Dunphie returned to Thala and phoned Anderson's chief of staff. He asked for authority to reinforce Stark's defenses and bring some order into the area.

The chief of staff said he would drive over to Thala and see for himself whether Dunphie's troops were needed.

Meanwhile, what Buelowius had failed to take by force, he set about to steal by infiltration. Small groups of soldiers working their way into the heights along both sides of the pass cut behind defensive positions and, around dusk, encircled and captured about one hundred Americans defending the Thala road.

Across the Hatab River, upon the approach of darkness, the inexperienced engineers began to show signs of what was sometimes called night fever — chattering teeth, knocking knees, and an inclination to run to the rear. As the German pressure finally began to take effect, one company broke and fled.

Moore radioed a report and an explanation. The infantry on the other side of the river, he said, had pulled back unexpectedly — he was undoubtedly referring to the encircled and captured troops — thereby exposing his flank. Then his supporting tank destroyers had moved back suddenly. The sequence of these two occurrences had demoralized the company of engineers. But he had reorganized what he could find of the fleeing men, and he had ordered the tank destroyers to return to their positions. He was setting up a counterattack to regain the abandoned defenses.

It would take Moore most of the night to get a counterattack ready, and in the end he would be unable to get it off.

As night descended over the Kasserine Pass, the situation was indecisive. Buelowius, despite his promise, had failed to take the narrows. Stark, despite the arrival of reinforcements, still lacked a solid defense.

Recognizing the confusion that the tactic of infiltration prompted among the American defenders, particularly along the Tebessa road, Buelowius ordered strong patrols to keep aggressive contact during the night. He placed his infantry well forward for pursuit operations in the event of American collapse or withdrawal.

Stark remained optimistic. After moving his command post back two miles to keep German artillery fire from breaking his wire communications, he asked for additional units — tanks, tank destroyers, infantry, and artillery, and for lots of air support in the morning.

Fredendall sent him a battalion of infantry under Lieutenant Colonel W. W. Wells, and a battalion of tank destroyers, and these units moved into Bled Foussana during the night.

Anderson's chief of staff, who came to Thala in response to Dunphie's report on the deteriorating conditions on Stark's front, found the situation rather quiet. Buelowius's attack having subsided, he saw no necessity to commit Dunphie's command. Stark seemed to have enough troops to "handle things as they are," even though he admitted that Stark seemed to lack a good "grip on things." Dunphie's brigade was to stay in reserve as long as the situation remained uncertain, for he wanted Dunphie to be available in case the Germans broke through at Sbiba.

At Dunphie's urging, he gave permission to move a light

detachment toward the pass. Under Lieutenant Colonel A. C. Gore of the 10th Battalion, The Rifle Brigade, a force of eleven tanks, a company of motorized infantry, a battery of artillery, and several antitank guns went forward from Thala during the night.

* * * *

Around nine o'clock that Friday morning of February 19, the 21st Panzer Division had started north from Sbeitla toward Sbiba. Wet ground delayed the approach march, and not until noon did the point of the armored column reach a narrow belt of mines across the road, about six miles below the village. German engineers opened a gap in the mine field, while artillery covered them by firing against the Allied forces on the heights. A short advance brought the column around 2 P.M. to a much better laid mine field, which was covered by Allied artillery, and the Germans were greeted by a hail of shells.

The German column stopped and pulled back. Then a group of about twenty-five tanks and some truck-borne infantry swept eastward out of range of the Allied artillery and cut north against Ryder's infantry.

A detachment of British Lancers sallied out to deter the attack, lost four light tanks to the heavier German guns, and retired.

The Germans then brought up several batteries of light field howitzers, got them into firing positions, and began to spray the Allied troops on the ridge, while infantry prepared to assault.

At this time, Rommel arrived at the division command post. From his observations, he gathered that the division commander, Colonel Hans Georg Hildebrandt, was readying a cautious frontal attack with tanks well spread to keep casualties to a minimum. Since this type of formation also diminished striking power, he urged Hildebrandt to concentrate his forces in depth on a narrow front and push with all his might for an immediate breakthrough.

The advice was good but too late. Allied artillery units had plotted more than one hundred targets in advance, and despite a lack of satisfactory observation on that cloudy day, they fired accurately and devastatingly on the German tanks and infantry.

After losing about a dozen tanks, Hildebrandt, with Rommel's consent, called off his attack before it was properly started. The waterlogged roads inhibited maneuver. And the defensive positions were well placed, stoutly defended, and heavily protected. Abandoning the disabled tanks, as well as other vehicles that had become bogged down in the mud, he pulled his troops back and dug defensive positions about seven miles south of Sbiba.

Koeltz, Keightley, and Ryder had won the first round, but a second was surely in the offing. After dark, the defenders at Sbiba redoubled their mine-laying efforts and stretched more barbed wire in front of their positions. They expected a resumption of the attack in the morning.

Disappointed by the check of the 21st Panzer Division before Sbiba, Rommel reflected momentarily on the opportunity lost at Tebessa. An offensive through Tebessa would probably have gotten well under way before meeting serious resistance. At Sbiba and Kasserine, the opposing forces had collided at once.

But the Tebessa possibility was gone. The chessmen were disposed, and the game was well under way.

The immediate problem was to decide where to make his main effort. The terrain at Kasserine was less favorable for offensive maneuver, but the defenses appeared weaker than at Sbiba. On this basis, Rommel changed his mind. Instead of merely sealing off the Kasserine Pass behind a feint toward Tebessa, he decided now to concentrate the weight of his effort at Kasserine.

The 10th Panzer Division was marching to Sbeitla, and there General Fritz Freiherr von Broich, the division commander, was to learn whether he was to continue westward to Kasserine or turn north toward Sbiba. The instructions were for Kasserine. He was to be ready at dawn of Saturday, the 20th, to push through the pass toward Thala, while Buelowius struck westward to block the defiles leading to Tebessa and Haidra.

It would be impossible for Broich to attack through the Kasserine Pass at daybreak. Retarded by the bad weather and the poor condition of the roads, he had gotten only advance elements to Sbeitla by Friday night.

Rommel chafed under the delay, for he believed passionately in the lightning thrust. Waiting impatiently for his forces to gather, he was aware of the frantic efforts on the Allied side to build a barrier along the Western Dorsale. He realized too that his time was limited — Montgomery's approach to the Mareth Line might be slow, but eventually he would get there. Yet everywhere Rommel looked, at Kasserine, where Buelowius had failed to take the pass, at Sbiba, where Hildebrandt had bogged down, and at Sbeitla, where Broich was moving ponderously, no one seemed to appreciate the need for speed.

The worst was yet to come. Broich's division, Rommel learned that evening, was only at half strength. Important elements, notably the heavy panzer battalion, which had almost two dozen Tiger tanks, were absent. They were still in Arnim's sector because he had refused to release them to Rommel's control.

To compensate for the late arrival of the 10th Panzer Division and its reduced power, Rommel brought forward tanks and *bersaglieri* from the Centauro Division. Coming up from the Feriana area, these units reinforced Buelowius's Afrika Korps Detachment at Kasserine during the night.

* * *

If a solid punch was still lacking at Kasserine, the flurry of short jabs that Buelowius was managing to throw during the hours of darkness was on the verge of achieving a knockout.

Stragglers in increasing numbers from the American infantry battalion along the Thala road indicated how well the Germans were succeeding in undermining the defensive positions by infiltration and encirclement: one of the three rifle companies was cut off, the battalion command post was surrounded, and the other companies were out of control.

By midnight of Friday, February 19, the situation was a perfect example of fluidity. Some troops were holding out, others were fleeing in panic, many were missing, and no one knew exactly what was going on and precisely how many troops were left to block the Thala road.

On the other side of the Hatab River, barring the Tebessa road, the engineers were still in position, remaining so despite steady pressure from German patrols, much nervousness and milling around, and some flight to the rear. Moore reported that he had lost two men killed, ten wounded, and forty-four who were missing; but these figures could be only the vaguest kind of approximation, and no doubt on the optimistic side.

Still trying to get a counterattack organized, he sent a lieutenant to guide several artillery forward observers to a good post. When the small group arrived, one artilleryman announced simply, "This place is too hot," and all departed.

He then attempted to direct artillery fire by map coordinates, but his efforts were in vain. The batteries were moving to the rear, and as a result of their haste all check points previously registered were of no value.

In contrast, the French battery of 75-mm. howitzers stayed in place and furnished solid support.

Moore canceled his plans when stragglers turned up and

announced the disruption of the infantry defenses along the Thala road. There was no point in counterattacking if the Germans were about to burst through the pass.

As for the other units, no one was quite sure what the battalion of the 39th Infantry was doing, but the tank destroyers, it appeared, had lost eight guns, more than half, to enemy fires.

The defense of the Kasserine Pass seemed about to disintegrate.

* * * *

Earlier that night, when Fredendall learned that the 16th Infantry was moving from Koeltz's sector toward Bou Chebka, he began to think of sending a portion of Ward's 1st Armored Division to reinforce the troops in the Foussana Basin. He sent word, not to Ward, but to Robinett, who commanded CCB.

The message that Robinett received an hour after midnight — at one o'clock on Saturday morning, the 20th — was garbled, without punctuation, composed in haste and transmitted in some excitement. After being straightened out, it read as follows: "General Robinett — Fight going on south. Stark has been attacked during the night by a small number of tanks, estimated 3 battalions infantry, and supported by artillery. Attack sometime during night resulting in some infiltration at flanks. . . . In the event of a penetration of the Kasserine Pass, you will be prepared to move a portion of your division" — Robinett was startled; was Ward relieved and was Robinett now in command of the division? — "to counterattack . . . [from Haidra or Thala]. The situation at this time is not serious. This is furnished only for your information and planning."

Robinett immediately alerted his subordinates and checked out the message with Ward's headquarters. Ward, so far as everyone knew, was still in command.

It was the old story. Fredendall was bypassing Ward. The relations between the two men had so deteriorated that Fredendall had telephoned Truscott to say that Ward "simply had to be relieved" of his command. Would Truscott talk to Eisenhower about getting a replacement?

When Terry Allen, commander of the 1st Infantry Division, arrived at Bou Chebka with the 16th Infantry Regiment, Fredendall gave him the broad mission formerly assigned to Ward — control of the defenses of the entire area south of Foussana: the Western Dorsale from Djebel Chambi to El Ma el Abiod.

* * * *

What kept the Kasserine defenses intact during the hours of darkness on the morning of Saturday, February 20, was the arrival of two units — Gore's small composite force of British tanks, infantry, and artillery, and Wells's battalion of American infantry.

Despite a spreading sense of uncertainty among the Allied troops in the basin, the exits from the pass leading northward to Thala and westward to Tebessa were, somewhat miraculously, still blocked at daylight of the 20th.

28

THE WEATHER was still bad on Saturday, February 20. A heavy, damp mist clung to the ground. Throughout the day, from time to time, a drizzle would dilute still further the consistency of the surface mud, penetrate men's collars and shoes, leave a thin sheen of moisture on gun barrels, and cloud the windshields of vehicles.

At seven o'clock on that foggy morning, Rommel drove to the village of Kasserine, where he saw Broich, who was bringing his 10th Panzer Division forward from Sbeitla, and Buelowius, who was preparing his second day's attack. To his practiced eye, neither officer was acting energetically. He wanted Buelowius to make room quickly on the Foussana Basin for Broich's troops and Broich to be ready for commitment. Becoming outwardly and visibly angry for show and effect, he berated his subordinates. Both jumped to.

On the other side of the pass, Stark was trying to hold things together. After a virtually sleepless night, he learned that Gore's troops had moved forward to re-establish blocking positions near the fork in the road. He ordered Wells to climb the slopes of Djebel Semmama and protect Gore's flank.

Buelowius's attack, which started at 8:30 with the crashing roar of a massive artillery preparation and the terrifying shrieks of Nebelwerfer, ran into Gore's detachment on the Thala road and slowed. But on the Tebessa road, Moore's engineers began to give way.

Apprised of the German pressure, Fredendall sent Robinett a message. He was to march his CCB without delay through Haidra to Thala and assume command of all the units defending the Kasserine Pass. Would he come ahead of his troops and report personally to Fredendall, who was going to be somewhere on the road south of Thala?

With a less than perfect understanding of the situation, Fredendall expected Robinett to clear the Germans from the narrows before the end of the day. The only question was where to get him started. Which road? The road from Tebessa, from Haidra, or from Thala? To find the answer, Fredendall drove from Kouif to Thala, then started toward the Kasserine Pass.

Buelowius, sensing the road to Tebessa opening in midmorning, committed tanks and *bersaglieri* of the Italian Centauro Division, plus more German troops in that direction. But on the Thala road he was unable to gain enough space to permit the commitment of Broich's forces and, as a consequence, the bulk of the 10th Panzer Division remained assembled and unemployed east of the Kasserine village.

After checking the progress of operations at Sbiba, Rommel returned to Kasserine before noon. He decided to apply more pressure to open the road to Thala, and he ordered Broich to wait no longer, but to commit part of his division to clear the bottleneck.

The need for a quick breakthrough had become overriding, not only because of the Allied buildup along the Western Dorsale but also because of a development far to his rear. Montgomery had that morning attacked the rearguards screening the Mareth positions and a violent struggle was taking place that would last all day long. Once the screening forces retired behind the Mareth Line outposts — an event that would take place that night — a major battle at Mareth could be expected within a matter of days. If Rommel was going to gain a decisive victory at the Western Dorsale and drive into the deep Allied rear, he would have to do so soon — before Montgomery attacked.

Kesselring was in Tunisia that day, and he came to Kasserine for lunch with Rommel. He agreed that the pass would have to be forced open rapidly if the operation was to have any chance of real success. Where was Rommel planning to make his main effort beyond the narrows? A feint toward Thala perhaps and a major strike toward Tebessa?

Rommel was undecided. A thrust to Tebessa had the disadvantage of taking his major forces away from the support of the 21st Panzer Division at Sbiba.

At Sbiba, Hildebrandt was trying for the second day to storm the Allied ridge positions. Infantry attacked with heavy artillery support to tie down the defenders while forty tanks made a wide sweep around the flank to envelop the village from the rear and cut the road leading north. The concept was excellent, but the execution poor. The fog and rain over the battle area and elsewhere in Tunisia deprived the German assault elements of preparatory air attacks and promised air support but had little effect on the Allied artillery, which fired with disturbing accuracy. When the enveloping force found its route of advance impassable because of the soft ground, the attack was as good as dead. Infantrymen pushed through the heavy Allied shelling and moved within range of small arms and mortar fires, but when Hildebrandt sent tanks to help, they were driven back and the attack collapsed.

Though German casualties were relatively slight, the offensive effort came to a standstill in the early afternoon. Ineffective and irresolute, mainly as a consequence of the volume and accuracy of the Allied artillery, the attack seemed tentative from the Allied point of view and reprehensible from Rommel's.

* * * *

The place where Rommel was succeeding was along the Tebessa road, where a relentless advance drove the American engineers out of their positions and sent them fleeing across Foussana.

"Enemy overrunning our CP," Moore radioed in some excitement exactly at noon. "Am moving CP and taking to high ground on our left."

He relocated his command post, only to come under machine-gun fire. Several minutes later, a tide of enemy infantrymen swept through the area and engulfed the installation.

Moore and his executive officer escaped. How they made it, they would never know. But an hour later they turned up at Stark's headquarters and announced that the 19th Engineers no longer existed.

With enemy fires coming in from their flanks and across their routes of withdrawal, the engineers fell back in disorder. Tank destroyers and artillery moved to the rear. The French battery of 75's, out of ammunition and unable to move because the gun carriages lacked traction, destroyed the howitzers. As the defense crumbled, small groups of men made their way to the rear as best they could. All afternoon long and into the night, the troops who had been blocking the Tebessa road scurried across the basin toward Djebel Hamra, fifteen miles away.

It would take several days to account for most of the men and total the losses. Then it would become evident that during the three days of combat between the 18th and 21st of February, the 19th Engineers had slowed Rommel's offensive at a cost of eleven men killed, twenty-eight wounded, and eighty-nine missing.

*   *   *   *

Shortly before noon of Saturday, the 20th, after getting CCB started toward Haidra, Robinett hurried off to meet Fredendall. As he ascended the steep grade into Thala past crowds of "uncommonly excited" Arabs, he wondered what special sources of information they had for knowing how the battle was progressing.

Beyond Thala, after turning toward the Kasserine Pass, Robinett met Fredendall, who was returning from his brief inspection tour. He had been about halfway to Stark's command post when he learned that the defenses covering the Thala road had collapsed. He had then started back to find Robinett more quickly.

During his short trip, Fredendall had decided it would be impractical to give Robinett command of all the forces in the basin. Instead, he would set up two distinct defensive sectors, with Dunphie to control all the troops north of the Hatab River, Robinett all those to the south.

This is what he told Robinett when they met and conferred at the side of the Thala road in midafternoon. "Head your column off at Haidra," he said, "and move southeast and secure the passes of Djebel el Hamra," — meaning the roads going around Hamra to Tebessa and Haidra — "stop enemy advance in that sector, drive him out of the valley, and restore our position in the Kasserine Pass."

It was a large order.

"If you get away with this one, Robby," Fredendall said, "I'll make you a field marshal."

Flattered by Fredendall's confidence, Robinett promised to do his best.

"Good luck," Fredendall said, and got into his jeep and drove away.

Robinett sent a staff officer to turn the CCB column at Haidra, get the troops into an assembly area near Djebel Hamra, and prepare for action.

As he assembled and briefed his unit commanders at Haidra on that cold and rainy evening, he had no idea that Anderson had inserted another link into the chain of command forged by Fredendall.

Anderson was dispatching Brigadier Cameron G. G.

Nicholson, assistant commander of the British 6th Armoured Division, from Sbiba to Thala with additional troops. He was to act as Fredendall's representative and, with a skeleton headquarters named the "Nickforce," take control of the operations of all the British, American, and French troops in the Bled Foussana south of Thala — the units commanded by Dunphie, Robinett, Stark, and others.

Then Anderson issued a directive for all the troops: "There will be no withdrawal from the positions now held by the First Army. No man will leave his post unless it is to counterattack."

* * * *

On the Thala road, Gore and his men made a valiant stand on the afternoon of Saturday, February 20. With mounting casualties, they fought until their last tank was destroyed before giving way, accompanied by five American tank destroyers left of forty.

Sensing the withdrawal and nagged by disturbing thoughts of the struggle along the approaches to the Mareth Line, Rommel galvanized the attack. Around 4:30 that afternoon he ordered all of Buelowius's and Broich's troops through the pass. As Germans and Italians poured through the Kasserine narrows, the exit fell completely into Axis hands. Engineers quickly repaired the Hatab River bridge, damaged by artillery, and a strong tank-infantry force broke up the Allied retirement along the Thala road. Overrunning half a dozen American tanks, Germans cut off Stark's and Wells's infantry on the heights of Semmama. They pushed small and by now scattered Allied elements back against the mountains and systematically destroyed them. All the armored personnel carriers of Wells's battalion that were parked near the base of Semmama were suddenly endangered, and most of the drivers had no choice but to take off on foot, leaving the dispersed riflemen to get out as they could. As

Rommel's drive picked up speed, about twenty Allied tanks and thirty troop carriers, many of the latter trailing a 75-mm. gun, fell into German hands.

In the midst of the excitement, Rommel found time to ponder briefly on the quality of the captured materiel. The Americans, he observed, were fantastically well equipped and organized. The standardization of their vehicles and spare parts was astonishing. The Germans, he reflected, had much to learn in this field.

* * * *

Around nightfall, it became apparent to Stark that enemy patrols were closing in on his command post. All afternoon, while enemy artillery had beat a tattoo along the left side of his sector, his own troops had dribbled down from the foothills in search of escape, and he had re-formed them and sent them back. Now, enemy rifle fire was extremely close. Unless he got out, he was sure to be overrun. Closing his headquarters, he and his staff members began to walk up the road toward Thala. Stragglers joined his party, some claiming that the Germans were only two hundred yards behind them. They walked on, all showing signs of exhaustion, but otherwise — so it seemed to Stark — displaying the same old fighting spirit.

He reached Dunphie's headquarters around midnight. A message awaited him. The enemy, Fredendall had informed him, was reliably reported in firm possession of the Kasserine Pass.

This was the least of Stark's worries. What concerned him was the virtual disappearance of the infantrymen who had fought along the Thala road. As near as he could tell, at least 150 officers and men were missing. Probably more. Many troops were still out on the hills, completely surrounded.

As it turned out, the losses among the American infantry

under Stark totaled about 30 killed, 100 wounded, and 350 missing.

The only satisfaction Stark had was his certainty that he had blocked the Germans for two days.

* * * *

Kesselring, who flew back to Rome that afternoon, stopped at the Tunis airfield, summoned Arnim to a meeting, and discovered that the Fifth Panzer Army commander was still suspicious of Rommel's intentions. Arnim believed that Rommel was eventually going to attack, not toward Le Kef, but toward Tebessa, and this would divert the main course of operations away from his own army. Again he urged an attack by the 10th and 21st Panzer Divisions toward Le Kef, not from the south under Rommel, but from the east under his control.

But Kesselring had come to Tunis for quite another reason. He censured Arnim bluntly for having withheld important elements of the 10th Panzer Division from Rommel's control, thereby weakening Rommel's attack.

Arnim replied that the accusation was unjust. The units he was charged with retaining against orders had not been in reserve and available; they were in close contact with Allied forces and virtually impossible to disengage from the front. He had sent, he said, what parts of the division he could.

Brushing aside his transparently poor excuse, Kesselring instructed him to send the remaining elements to Rommel at once. He ordered him to make an immediate diversionary attack north of Pichon. Very specifically, almost insultingly, he advised him to keep a tank battalion in reserve to exploit success.

That evening Arnim obeyed, but only partially. He called together his subordinate commanders and instructed them to be ready to attack on Monday, February 22, and to pursue at the first indication of an Allied withdrawal. But he stubbornly retained what he had of the 10th Panzer Division, most significantly a battalion of the tremendous Tiger tanks.

At Tunis, Kesselring also saw a Comando Supremo representative, an Italian general. "In order to guarantee co-ordination of these operations by unified command," Kesselring told him, "I shall recommend to Comando Supremo [in Rome] that Field Marshal Rommel assume command of Fifth Panzer Army in so far as elements of that army are, or will be, participating in the drive."

It was somewhat late to set up a unified command. But perhaps still worth doing.

At Kasserine, Rommel suddenly became cautious. Though tankers of the Italian Centauro Division rolled for five miles down the Tebessa road without meeting opposition and reconnaissance troops radioed that organized resistance along the Thala road had disappeared, he halted their advances. Expecting a counterattack on the following day, he wanted the units held well in hand, ready to crush the Allied onrush. After that, the roads would be altogether open for the subsequent thrust to Le Kef. Or perhaps to Tebessa. He still hadn't decided.

29

AROUND 11 P.M., Saturday, February 20, Robinett received a message telling him to go to Thala, there to meet at midnight with Nicholson, who was taking command of the troops in the Foussana Basin. He departed at once.

At Thala, in the dimly lighted hallway of the French post office that served as Dunphie's command post, he saw Stark, who appeared exhausted. Anderson's chief of staff, Brigadier C. V. O'N. McNabb, in striking contrast to the others in the building, was well groomed, freshly shaved, relaxed, a model of the self-reliant and confident British General Staff officer. Sitting at a table on which a map of the area had been spread, he sipped his tea.

Nicholson, who was struggling through the mire of a mountain track from Sbiba to Thala, was still absent at midnight.

A few minutes beyond that appointed hour, McNabb asked all staff officers to leave the room. Then to Dunphie, Robinett, and Stark, who remained, he announced, "Since Nicholson has not arrived, the II Corps will be responsible for the coordination of forthcoming operations."

No one seemed to notice the lack of representation from Fredendall's headquarters.

McNabb proceeded to outline the state of affairs in Tunisia. Speaking slowly and with measured words, he characterized the situation as "desperately critical." Most of the tanks of the 1st Armored Division, except those of Robinett's CCB, had been destroyed, and the 6th Armoured Division had not yet received its new M-4 tanks. Matters had deteriorated far too much, he believed, to think of retaking the Kasserine

Pass during the next twenty-four hours. The Allies could remain in Tunisia only if they held the passes leading to Tebessa and Le Kef.

What should be done? he asked. Were there any suggestions?

Robinett spoke up. Everyone, he proposed, should remain first on the defensive — Dunphie to meet the enemy in front of Thala, while he covered the roads to Tebessa and Haidra. After stopping and disorganizing the enemy assault units, they should both attack toward the Kasserine Pass. Acting together, they could force the enemy out of Foussana.

After some discussion, McNabb approved this plan. They would await attack, then counterattack at once, making their main efforts on the outer flanks.

He added a cautionary word. The commanders in both sectors were to conserve their tanks as much as possible by advancing to the narrows with infantry moving across the high ground enclosing the basin.

Dunphie, whose main line of resistance was now nine miles north of the Kasserine Pass and on the second lateral ridge about halfway between the narrows and Thala, was to fight a delaying action to the third and last lateral ridge. There, three miles below Thala, a battalion of the 5th Leicesters, which had arrived from Sbiba that evening, was erecting a final defensive line. If the Germans penetrated these defenses, the road to Le Kef would be open and the Allied forces would probably have to start evacuating all of Tunisia.

Stark was to form a straggler line at Thala and send all the troops he gathered to reinforce the Leicesters.

Shortly after the conference was over, Nicholson arrived and confirmed the plans. He opened his "Nickforce" headquarters next door to Dunphie's.

Though Anderson had sent Nicholson to coordinate the operations in the Foussana Basin, and though McNabb had nominated Fredendall to exercise coordination, neither, it would turn out, would have much influence on developments. Nicholson had contact only with Dunphie, and they would work well together. Fredendall had intermittent communications only with Robinett, who would operate independently for the most part. And perhaps this was just as well, for at least three visitors to the II Corps headquarters on Sunday, the 21st — Robinett, Welvert, and Terry Allen — would find the atmosphere in the command post harassed, worried, and fearful. None of the three commanders, all subordinate to the corps, would receive either information or instructions that day, and Robinett would later reflect that it was just as much a mistake for Fredendall to remain closeted in the mining school at Kouif as to have stayed in the dugouts near Tebessa.

Returning from the conference at Thala, Robinett found the units of his CCB struggling over the increasingly churned-up, rain-soaked road leading from Haidra to Djebel Hamra to plug the hole opened by the disintegration of the engineers. Though he lacked knowledge of the exact locations of all his troops, he had the feeling that the units were retaining their cohesion, finding assembly areas despite the darkness and the wet ground, and establishing a light screen along the eastern face of Hamra.

Many stragglers from Kasserine, some even from as far away as Djebel Ksaira, were being assembled at a line along the eastern base of the Hamra Ridge. Someone was distributing rations, weapons, and ammunition to them and organizing them into provisional companies for defense.

Upon the approach of dawn, Robinett felt confident that the Tebessa and Haidra routes were covered, even though a shortage of mines and wire prevented the defense from being as secure as he might have wished. Behind these positions, someone had put small groups of engineers to work on the roads.

When he inspected his troops after daylight on the foggy

morning of Sunday, February 21, he found a tank destroyer battalion in need of ammunition, rations, and gasoline, a situation he remedied at once. The artillery was all right. The battalion of the 39th Infantry had suffered serious losses but could be used to plug gaps in the defensive line. A battalion of the 16th Infantry and a French Senegalese unit protected his right flank on the south, somewhere off toward Bou Chebka.

During the day he would receive word from Fredendall that the 16th Infantry — all or part? — was attached to his command. But he was never sure that the units concerned had received the order.

As Robinett studied the map, he concluded that the situation was far from hopeless. Though Rommel had gained undisputable possession of the Kasserine Pass, his advance beyond the fork in the road would diverge. Eventually, his forces would be too widely separated to give each other mutual support.

* * * *

Without sufficient troops for strong thrusts along both roads inside the Foussana Basin, Rommel had to decide where to block and where to push. What was his major objective? Tebessa or Le Kef?

Still hesitating, he sent reconnaissance forces out along both roads to discover where the prospects appeared brighter. Perhaps he should, as Kesselring had suggested, strike toward Tebessa after all. He ordered Buelowius and Broich to move cautiously toward Djebel Hamra and Thala, respectively, ready to strike hard in either direction on order.

To give the 10th Panzer Division additional mobility, he virtually halted Hildebrandt's operations at Sbiba and instructed him to send his reconnaissance battalion to Kasserine. He wanted activity at Sbiba, but only enough to pin down the Allies.

Inside the Foussana Basin, the elements feeling out the Allied defenses reported excellent progress along both roads. On the left they ran into retiring engineers, infantrymen, and tankers and hastened their flight. Then, seven miles west of the pass, about eight miles short of Hamra, they stumbled into American troops who were turned the other way, facing them, and firing too — Robinett's screening forces. The pursuit came to an end. Instructed to avoid ambush, the reconnaissance elements pulled back out of range and awaited the arrival of reinforcement.

On the right, Broich's armored cars and self-propelled guns pushed Allied rearguards to the north. About nine miles beyond the narrows, they encountered defenses that barred further pursuit — Dunphie's main line of resistance. Before breaking contact to await additional forces, they knocked out six light British Crusader tanks.

Because the weather had improved — the sky remained covered, but the ceiling was higher and the wind less violent — and planes were taking to the air, Rommel postponed offensive action until he had pilots' reports on whether the Allies were massing for a counterattack.

While waiting, he drove into the Kasserine Pass to confer with Buelowius and Broich. They guessed that the Allies planned to remain on the defensive. All signs pointed only to light delaying opposition. Though Rommel's forces would diverge beyond the fork in the road, they might split the Allied defenders far more than their own offensive units, and on this basis the two commanders favored continuing the drive, particularly since Arnim was supposed to launch frontal attacks and pin down the Allied forces in northern Tunisia.

Rommel vacillated. Though Arnim was apparently preparing to carry out Kesselring's instructions, he still, despite Rommel's specific request, refused to release the Tiger tanks of the 10th Panzer Division. His latest excuse was that the tanks were undergoing maintenance and repair and were in no condition to be transferred.

As Rommel awaited word from the pilots of the reconnaissance planes, he felt depressed. Two days of attack had produced no decisive result. Was the operation about to break open? Or about to fail?

* * * *

Anderson that morning was preoccupied with the problem of finding reserves for the defenders at Thala. He told Koeltz that the only way he saw of getting more troops was to pull back the Sbiba defenders to a narrower front, thus creating excess forces. Would Koeltz please start thinking about how he wanted to shorten his line?

Koeltz objected to any withdrawal. Breaking contact with the enemy was always delicate and risky. Forcing the 34th Division to give up excellent positions, from which the men had repulsed the enemy, would make the splendid defense seem useless. Abandoning Sbiba would be interpreted by the Germans as a sign of weakness and probably lead to a massive attack.

Anderson said no more. But only for the moment.

* * * *

At Kasserine, while Rommel awaited reports from reconnaissance pilots, his advance elements continued to report an absence of opposition. At 11:30, he at last ordered the attack to continue. Despite the opportunity to slash through Hamra and attain Tebessa quickly, he finally decided to make his major effort through Thala to Le Kef.

Telling Broich to get started toward Thala, he instructed Buelowius to move to Djebel Hamra, block the road to Tebessa, and thrust to Haidra. This would keep the separation of his forces inside the basin to a minimum, and from Haidra,

Buelowius could move, if necessary, to Thala and facilitate Broich's progress.

Since Buelowius had to wait until Broich cleared the Kasserine Pass, and since the pass was jammed with this traffic until about 2 P.M., the attack to the west started about 4:30 P.M. It struck American tanks dug into excellent defensive positions, tanks belonging to Gardiner's battalion, which had given a good account of itself at Sbeitla and which had arrived at Hamra less than twenty-four hours earlier.

* * * *

"We were a pretty glum lot," Gardiner later said, as he recalled the march of his men from the Bou Chebka area toward Thala on Saturday, February 20. So far as he knew, he had the only medium tanks in the division that were in any shape to fight. And here they were, strung out along the road and heading toward trouble. The men had been lucky to get off lightly at Sbeitla. He was far from sure their luck would hold. A cold rain that began to fall hardly improved his outlook or his disposition.

En route to Thala, Gardiner received word by radio of a change in destination, and a guide in Haidra waved the column down the road toward Kasserine, while Gardiner himself went to see Robinett for instructions.

In his command post tent a short distance off the road, Robinett explained the situation. He believed that the Germans would try to take Tebessa, then go on to the airfields at Youks-les-Bains, ten miles farther west, where Allied bombers were based. He told Gardiner to dig in just east of Hamra, where the road coming from the Kasserine Pass split. At daylight, he was to move forward cautiously to meet the enemy. He was to be careful to preserve his tanks.

Rejoining his unit, Gardiner found the troops at the designated road junction, stopped there by a guide sent by Robinett. Out in front of everyone and seemingly isolated in the midst of unreconnoitered territory, with no exact knowledge where he was, his sole map of the area too large in scale to give him a detailed appreciation of the terrain, his advance party having reached the spot after darkness, Gardiner sent his reconnaissance platoon out to probe cautiously toward the pass. Then he formed the battalion into what he called "a sort of covered wagon formation," with the tanks in a ring protecting the half-tracks and jeeps in the center. He had the tankers place one man on guard in the turret of every other tank. He sent a detail out on the road to check the stragglers coming back, exhausted and disorganized infantrymen and engineers who reported that things were really bad.

Up ahead, a fight was apparently still in progress, for Gardiner could see frequent gun flashes about twenty miles away and on the floor of the basin numerous burning vehicles that glowed like red-hot lumps of coal.

The only news he received during the night was that the artillery normally in support had come up and was somewhere behind him.

At the first light on Sunday, February 21, Gardiner discovered to his dismay that his battalion was right out in the flat. The country was open for miles, and his troops were cruelly exposed.

Several American tanks appeared out front, heading toward him. They had supported the engineers, and so far as the tankers knew, there were no friendly troops between Gardiner and the Kasserine defile.

When his reconnaissance platoon reported an excellent place to establish a defense, he moved his command several miles forward to a wadi that was perfect, just deep enough for the tanks to get under the cover of the bank and the guns to fire above. Off to the right in a cactus patch at the edge of several hills, he set up his assault guns and mortars. An artillery forward observer joined him and promptly registered in the howitzers.

Then everyone waited.

Nothing happened. The Foussana plain lay motionless under an enormous leaden sky. Not a speck of movement disturbed the tranquillity. Only the distant thunder of cannons suggested the presence of combat too far away to matter.

In midafternoon, a column of trucks appeared on the horizon. Several miles in front of Gardiner, the vehicles came to a halt. Men began to unload. Tanks came into view heading toward Hamra. All were enemy, and Gardiner's howitzers opened fire. The shells scattered the troops, sent the trucks back in panic, and prompted the tanks to seek cover in broken ground.

Again there was a long wait.

Finally, at 4:30, about forty tanks, accompanied by infantry — Buelowius's main forces — started toward Gardiner's defensive line with guns booming. Ten Stukas zipped over, circled, then dived on Gardiner's artillery. The aircraft knocked out one half-track, killed a man and wounded eight, but lost two planes to the streams of bullets sent up by troops manning new .50-caliber, synchronized machine guns that would spell the doom of the dive bomber.

So exhilarated were the antiaircraft gunners by the excitement of their kills and so accustomed were they to expect only enemy planes overhead that they became trigger-happy. Without attempting to identify the planes, they fired on and turned back two American flights, damaging five aircraft beyond repair.

On the ground, a firefight at long range lasted about an hour. The enemy then quit.

Rommel was on the Thala road at this time, and he saw the tank and artillery duel. He had the impression that the Italo-German forces had made little progress toward Hamra. That evening Buelowius confirmed his suspicion. The troops, he said, were astonished by the flexibility and accuracy of

American artillery, which knocked out a good many — he didn't know the exact count — German and Italian tanks.

Gardiner's battalion had turned back the attack without losing a single man or piece of equipment. His outfit was still lucky.

When nightfall came, he figured he would be too vulnerable to night infiltration, so he pulled his troops back several miles. Once again he set up his covered-wagon formation, established outposts, received ammunition and gasoline, and awaited the next day's battle. During the night a company of about fifteen tank destroyers came up to give him additional security.

Robinett sent word, for Heaven's sake, to hold all antiaircraft fire until planes were positively identified. German and Italian aircraft had white or yellow noses; all American planes had their noses painted a dark color and the pilots were going to rock their wings over Allied positions instead of gliding in a chandelle or diving like the enemy. Watch it, he warned.

Surveying his front at the end of Sunday, February 21, Robinett, somewhat perversely, was disappointed despite Gardiner's repulse of the enemy. If German planes had been able to harass his troops, why hadn't more Allied planes appeared? And why had the British failed to keep him informed of what was happening around Thala? He had no idea whether to launch a counterattack toward Kasserine according to the plan formulated with McNabb and Dunphie. Who was coordinating the operations?

Not until late that evening, when a liaison officer came from Thala, did he learn that the British had suffered serious losses along the Thala road. They still held the village, but barely. A counterattack, then, he decided, was unwarranted. The major Axis attack, he figured, was yet to come. And on this basis, he looked after the resupply of his combat elements, had all the troops pack and stow their tentage, and sent all administrative vehicles and kitchens well to the rear.

He then waited for the enemy to reappear on the morning of the 22d.

* * * *

Dunphie had understood, as a result of the midnight conference, that he was to defend at all costs in order to gain time for the Leicesters to prepare strong defenses along the ridge immediately south of Thala. How could he gain time at all costs while conserving his tanks? His tanks were so light and their guns of such short range that he would be able to delay the Germans only, on the contrary, by expending them. Since they were about to be replaced by American Shermans, he figured his tanks were doubly expendable. On this basis, he planned a stubborn defense for Sunday, the 21st.

The Germans gave him the whole morning. Absolutely free.

Around noon, as he watched from the second lateral ridge across the Thala road, the Germans formed up for attack out of British artillery range. Dunphie braced himself and his men. They would have to pay now for the time they bought for the Leicesters.

Broich assembled about thirty tanks, twenty-five self-propelled guns, thirty-five half-track carriers, and two companies of infantry, and this task force advanced in an extremely deliberate manner, their weapons firing. Soldiers on foot searched carefully for mines along the routes. Vehicles moved slowly, seeking cover. Infantrymen skirted open spaces.

Dunphie's tankers, protected by skins of armor too thin to withstand the enemy shells, their guns outranged, tried to use the shelter of each wadi, each fold in the ground, each cactus patch for concealment, hoping they could remain hidden until the Germans came close enough for them to come out and inflict a wound.

KASSERINE 269

In an hour the Germans overran a stubborn group of defenders on the outpost line. After two hours, they had destroyed more than fifteen of Dunphie's tanks and dislodged the outposts.

The British who survived withdrew under the cover of smoke to the main positions on the ridge halfway to Thala.

Rommel, who had spent much of the early afternoon with the spearheads, finally became disenchanted with Broich's leadership. Around 4 P.M., he took personal command of the assault. Brushing aside all difficulties, he moved directly into Dunphie's main positions.

About to be overwhelmed after battling at close range on the ridge for more than an hour, Dunphie called for smoke to cover a withdrawal. He had bought all the time he could. He began to retire to the last ridge south of Thala, where the Leicesters held the final line of defense.

Rommel ruthlessly ordered pursuit, and the advance continued, this time unopposed except for long-range shelling.

What remained of Dunphie's unit passed quickly through a gap in the defensive line held open. About 7 P.M., his command vehicle, last in his column, followed the men into the security of the positions he had given the Leicesters time to erect.

The security was short-lived. The Germans had placed a captured British tank at the head of their column, and they followed Dunphie into the British positions. When the stratagem was discovered, the Germans were well within the final defensive line.

The darkened ridge three miles south of Thala now became the scene of a wild melee, an extravaganza in technicolor of burning vehicles, singeing flares, and flashes of fire. For three hours bedlam boiled over the ridge. And with both sides finally exhausted and seeking brief respite, the fighters parted and stood back, the Germans going a thousand yards to the south, the British ceding the same distance to the north. The final defense line lay abandoned, occupied only by the unconscious and the wounded. A hushed stillness replaced the madness.

The 10th Panzer Division that day took 571 prisoners, destroyed 38 tanks and 28 cannons, but failed to get into Thala.

Why did Rommel refrain from pressing the attack into the village? Were his troops exhausted? Did they lack ammunition? Or was he the victim of his own hesitation? Had he persisted, he would have encountered only a French battalion performing routine security duties, soldiers who had no weapons capable of opposing tanks.

He later said that he believed strong Allied units were coming into Thala and that he feared his assault troops would be crushed. Was this a *post facto* excuse or a bona fide reason?

Accompanying the combat troops had enlivened him, but he had gone back to Kasserine after the capture of the ridge halfway to Thala, believing that the momentum of that triumph would carry the troops into the village. The inevitable aftereffect of the battle, the letdown, left him tired, washed out, discouraged. Perhaps it was already too late to hope for further success. He had lost much time. His forces were fatigued. His confidence in the operation and his vision of triumph and glory faded.

He shook himself out of his doubts. One small burst of energy would get him into Thala and on the road to Le Kef. One extra effort. He ordered the attacks continued the next day.

Buelowius had a special problem. Djebel Hamra, he explained interminably, was on a flat plain almost devoid of cover and directly under Allied observation. A frontal attack would be out of the question in daylight and extremely difficult at night. A direct thrust to the base of Hamra and a march along the Haidra road would open the forces to prolonged flanking action. The only solution was an operation during the hours of darkness. Perhaps a successful advance along the road going around the southern side of Hamra to Tebessa could be followed by a cut across the Hamra Ridge to the Haidra road.

Rommel seemed hardly to be listening. Absent-mindedly, he gave his assent.

That Sunday night, while Buelowius started a battalion in a wide enveloping movement designed to sweep around the Tebessa side of Djebel Hamra, Broich consolidated his forces and prepared to take Thala.

Barely in front of Thala, the Allies still had a defensive line of sorts. The valiant stand of Dunphie's brigade was an outstanding victory won by the courage and devotion of dedicated and proud men who had bought time at a high cost.

But the time had not been purchased, it would turn out, for the Leicesters. Dunphie had made it possible for a reincarnation of Frank Merriwell, a tall, red-haired American brigadier general named Irwin, to arrive with help in the very nick of time.

30

EXPECTING a German breakthrough at Thala on Sunday evening, February 21, Anderson told Koeltz he would have to abandon Sbiba and pull back to the northwest for forty miles to the heights around Le Kef.

As usual Koeltz protested. A retirement across open terrain that was perfect for the operations of enemy tanks and dive bombers would bring the French forces to disaster. His troops lacked motor vehicles; three-quarters of their equipment was mule-drawn, their antitank guns were ludicrous, their antiaircraft weapons ridiculous. If a withdrawal was really necessary, why not move the French northeast to block Arnim?

How would that help Thala?

The Germans at Thala, Koeltz pointed out with Gallic logic, were in a pocket. All their supplies had to come through the Kasserine Pass. When good weather returned, Allied planes could destroy the German supply columns, cut off sustenance to the forward combat elements, then inhibit their attempts to get out.

But this was no solution to the immediate problem. As a temporary expedient, Anderson told Koeltz categorically to send a battalion of infantry and whatever else he could spare to Thala.

Because Ryder had again repulsed Hildebrandt's attack that afternoon and was making some local readjustments, Koeltz asked Keightley to fulfill the request. A battalion of British infantry and some tanks were soon marching westward over the mountain trail.

While Anderson was concerned with Thala, Koeltz was

watching his sector to the northeast. All day long enemy patrols had probed that front as though looking for a soft spot. Did this presage an attack? An operation by Arnim, Koeltz figured, would facilitate Rommel's progress at Thala.

That night, when a battalion of French infantry arrived from Constantine, he sent the troops to the northeast to reinforce the positions facing Arnim.

* * * *

The newly arrived French battalion was part of a mass movement of Allied units coming from Algeria and other areas west of the Tunisian front, some from as far distant as Morocco. Thirty-five M-4 tanks and crews were traveling by rail, and seventeen more were en route by sea and rail to Tebessa. A provisional British tank unit with twenty-five new Churchill tanks had rolled through Le Kef on Saturday night, the 20th, to bolster the Sbiba positions. At midnight of the 20th, at Oran, when the 47th Infantry Regiment of the 9th Division received urgent orders to march at once by truck to Tebessa, the men struck their tents, loaded their equipment, and started at dawn in a blinding rain and hail storm along the narrow, winding mountain roads toward Tunisia.

Of all the units making their way to Tunisia, the 9th Division Artillery, commanded by Brigadier General S. LeRoy Irwin, reached the vital point at the decisive moment and exerted the conclusive influence on the Battle of Kasserine.

At Tlemcen in western Algeria on Wednesday, February 17, Irwin had received a message in the morning to take three of his four artillery battalions, plus two cannon companies, by forced marches to Tebessa, 735 miles away. Half an hour afterward, he issued his orders. Five hours later his command was on the way. Traversing the extremely rugged country over poor roads shrouded in fog and made slippery by rain and hail, Irwin's convoy, averaging better than 180 miles per day, reached Tebessa at 2:10 P.M., Sunday, the 21st. An hour and a half later, he had word to come in all haste to Thala. As his dead-tired men continued, Irwin went ahead to Kouif, where Fredendall briefed him.

At 8 P.M., in the midst of the murderous battle on the ridge barely three miles south of Thala, Irwin's howitzers were rolling into the village and he was conferring with Nicholson on how best to reinforce the defenses. The appearance of the guns brought a surge of confidence to the embattled defenders and stopped frantic preparations for an exodus. Placed in command of all the artillery at Thala, Irwin told his subordinate commanders they would have to be ready to fire at daylight despite the fatigue of the men. While he placed his forty-eight guns into position, Dunphie led a small group of tanks in a sortie around midnight to distract the Germans.

Already in place were about 36 artillery pieces — 12 Bofors guns, 2 batteries of antitank weapons, 12 light destroyers, and twenty-two 25-pounders of Royal Artillery. To bolster these British cannons, Irwin put the twelve 155-mm. howitzers of his 34th Field Artillery Battalion along a trail running westward from Thala, where they could partially enfilade the road coming up from Kasserine. He sited the six 75-mm. howitzers of the 47th Infantry's Cannon Company to protect their western flank. Still seeking the advantage of enfilading fires, he located the twenty-four 105-mm. howitzers of the 60th and 84th Field Artillery Battalions about a mile to the south, with the six 75-mm. howitzers of the 60th Infantry's Cannon Company on their right.

Scarcely one thousand yards away was the new main line of resistance, inhabited by a small but gallant band. The Leicesters were down to three platoons — about one hundred men, augmented by a handful of stragglers rounded up by Stark. Dunphie's brigade had perhaps twenty tanks — but the 17/21 Lancers and the 2d Lothians had been keeping them in continuous operation for twenty-four hours, and the mechanical strain was beginning to tell. Adding some strength to this slender line were two new arrivals sent from Sbiba by Keightley — the infantry troops of the 2d Hampshires and the tankers of the 16/5 Lancers, some of them equipped with new Shermans.

No more than 1,200 yards — less than a mile — below the main line of resistance, on the dominating ridge formerly held by the Leicesters, were the Germans, with at least 50 tanks, 2,500 infantrymen, 30 artillery pieces, and numerous weapons of smaller caliber.

Having situated his guns by map and his men having put them into firing positions during the night, Irwin was unable to estimate how effective his fires would be. But there was nothing to do except wait for daybreak.

The pieces were ready by five o'clock on the morning of Monday, the 22d, and shortly afterward, when daylight came, the gunners started their registration fires. Irwin saw at once that he was at a disadvantage. The ground he occupied was lower than the height held by the Germans. His troops would be under enemy observation, and they would have to expect communication wires to be cut, radios jammed, and a heavy toll among gunners and message bearers.

As the morning mist rose, the enemy-held ridge came into view. Firing at targets of opportunity, most of them German tanks, Irwin's artillerymen, exhausted but game after their long journey, made their guns sing out. The earsplitting cacophony brought smiles to the faces of those who defended Thala.

* * * *

At seven o'clock, Monday, the 22d, Broich was ready to start his final advance into Thala when a volley of shells from Irwin's howitzers struck among his troops. This was something new, and he was startled. Judging the bombardment to be the prelude to a counterattack, he checked with Rommel by phone. Might it be better to wait before launching the assault?

Rommel thought so. He said he would drive up to see for himself.

While he was coming up the Thala road, British tanks left their positions and headed toward Broich's line, confirming his expectation of a counterattack.

Actually, Nicholson had sent the few remaining tanks of Dunphie's brigade in a foray to discourage the German attack that he anticipated. Five British tanks were quickly knocked out, but their sacrifice bluffed Broich.

When Rommel reached the scene, he saw in the renewed action a confidence that he estimated came from the arrival of strong Allied reinforcements during the night. He too remarked the increased volume of artillery shelling. He approved Broich's decision to postpone the offensive until the Allied thrust was contained. Broich was then to lunge forward through Thala and head north.

And thus Broich let the morning pass. There was no Allied attack. There were air strikes, artillery exchanges, and what Broich misinterpreted to be aborted preliminary probes.

Nothing of importance having developed by noon, he informed Rommel he would get off his attack at four o'clock.

* * * *

About the time that Nicholson was sending Dunphie's tanks out on their suicide mission, he sought help from Fredendall, asking whether the Americans could do something to divert the pressure at Thala. Anderson soon telephoned to support the request. As he saw it, the British were bearing the whole weight of the German armor. Why weren't the Americans helping out?

Fredendall turned to Robinett and ordered him "to bring all possible forces to bear in order to assist."

Robinett was having trouble enough of his own. His whole right rear seemed about to be uncovered by what appeared to be a lightning enemy stroke toward Bou Chebka, and he warned Gardiner to take care.

Gardiner had advanced his battalion to the wadi he had occupied the day before, but found an enemy tenant who was in no mood to share the place. An argument resulted in an exchange of fire. Making no headway, he decided he would have to pry the enemy out of the ditch. While his mortar platoon laid down a smoke screen, he sent a tank company around the flank to edge into the wadi. Just when success seemed sure, he learned the bad news from Robinett — enemy troops had captured some American howitzers somewhere off his right flank and were about to turn the guns on him and enfilade his force. He held up his attack.

The guns were lost to the battalion that Buelowius had sent on a wide sweep to the left of Djebel Hamra and a subsequent thrust toward Tebessa. Starting their movement during the night, the men ran into a violent rainstorm and became lost in the darkness. Instead of taking the road leading westward to Tebessa, they followed a camel trail going south. Marching slowly over an increasingly difficult track made almost impassable by recurring downpours, they were almost seven miles south of Hamra and near the Bou Chebka pass at daylight of Monday, the 22d.

They were also in the midst of a miscellany of Allied forces — troops of the "Constantine" Division, units of Ward's 1st Armored Division, a tabor of Goums, a group of Spahis, some armored cars of the Derbyshire Yeomanry, a handful of American Rangers, part of the 16th Infantry, and the 33d Field Artillery Battalion. But hidden by a blanket of morning mist, they infiltrated into the artillery positions and overran and captured a battery of howitzers and several antiaircraft guns.

Since the Allied troops were guarding the Bou Chebka Pass against attack from the south, the appearance of enemy coming from the north provoked considerable doubt, anxiety, and confusion.

It took most of the day to restore order, regain the guns, and drive the enemy battalion back up the camel trail.

Worn out by their long day of exertion, a large group of stragglers stumbled into a wadi and found themselves near a company of American tanks. The Americans decided that the opportunity was too good to waste.

A radio message that enemy soldiers were surrendering in droves brought Gardiner to the spot in time to see one of his tankers with a tommy gun nestled in his arms come around a bend in a wadi followed by a procession of prisoners. He thought there must be at least a thousand. The actual count showed just under three hundred — a few Germans wearing uniforms of the Afrika Korps and quite a few Italian *bersaglieri*, their uniforms topped by traditional pith helmet and plume.

Buelowius's attack had foundered, but this was far from clear to the Allies.

* * * *

Things had gone badly all day long at the II Corps command post. A hectic week of nervous tension and little sleep had made many headquarters personnel jumpy. They expected the worst, and every sign seemed to bear out their impression of approaching disaster.

The first note, sounded at the beginning of the day, was in tune with the general air of nervous expectation. Nicholson's phone call indicated the imminent loss of Thala, and Anderson's soon afterward seemed to substantiate a continuation of the defeats at Faid, Sidi bou Zid, and Sbeitla. What would the corps do if the Germans broke through Thala?

When news came of Buelowius's penetration to the Bou Chebka area, the passes of Dernaia and El Ma el Abiod seemed as good as lost.

Under the impression that the Allied defenses were caving in everywhere, Fredendall went to see Welvert just before noon of Monday, the 22d. He asked that the "Constantine" Division be ready to withdraw to the heights around Tebessa.

Robinett was visiting the II Corps command post to lodge a blunt complaint. To a staff member, he presented a list of inexcusable and unforgivable blunders. No one was coordinating the units in the battle area, and coordination was badly needed. No one in the field knew what unit boundaries had been assigned by higher headquarters, and specific areas of unit responsibility were urgently required. No one knew who was on the flanks or in support, and the piecemeal commitment of small units from different organizations was causing untold confusion. No one was coordinating defensive fires or providing military police and transportation to take charge of evacuating prisoners to the rear. Why wasn't the corps exercising the proper control?

Soon after Robinett departed, someone at the corps headquarters decided that the command post had to move from Kouif to avoid being overrun and captured.

When Fredendall returned from his visit with Welvert, he found the command post half abandoned, many personnel moving, apparently to Le Kef or to Constantine. He tried to round up and call back the headquarters clerks and radio operators, but many had already gone.

Apprised of Robinett's complaint, Fredendall decided that the dissolution of his command post prevented him from taking the requisite control. He gave Ward and Allen responsibility to coordinate the units along the front — to Ward the task of holding at Thala and Hamra; to Allen that of retaining the passes in the south.

Learning that the 47th Infantry, which was on its way to the front, was about thirty-five miles south of Constantine on the road to Tebessa, Fredendall instructed the regiment to remain where it was until the situation cleared up. If the enemy broke through Thala and Tebessa, the regiment would be in position to protect Constantine.

Shortly thereafter, Juin, who had been told by Welvert that Fredendall was thinking about withdrawing, came to Kouif. He found the corps commander sitting on a box in his empty office.

Was it true, Juin asked, that he was considering a withdrawal?

Fredendall nodded.

Why withdraw, Juin asked, when Tebessa was the best place to defend?

Fredendall said he shared Juin's view, but he had to be prepared for the worst.

How about Fredendall's reserves?

He had none.

If a withdrawal became necessary, Juin asked, in which direction would Fredendall go?

To the north. He could not abandon the British.

To Juin, this meant that Fredendall had already as good as renounced a defense of Tebessa. If the Germans took Tebessa, they as good as had Constantine. Having been anxious about this for some time, Juin tried to get Fredendall to reconsider. Leaving Tebessa, he told the American, meant abandoning his base of supply and being cut off from Algiers.

Fredendall made a hopeless gesture.

Judging that technical and military arguments would have little effect, Juin tried a sentimental approach. If Fredendall had no desire to defend Tebessa, he said emotionally, he would detach Welvert's division from the II Corps. The French alone would fight for Tebessa until the death of the last man.

The appeal was effective. Fredendall was visibly moved. He swore he would not abandon Tebessa.

Hardly reassured by the promise, Juin sent Giraud a message that evening. If Thala fell, he wrote, Tebessa would certainly be abandoned, like Gafsa.

Welvert was being a realist. At nightfall he sent several units to dig defensive positions around Tebessa. He moved his command post to Youks-les-Bains.

Anderson also shifted his command post during the night of Monday, the 22d — from Rohia, nine miles above Sbiba, to the north, behind Le Kef.

Koeltz was tempted to withdraw his headquarters too, but at the last moment he decided to remain where he was.

Though Arnim had attacked the center of his sector and seemed about to make a breakthrough, the German had, for unknown reasons, canceled his offensive and pulled his troops back toward Pichon.

But since German planes had for the first time bombed and strafed the route between Thala and Le Kef, Koeltz implemented Anderson's instructions to abandon Sbiba. That night Keightley's 6th Armoured Division and Ryder's 34th Division drew back toward Rohia to be ready to repulse a penetration through Thala.

The 21st Panzer Division could have entered Sbiba unopposed that night, but, inexplicably to the Allied commanders, the Germans remained where they were and watched the Allied troops go.

* * * *

At Thala, the situation had remained unchanged all day long on Monday, the 22d. Broich still seemed to be on the verge of cranking up an attack. His troops appeared poised for an offensive. Yet he made no move.

The British and American commanders, who were anxiously watching, ascribed his failure to attack to two events. Irwin's stalwart artillery, under attack by Stukas throughout the day and under intensive shelling, had apparently put out enough fire to discourage a renewal of the German effort. Working in their exposed positions, ready to drop from fatigue, the artillerymen had lost seven men killed and twenty-one wounded, plus four howitzers, but they kept pumping out the shells.

The second occurrence that seemed to deter Broich was an air strike that appeared to tear his units apart. The rain of the past few days had turned into mire all the airfields except the base at Youks-les-Bains, where a steel-planked air strip permitted planes to operate. From that field, 114 sorties were flown over the Thala area alone.

For the jittery American ground troops, who had begun to

believe that only German planes were able to fly, the appearance of the American craft triggered an immediate reflex. Antiaircraft gunners shot down five American P-38's. This was nervousness plain and simple, for the distinctive double fuselage had no counterpart in the German or Italian air forces.

Eisenhower, who was watching the battle from afar, had good perspective. It seemed clear to him that the German offensive had reached flood tide and was on the point of ebbing. Attack at once during the night, he urged.

Anderson and Fredendall took exception to his counsel. The tension continued in all the Allied command posts as everyone awaited a continuation of the German effort that, this time, would surely push the Allies into further retreat.

To Ward, who was active all afternoon long as he drew together the strings of control, the situation seemed to be improving. He was on the point of issuing an order to counterattack, when he learned of two new developments, both affecting his exercise of command.

First, though Fredendall had given Ward responsibility for both Thala and Hamra, Anderson now put Nicholson directly under Keightley, whom he detached from Koeltz and placed under Fredendall. This took the Thala forces away from Ward and restored coordination to Fredendall, who, because of the disintegration of his command post, was in no position to exercise it.

Second, an American officer was arriving to take hold of the situation. No one knew exactly what his place in the command structure would be — would he take command of the corps, become Fredendall's deputy, or replace Ward?

In deference to these changes, Ward withheld his instructions. The only thing he did was to move CCA from El Ma el Abiod to Haidra, where the troops would be ready for use at Thala or Hamra, depending on what happened.

The American officer about to arrive was barrel-chested Ernie Harmon. He would blow in like a whirlwind. He would set things right.

31

When Rommel drove up the Thala road on Monday morning, February 22, to check Broich's impression of the increased Allied strength, he came to the conclusion that the flow of Allied reinforcements nullified all hope of further success. But beyond telling Broich to go over temporarily on the defensive, he said nothing, for he was to meet that afternoon with Kesselring, who was coming to Tunisia.

The reports that Kesselring had received in Rome late the night before were more than satisfactory and promised further triumph. Rommel held the initiative. Thala was virtually captured, Tebessa within easy reach. The inability of the 21st Panzer Division to get through Sbiba could be only a temporary check. Once Rommel got through Thala, which seemed likely at any moment, the opposition at Sbiba would collapse.

Since penetrations through Thala and Sbiba would completely disarray the Allied dispositions and open a multitude of opportunities, Kesselring decided to go to Tunisia not only to give counsel but also to insure effective cooperation between Rommel and Arnim. The situation at the Mareth Line seemed quiet, and while Montgomery slowly completed his preparations for attack, the Axis forces could exploit their victory.

Landing at Tunis on the morning of the 22d, Kesselring was briefed by members of Arnim's staff. Uneasily, he began to have vague apprehensions that all was not going as he believed.

He flew to air force headquarters near Sfax, and from there took a small Storch plane to Kasserine, where Rommel's

Volkswagen met him at the air strip. He arrived at Rommel's command post at one o'clock.

Rommel seemed depressed. Complaining that Arnim was withholding forces he needed, he gave no indication that he had exercised the full authority of his rank and prestige to demand their transfer to his front. Criticizing Hildebrandt's leadership of the 21st Panzer Division at Sbiba, he made no mention of having threatened to relieve the division commander or of having changed the composition of his attack formations.

Kesselring tried to cheer him up. Nothing was settled, he said. Affairs could still go either way. One small push was all that was needed.

Rommel thought not. In a tired and discouraged voice, he said that he lacked enough force to obtain a decisive breakthrough before Montgomery became active at the Mareth Line.

Kesselring tried again to raise Rommel's spirits, pointing out the importance of Tebessa, promising reinforcements, endeavoring to dispel concern over Mareth.

It was no good. And as he presented a detailed estimate of the situation, Rommel showed why.

The only favorable condition was the status of his supplies. He had enough fuel up forward to sustain two days of offensive operations and in reserve at Sousse, Sfax, and Gabes enough for two days more; plenty of rations; and adequate ammunition because of captured shells.

Everything else was unfavorable: The rain and fog impeded air support. The mud and mountains inhibited tanks. His units were fatigued. Air reconnaissance revealed that he was having no effect on the British in the north or on the French in the center. Neither had been seriously weakened or deprived of local reserves. On the contrary, a large body of reinforcements approached Thala and Tebessa. He could discover no precipitous Allied movements to the rear, no signs of panic. The Allied units seemed to be holding firmly.

The operation, he believed, had reached a state of equilibrium. He had prevented the Allies from driving to the sea near Sfax and coming between his and Arnim's armies. But at the same time they had blocked his thrust to Le Kef.

Weighing the strength of the Allied reinforcements against his own limited and now depleted resources, he had to conclude that further effort was useless. He had taken too many casualties. The opportunity for exploitation had passed.

After a short silence, Kesselring bowed to the inevitable — who else could take charge of the offensive? He accepted the review and the implicit decision.

The commanders agreed quickly that Kesselring would inform Comando Supremo and Rommel would withdraw from Kasserine and shift to the south to oppose Montgomery.

Kesselring asked Rommel whether he would like to have command of the army group in Tunisia.

He declined. He saw no further glory to be won in North Africa.

As Kesselring returned to Sfax, he reflected that Rommel had displayed "a scarcely concealed desire" to get back to the Mareth Line with unimpaired forces. The Kasserine operation had fizzled — or had it? — but Rommel seemed anxious, above all, to preserve his troops for a showdown with Montgomery. Had the Americans failed to challenge his leadership? Did he consider Montgomery a more worthy opponent? Was there a personal score — the defeat at Alamein and the retreat across Libya — to settle?

Whatever the reason, the impending clash at Mareth, Kesselring believed absorbed too much of Rommel's attention. Or perhaps he was simply exhausted, physically and morally. "Nothing of his usual passionate will to command," he later remarked, "could be felt."

Before flying to Rome, he stopped at Bizerte and saw Arnim. He reproved Arnim severely for having withheld forces from Rommel, blamed him for the disappointing conclusion of a promising opportunity that would never again appear, and instructed him to apply pressure in the north to help Rommel regroup in the south.

After Kesselring left, Arnim halted the attack he had somewhat unwillingly launched against Koeltz's front. If Rommel was calling off his offensive, he figured, his own effort had no point. The good chance he had of disrupting the French sector and of taking Le Kef himself — from the east — escaped his notice.

As Kesselring flew across the Mediterranean to Rome, he concluded that he should have insisted on a single command for the Kasserine operation. The failure was as much his fault for letting Comando Supremo stand in the way of giving the overall Tunisian command to Rommel. It was probably too late now. He had the impression that a strategic victory was out of the question.

Yet perhaps he ought to insist on the apointment. Rommel had more experience in North Africa than anyone else. The promotion might give him confidence, stimulate his imagination, make him feel that his talent was recognized and appreciated.

He would see when he got to Rome.

In Tunisia, Rommel told Broich to remain in place in front of Thala and Hildebrandt to stay where he was in front of Sbiba. That night, without waiting for a directive from Comando Supremo, he ordered his forces to prepare for withdrawal. Buelowius was to pull out first and go to Thelepte and Feriana, while Broich stood guard at the Kasserine Pass. Then the Afrika Korps was to go to Gabes, while the Centauro Division covered Gafsa. The 10th Panzer Division was to move through Kasserine to Sbeitla and there join the 21st Panzer Division withdrawn from Sbiba. Both armored divisions were to go through the Faid Pass, the 10th turning north to Pichon, the 21st south to Sfax.

Shortly before midnight of Monday, the 22d, Comando Supremo confirmed his arrangements, adding that he was to use demolitions and mines in abundance to obstruct Allied pursuit. Instead of sending the 10th Panzer Division to Pichon, he was to keep it near Gabes for use against Montgomery. In the north, Arnim was to prepare an attack designed to prevent an immediate follow-up of Rommel's withdrawal. The airborne and amphibious operations, projected so hopefully five days earlier, were canceled.

The battle of the Kasserine Pass had ended that Monday morning of the 22d with the opening volleys of Red Irwin's artillery pieces.

But no one on the Allied side of the front could know this. Tension remained at a high pitch. And Ernie Harmon arrived to add a significant and dramatic postscript to the experience.

32

HARMON WAS IN TUNISIA because the relationship between Fredendall and Ward had gotten worse. The two men were strictly on "official" terms, barely speaking to each other except in line of duty.

For some time, Eisenhower and Truscott had talked of bringing Major General Ernest N. Harmon from Morocco, where he headed the 2d Armored Division under the overall command of Major General George S. Patton, Jr. On Saturday, the 20th, Eisenhower decided to do so. His first thought was to relieve Ward and give Harmon the task of rehabilitating the 1st Armored Division. But his principal subordinates pointed out that Fredendall had hobbled Ward.

Concluding that a change in the midst of battle would be, in his words, "inexpedient," Eisenhower determined to send Harmon as "a useful senior assistant" to Fredendall in "the unusual conditions of the present battle." Fredendall was to use Harmon any way he wished except to relieve Ward. In effect, Harmon was to be Fredendall's deputy commander or Eisenhower's personal representative at the front.

Harmon was summoned on Sunday, the 21st. He flew to Algiers. Arriving late, he saw Eisenhower, who brought him up to date on developments in Tunisia, then went to a hotel for a few hours' sleep.

Early on Monday, the 22d, a chauffeur called for him, then picked up Eisenhower and several others who were to drive to Constantine. An air raid over Algiers held up their start, and they reached Constantine late in the afternoon.

After a short discussion with Truscott, Harmon left by jeep

for Tebessa. All along the road, he bucked heavy traffic moving the other way.

At Tebessa, he tried to find the II Corps rear headquarters. No one knew where it was. Everyone seemed to be gone or going to Constantine.

He finally located the place where the corps rear headquarters had been. A telephone was there, and it was working. He bulled his way past several operators to get Fredendall on the wire.

Were they moving? Harmon asked. And if so, where?

They were not moving. They were waiting for him to arrive at Kouif.

He reached Kouif around three o'clock in the morning of Tuesday, the 23d, a few hours after Rommel had ordered his forces to start withdrawing.

He found Fredendall and two of his principal staff officers, he later remembered, "sitting around looking very glum." He thought Fredendall was drunk, but he was only groggy from nervous tension and lack of sleep.

The first thing Fredendall did was to ask whether Harmon thought the command post ought to move.

Harmon found that a hell of a question to ask someone just arriving. Instinctively he said, "Hell, no."

Fredendall turned to the two staff officers. "All right," he said, "that settles that. We stay."

Returning to Harmon, Fredendall asked whether he had come to relieve Ward.

Harmon said no to that too.

Fredendall then handed him an envelope and said, "Here it is. The party is yours."

Somewhat startled, he opened the envelope and found a typewritten order placing him in command of "the battle then in progress."

What the hell did that mean?

It meant that he was in direct command of the 1st Armored

Division and the 6th Armoured Division, and his mission was to hold the Germans, then drive them out. The Germans, Fredendall said, were about to crash through Thala.

The phone rang, and Fredendall answered. It was Ward's chief of staff, and Fredendall told him to hurry up those thirty-three diesel tanks he was getting into shape. He had some difficulty getting the message across, for after a while he looked over to Harmon and made a gesture of disgust. He couldn't do a damn thing with Ward, he said.

What was the trouble?

Fredendall explained. A whole bunch of new Shermans had been sent from the United States for the British, and the British had turned some back to Ward, who really needed them. He had formed a provisional tank unit under Hains and Hightower. But the crews had come out of light tanks and were unfamiliar with the Shermans. They had never fired the guns. Ward wanted to give the troops some experience before he committed them.

The hell with that, Harmon thought. The tanks were too good to waste. Their presence at Thala would at least raise morale.

"Am I in command?" he asked.

"Yes," Fredendall said.

"Well, here, give me that phone."

Harmon told Ward's chief of staff to get those tanks to Thala by daylight, and that was an order.

Yes, sir, the chief of staff said, but he wanted Harmon to know it was a wrong order.

Harmon said he didn't give a damn whether it was wrong or not. The tanks were doing nobody any good if the Germans got to Thala. He wanted those tanks there by daylight.

Now, he asked Fredendall, what help could he expect?

Fredendall gave him a jeep with a radio and an operator, plus a driver who knew the area, and an assistant operations officer. Turning over to Harmon the job of running the battle, he went to bed.

Harmon drove to Haidra and found Ward's command post. Ward was asleep, but he got up at once.

"Ward," Harmon said, "I'm about one thousand files behind you" — meaning he was quite junior to Ward on the rolls of the Regular Army — "but these are my orders and that's how it is."

He was most cooperative. He turned out his staff officers, who quickly briefed Harmon, he said he would get those diesels up to Thala as fast as he could, and he issued an order to his subordinate commands: "All units will be alerted at dawn for movement in any direction except to the rear."

Satisfied that Ward had everything under control, Harmon went on to Thala, where he found Nicholson in a cellar.

Nicholson was all right. He said, "We gave them a fucking bloody nose yesterday, and we'll do it again this morning."

He liked Nicholson.

When he learned that Anderson had ordered Irwin's artillery to move out of Thala to Le Kef, he said, "To hell with that." He countermanded the order and took responsibility for holding the artillery where it was. He figured that if the Allies won, nobody would mind; if they lost, nobody would care.

Harmon told Nicholson to hold all day long, to make no move until nightfall. Then he was to send infantry forward along the ridges and give all the artillery support he could throw in. The troops were to stay on the high ground all the way to the shoulders of the Kasserine Pass.

He looked over Irwin's artillery positions and found them pretty good.

He prayed for Ward's tanks to get there. He really didn't expect them by daylight. They arrived around ten o'clock, which was pretty fast. He personally placed the tanks into position.

Then he went to visit Robinett, who was glad to see him. He said he had forty-eight tanks in operating condition, and that was all. But there was no question about the ability of CCB to hold. He was sure he could hold.

"We are not only going to hold," Harmon told him, "but we are going to drive the damn bastards back."

Satisfied that Robinett had his outfit well in hand, he drove to Haidra for an hour or two of sleep. He was worn out. But he knew he could bounce back.

Bounce back he did, and he took over Ward's command post, his staff, and his facilities. Fredendall's installation was still being manned on a skeleton basis.

Uninformed of Harmon's exact role and believing his own relief to be only a matter of time, Ward took his operations officer and his aide to Robinett's command post, where they pitched their tents. He soon learned that he was not to be relieved, and he returned to an active role, ably seconding Harmon's efforts designed to make sure that the troop units remained firmly in place.

* * * *

Along the Kasserine front that day, Tuesday, the 23d, no one on the Allied side could believe his eyes. At Thala, Dunphie's tankers opened fire at daylight, Irwin's artillery delivered several concentrated volleys, everyone stood ready to repulse an enemy attack, and there was no reaction from the Germans.

At 2:45 that afternoon, Nicholson ordered all fires to cease and reconnaissance parties to advance. Discovering that the Germans had gone, British troops moved forward and reoccupied the main ridge three miles south of Thala. They had lost contact with the enemy.

For Irwin, the firing had come to an end just in time. Though his 155- and 75-mm. howitzers still had shells, his two battalions of 105-mm. howitzers had fired so furiously that they had enough rounds on hand for only fifteen minutes longer. In less than two days of action, he had lost eight men killed, thirty-six wounded, and one missing; five trucks had been destroyed, four howitzers were put out of commission, and three were damaged. Yet he had delivered the knockout, and he complimented his troops for their fine demonstration of stamina, courage, and coolness.

Just above Sbiba, Ryder began to believe that the Germans were withdrawing. He ordered his regimental commanders to send out patrols and prepare to move forward. Koeltz seconded the instruction: "Enemy appears to be withdrawing Thala pocket. Launch strong reconnaissance very aggressively with tanks and guns." Small groups confirmed the enemy departure as night was falling, and the commanders decided to wait until morning to pursue. Ryder's troops had had no easy time — the 34th Division had lost approximately 50 men killed, 200 wounded, and 250 missing.

At Hamra, Robinett pushed his forces forward slowly as enemy pressure decreased, then vanished. A field artillery battalion that had fired fifty-one missions and expended more than two thousand rounds on the previous day, fulfilled two missions and delivered only thirty-seven rounds for lack of targets. Even after moving forward four miles, the firing batteries found the enemy out of range.

Gardiner's men advanced cautiously about eight miles. They had plenty of time to pick up a souvenir from a wide selection of equipment and supplies abandoned by the enemy. One of the better finds was a truckload of American Air Corps rations that the Germans had obtained at Feriana; the food was more than tasty after a week of cold C rations.

Near Bou Chebka, when Allen's battalions reported they were out of contact with the enemy, he ordered "very active patrolling."

Despite the relaxation of German pressure, Harmon, with Fredendall in agreement, was suspicious of Rommel's intentions. Perhaps he was only regrouping for a sudden lunge to the left, toward Tebessa. Was anything in reserve and available to block a thrust in that direction? Yes, CCA, which Ward had moved from the Tebessa area to Haidra only the night before. Harmon directed CCA to march back and protect Tebessa against attack from the south. The command returned, and the men took the same positions they had vacated twenty-four hours earlier.

That afternoon of the 23d, Eisenhower and Truscott drove to Tebessa, where they met Fredendall and Allen. For the first time, Truscott later recalled, there was "a distinct note of optimism." Though Eisenhower suggested that every effort be made to destroy the Germans before they could escape, the field commanders cautioned against reckless action — better wait to see whether the enemy withdrawal was real.

It was real. Making lavish use of the big plate-shaped Teller antitank mine and of the bounding antipersonnel mine named "Bouncing Betty," the Germans left thousands of mines and booby traps as they pulled back, the sand-colored trucks of the Afrika Korps with the small green palm tree painted on the doors heading the procession. As Broich's rearguards came through the Kasserine Pass, Rommel set up his headquarters near Sfax.

There on the afternoon of Tuesday, February 23, he received a message from Comando Supremo announcing his temporary appointment as commander of Army Group Afrika, with authority over Arnim and Messe. His mission was to destroy the advancing columns of the British Eighth Army in the south and to prepare an offensive against the Allied army in the north.

He was too weary to care. He was really not feeling well.

* * * *

Short of reserves and mindful of the losses Rommel had inflicted, the Allied forces in the Foussana Basin carefully

13. The village of Kasserine, a border town during antiquity, a place of vital encounter during World War II. *U.S. Army Photograph*

14. Kasserine Pass, the German view. "To enter the Kasserine Pass from the south, take the black-topped road out to the village of Kasserine, and head for the midnight-blue mountain range of the Western Dorsale. . . . Suddenly, a small opening appears between two looming hill masses. . . . On the left is Djebel Chambi. The one on the right is Semmama. The road runs between them . . . and this is the Kasserine Pass." *U.S. Army Photograph*

15. Major General Ernest N. Harmon, who took command of a battle instead of a corps. *U.S. Army Photograph*

worked their way toward the narrows of the Kasserine Pass on Wednesday, February 24. The infantry kept to the high ground, the tanks and artillery stayed on the floor of the plain. No enemy units, only an abundance of demolitions, mines, and booby traps, as well as occasional rounds of the 210-mm. "ash cans" that came whining in, impeded the advance.

From their positions just north of Sbiba, a Franco-American force moved south and re-entered the village. They found a plethora of mines and booby traps, all the bridges destroyed, and Arabs burning and looting Sbiba. The French, who knew how to handle Arabs, stopped the disorder. The American report of the French method was matter-of-fact: "They shot some and took others prisoner."

Daylight on Thursday, February 25, came with a dense fog. As infantry and tanks inside the Foussana Basin continued toward the pass, Americans pushing on the Hamra side, the British on the Thala side, Colonel C. C. Benson disappeared into the mist on foot. Sure that the enemy was gone, he preceded the march and was the first to arrive at the fork of the road just above the defile.

An artillery preparation by CCB into the narrows fell into an undefended passage. Not a bit of resistance, not a single shot greeted the troops of CCB and of the 16th Infantry, who retook the pass that day without having to squeeze a trigger or pull a lanyard. The only thing they had to do was to dig mines out of the ground everywhere.

In the middle of the Kasserine Pass, Gardiner was sitting on the deck of his command tank and enjoying the luxury of having his shoes off for the first time in six days when Ward drove up and asked to use his radio. Since it was not working well, Gardiner, still in his stockinged feet, took Ward to one of his company commanders. From that tank, Ward sent a message to Fredendall: "The pass is ours."

By sunset, American troops were in the village of Kasserine, and by darkness in Feriana. The Germans and Italians were gone. Only the clutter of wreckage remained, burned-out vehicles, abandoned guns, scattered shell cases, gas cans, and miscellaneous rubbish.

The Allies soon regained the wrecked town of Sbeitla, thoroughly mined and booby-trapped, and Sidi bou Zid, altogether deserted and in ruin. All nine bridges between Sbiba and Sbeitla were demolished, and the possible bypasses were heavily mined. "We encountered mines and demolitions on such a scale," Eisenhower later wrote, "as to suggest virtually a new weapon in warfare, and as a result, our progress was delayed and contact with the enemy lost."

Koeltz had a different explanation. The Allied units were in such disorder and their commanders so shaken that only aircraft could strike at the enemy in retreat.

Within a few days, the Germans were back where they had begun operations on February 14, less than two weeks earlier. Rommel had accomplished little in the way of gaining elbow room in Tunisia, but he had thrown a scare into every Allied headquarters in North Africa and had taught the Allied forces much about the art of war.

With Allied troops streaming through the Kasserine Pass, this time in the right direction, Harmon returned to Kouif. He found everyone at the corps headquarters, he later said, "very jovial and happy" and "pleased about everything."

In the midst of the mutual congratulations and backslapping, Fredendall suddenly asked, "Are you going to relieve Ward?"

"No," Harmon said, "I think he did pretty well."

"Then I guess we won't need you any more," Fredendall said.

So Harmon headed back to Constantine, where he admitted to Truscott that the Allied follow-up had been slow. "We let them get away," he said, shaking his head. Had the Allied troops pushed ahead twenty-four hours earlier from Hamra and Thala, he mistakenly believed, they would have been able to cut off Rommel and "make it cost him a hell of a lot more than it did."

Obviously disappointed because he had commanded "the battle" rather than the corps, Harmon told Truscott he wanted to get back to his 2d Armored Division and teach his troops some of the lessons he had learned. "Of course," he added, "if the Army needs me again, I would be very glad to . . . do the same thing again."

He stopped at Algiers to see Eisenhower and give him his impressions of the front. They were brief. Ward was all right, but not Fredendall.

Eisenhower offered Harmon command of the II Corps, but he refused it. He could not, he said, take the corps after recommending Fredendall's relief. It would look as though he were motivated by his desire for the command.

He suggested, instead, Patton.

Then he returned to Morocco and his division.

He had arrived in Tunisia after Rommel had made his decision to withdraw. But he had had a considerable effect on the battle, and his presence had been invaluable. He may not have prevented Rommel from winning, but he prevented the Allies from losing. His exertions had made possible the birth of a legend — that the Americans had, in the end, defeated the master of desert warfare in North Africa and driven him back. And this, above all, would destroy the sense of inferiority that Rommel had sought to impose.

33

AFTER APPROVING Rommel's decision to break off the Battle of Kasserine on February 22, Kesselring instructed Arnim to apply pressure in the north to enable Rommel to regroup and array his forces against Montgomery.

As Arnim assembled his units, he kept wishing he had the 10th Panzer Division. Though Rommel controlled the division and as army group commander was now his immediate superior, Arnim flew to Rome at dawn of the 24th. A conference with Kesselring produced a new plan for a major offensive along virtually his entire front.

While Kesselring explained the operation to Comando Supremo, Arnim returned to Tunisia that afternoon to attend a meeting with Messe that Rommel had called. Full of enthusiasm, Arnim took the initiative in the discussion. How could the Axis guarantee a lengthy defense of North Africa? he asked. By keeping the Allies off balance? That would only postpone the inevitable decision to withdraw. No, by putting one or the other of the Allied armies out of action for at least six months. That was his intention. After he destroyed the Allied forces in the north, he would lend a hand to take care of Montgomery in the south.

It all sounded familiar to Rommel.

Messe did little more than lament his shortages in men and materiel. He looked for the Allies to attack his Mareth positions from all directions — everywhere except from the north, where he was connected with Arnim's army, and the east, where the sea protected his flank. He recommended a withdrawal in order to draw closer to Arnim's forces. There was little point, he felt, in getting his army inextricably engaged and irretrievably lost.

This too was old hat.

Rommel said little.

That evening, when Kesselring's chief of staff arrived to explain to Rommel the newly projected offensive in the north, he made a preposterous request: could Rommel support Arnim by keeping the 10th and 21st Panzer Divisions in position at Thala and Sbiba where they would continue to threaten Le Kef?

Rommel was flabbergasted by what he termed a "completely unrealistic" concept contrived by the "nincompoops at Comando Supremo." Didn't Kesselring know that the panzer divisions had already departed the Kasserine area and were on their way to Gabes and Sfax?

Apparently Kesselring had forgotten.

Arnim opened his large-scale attack against the British on the 26th. His offensive lasted three weeks. Though he took 1,600 prisoners and destroyed or captured 30 guns, 16 tanks, and 70 vehicles, he lacked the strength for a decisive exploitation.

Had his effort been coordinated with Rommel's drive at Kasserine, a strategic victory in Tunisia would undoubtedly have been won.

As early as the third day of Arnim's attack, Rommel visualized its futility. A memo he sent to Kesselring illuminated his discouragement. He believed that his long front of almost four hundred miles could be penetrated and broken at any point. He therefore proposed that Arnim launch limited, spoiling attacks while Messe moved his army toward the northeastern portion of Tunisia, the original bridgehead area, in order to shorten the front by one hundred miles.

To Rommel's suggestion, which seemed like the first step toward an evacuation of North Africa, Kesselring and Comando Supremo said no. Instead of withdrawing Messe from the Mareth Line, Rommel was to assist Arnim by attacking Montgomery.

Messe launched his attack on March 6, and the superiority of Montgomery's forces quickly became evident. A heavy gloom settled over Rommel. The days of Army Group Afrika in Tunisia, he felt, were distinctly numbered.

Could he save Messe's strength, he asked Kesselring, by withdrawing before Montgomery attacked? Could he have permission to form a more solid bridgehead that could not be cut off? Could he start making preparations to evacuate North Africa altogether? Could he save the troops even if he had to sacrifice their equipment?

Kesselring referred the questions to Mussolini and Hitler.

Both replied in the negative.

Believing that further resistance in North Africa was useless, Rommel turned over to Arnim temporary command of the army group on March 9 and departed for Rome. He tried to get Kesselring, Comando Supremo, and Mussolini, in that order, to understand the hopelessness of the situation. All referred him to Hitler.

On March 10, after flying to Hitler's headquarters, he saw the Fuehrer.

Hitler was no more sympathetic than the others. He ordered Rommel to go on extended sick leave.

Rommel said he had every intention of returning to Tunisia. He could not abandon his troops. He could at least try to save as many as possible from destruction. Wasn't he still the most knowledgeable commander in Africa?

No, Hitler said. He was too ill to return.

Part VI

THE AFTERMATH

34

IN TUNISIA, Hanson Baldwin once wrote, in that "strangely beautiful," "strangely melancholy" land, depressed and arid, roamed by nomadic Arabs, strewn with the vestigial remnants of former glories, in that country where the "perfect symmetry of an ancient Roman temple, . . . the broken mosaics and the marble columns, the statuary and the relics of an age gone by" stand among the stark djebels and deeply bitten watercourses, in the sand and mud and shivering cold of winter, the Americans at Kasserine "paid in blood the price of battlefield experience."

The judgment is just, but, like most epitaphs, too brief.

* * * *

The Kasserine operation cost the Germans, according to their figures, 201 men killed, 536 wounded, and 252 missing — a total of 989; 14 guns, 61 motor vehicles, 6 half-tracks, and 20 tanks. Add to that the Italian losses. Prisoners taken by the II Corps numbered 73 Germans and 535 Italians.

In contrast, the Germans reported they captured 4,026 prisoners, 61 tanks and half-tracks, 161 motor vehicles, 36 guns, 45 tons of ammunition, a large amount of gasoline and lubricants, and much engineer equipment.

The actual Allied losses were much higher. Of the 30,000 Americans engaged in the Kasserine battle under the II Corps, probably 300 were killed, almost 3,000 were wounded, and nearly 3,000 were missing in action — more than 20 percent. The corps had been doubly decimated. It would take more than 7,000 replacement troops to refill the depleted American ranks.

The II Corps alone lost 183 tanks, 194 half-tracks, 208 pieces of artillery, 512 trucks and jeeps, and large amounts of fuel, ammunition, and rations — more materiel and supplies than the combined stocks in the depots of Algeria and Morocco. As logisticians rushed forward equipment by every available means of transportation, they emptied their reserves.

The situation improved early in March. Trucks were coming off assembly lines in Casablanca and Oran, and a special shipment of more than four thousand five hundred 2½-ton trucks and other wheeled vehicles arrived from the United States. Railway cars reached the theater in sufficient quantities to enable forty trains to run daily between Constantine and Tebessa, delivering more than ten thousand tons of equipment and supplies for the American combat troops — more materiel than all the Axis forces in Tunisia were receiving. As additional service troops were sent from the United States and the United Kingdom, they kept the roads and railways in a better state of repair, gave motor vehicles adequate maintenance, enlarged depots and airfields, and constructed ten pipelines to carry fuel directly from North African ports to Tunisia.

Paralleling the increased efficiency of the American supply establishment were similar reforms by the British, who expanded their administrative tail and discovered that their teeth were sharpened in the process.

The improved logistical structure benefited the French. Despite many competing claims for cargo space, the rearmament of the French military forces, agreed to at the Casablanca Conference, got under way as a special convoy of fifteen ships left the United States for North Africa in March, the first of many that would bring a stream of the latest models of weapons and equipment. As American arms reconstituted and restored French power, Giraud liberalized his administration, renounced all ties with Vichy, released from detention political prisoners and refugees, and opened negotiations to merge the forces in North Africa with De Gaulle's Free French.

* * * *

Alexander, who had arrived in Tunisia during the Battle of Kasserine, played an indirect role during the crisis. While trying to spur Montgomery's advance into southern Tunisia to alleviate Rommel's pressure, he toured the battlefront constantly, showing himself to troops and commanders, and bringing, like Harmon, a feeling of confidence. All who saw him — handsome, alert, approachable, unpretentious, open, and quite sure of himself — had the impression, somehow, that everything was now going to turn out all right.

His influence soon became direct and profound. Every day after his assumption of command, Eisenhower later acknowledged, there was a noticeable improvement in the coordination of tactical activity, in the readiness of the British, French, and Americans to accept orders without regard to nationality, and in the growth of mutual understanding.

There were other changes. Eisenhower's intelligence officer was fired for what was called his excessive reliance on one type of information. Having misinterpreted the enemy's intentions, he had diverted Anderson's initial attention from the south to the north. For this error, the staff officer was removed and replaced.

But Anderson too had been at fault. He had failed to verify by active ground patrolling the location of the enemy strength. Too firmly fixed in his conviction that the enemy effort would come in the north, he reacted too slowly to the German thrust beyond Faid in the south. As the American defenses crumbled, he lost his poise. Ready to give up, he had abandoned Sbiba, and he had instructed Irwin's guns to be moved back, an order that would have surrendered Thala had not Harmon countermanded it. Though Anderson's concept was to roll with Rommel's punch, the Allies were on the ropes at Thala and a further withdrawal would have put them out of the ring — probably out of Tunisia. The irony was that the battle was already over.

These damaging mistakes, plus Anderson's inability to inspire his American subordinates with confidence, might have prompted his dismissal. But Eisenhower's foremost concern was to foster Anglo-American unity, and he feared that calling for Anderson's ouster might disturb the harmony. Anderson remained in command of the First Army. At the end of the North African campaign, he seemed to drop out of sight.

Alexander judged Fredendall's performance to have been deficient, and he informed Eisenhower that he would welcome a new corps commander. The recommendation cinched the case that had been building up against him. His subordinates too had lost confidence in his leadership, pointing out that he had assigned tasks to units beyond their means — the 168th Infantry lost on Ksaira, for example, CCA cut to pieces at Sidi bou Zid. Since he disliked and distrusted the British and would never get on well with Alexander and Anderson, and since he had made it quite clear that if he or Ward were retained, the other would have to go, Eisenhower removed him.

Ordered home ostensibly because of his ability to train troops, Fredendall received a hero's greeting, a promotion to the three-star rank of lieutenant general, and command of the Second Army, a training organization. Few suspected that his performance at Kasserine had been less than adequate. Eisenhower's aide, as he later wrote, explained to President Roosevelt, "the reluctance Ike had in relieving Fredendall, and his hope that . . . Fredendall's fine qualities, particularly for training, would not be lost to the Army."

For his new corps commander in Tunisia, Eisenhower chose

Patton, a man he termed a "tank expert." Coming from Morocco, he took command of the II Corps on March 6. Major General Omar N. Bradley, who had recently arrived in North Africa as a War Department representative, was appointed his deputy.

Eisenhower instructed Patton first to rehabilitate the American forces — reorganize, re-equip, and retrain them. There had to be careful logistical planning; all combat troops, not only the engineers, had to know how to use mines properly and how to detect and remove enemy mines; and everyone had to have a spirit of genuine partnership with his allies.

Setting about to transmit an aggressive spirit to the corps, Patton drove his subordinates hard, put the troops through a rigorous program of training and hardening, and moved through his area with restless energy. His high-pitched voice soon became familiar to the troops, and his adroit mixture of profanity and vulgarity on the one hand and of sentimentality on the other, so transparently soldier talk and manipulative in design, had an initial effect of shock that soon turned to awe. He substituted military decorum for casualness, required spit and polish as an antidote against carelessness, clamped helmets on everyone, tightened up regulations on dress and personal appearance, reamed out soldiers who failed to salute, and insisted that everyone wear a necktie. Loaded down with pistols buckled around his waist, carrying on his shirt collar, on his shoulders, and on a metallic flag welded to his scout car the largest general's stars he could find, he raced through the countryside radiating glamor, action, and determination. The Regular officers who knew him as Gorgeous Georgie or Flash Gordon felt a surge of confidence spread through the ranks.

Underneath the carefully calculated show was a soldier of genius, who had prepared himself from boyhood for leadership in battle and for the high military responsibility he never doubted would some day be his. A hero with Pershing in Mexico and again in France during World War I, Patton had conscientiously worked hard to create an image that would become a legend.

As the troops worked hard, received new equipment, and refurbished the old, they also had time for creature comforts and relaxation. Instead of cooking C rations on a desert stove, a small hole dug in the ground and half filled with water topped with gasoline, or heating their food on the exhaust-manifold of an engine, they were served hot meals. They were issued new clothing. They attended ceremonies for the award of decorations. They listened to band concerts and heard on their radios the sexy programs of swing music furnished, along with a propaganda line, by Axis Sally and Dirtie Gertie from Bizerte.

Contact with native adults was negligible, and Arabs who were picked up on suspicion of questionable activities were usually turned over to a nearby French unit for disposition. But the Tunisian children were everywhere among the soldiers, who fed and clothed them, gave them affection, along with the chewing gum, candy, and sugar of the K ration.

Mail usually arrived once a week, sometimes after a two-week interval. A letter home took twenty to thirty days for delivery. Since the men had little stationery, they used toilet paper, wrappings from rations, the backs of old letters. Many tried to send souvenirs home, and among the packages opened by the base censor were found hand grenades, helmets, bayonets, and rifles.

In the 34th Division alone, the soldiers purchased more than $26 million of National Service Life Insurance during the first four months of 1943. Of the more than $4½ million they earned in pay during the first five months of the year, they allotted 50 percent to dependents and 4 percent to purchase War Bonds; of the 46 percent they received in cash, they used 20 percent for money orders sent home, 18 percent for savings in the form of Soldiers' Deposits, and 8 percent for local expenditures, crap games, and poker.

Replacement troops, who usually came in groups of 125

to 275 men, were generally below average in physical fitness, training, and mental capacity. Many had never participated in field maneuvers or fired a weapon. Some were improperly equipped. Commanders suspected that units in the United States were unloading disciplinary cases by shipping them overseas.

As reports clearly categorized the individual replacements as unsatisfactory in the main, and as specific weaknesses of soldier performance at Kasserine became known, the Army lengthened the thirteen-week training cycle in July, 1943, to seventeen weeks. Six months later, the most glaring training deficiencies seemed to be remedied. An Army Ground Forces staff officer expressed in a letter to a friend his confidence in the program. "While we have many weak spots," he wrote, "and a hell of a lot remains to be done, yet in general, I am convinced that we have been turning out soundly trained and well trained divisions. Some of them, I believe sincerely, equal anything the Germans ever turned out, at least so far as training is concerned. Lacking the necessity for defending our homes and [having] a certain national softness that does not develop a keen desire to fight, our individual fighting spirit may not be too hot, but I still think the training is there."

Weaknesses in American weapons had also become evident at Kasserine. The light M-3 tank was suited only for reconnaissance. The half-tracks, called "Purple Heart Boxes," were insufficiently armored. The 37-mm. antitank gun was effective only at very close range against scout cars and other light vehicles.

Sherman tanks would be produced in increasing numbers, and they would become the workhorses in the European theater. Improvements in guns would result in the development and extensive use of 76-mm. high-velocity tubes for tanks and 90-mm. guns for antiaircraft and ground fires.

Commanders on all levels met in conference to exchange ideas gained from the Kasserine experience. They tested new and improved techniques in fire direction control. They discussed procedures to obtain better intelligence and more effective air support. All agreed that divisions had to be fought as divisions instead of in small, separate pieces. Ryder had early concluded that he would "cut out that combat team stuff" and keep his 34th Division concentrated. After Kasserine, the Americans would hold their large units together rather than parceling out segments. The division had been organized as a self-sufficient and powerful combat force, and this would be the way it would be used in the future.

Under Alexander's direction, the ground forces reorganized their sectors. The emergency at Kasserine had required the hasty dispatch of units to positions on a shifting front and the hurried improvisation of *ad hoc* units to meet the demands of a rapidly changing situation. The results had been an inevitable separation of units from their parent commands and an intermingling of the troops of all three nations, which had intensified the confusion of combat. Immediately afterward, detached brigades, regiments, and combat teams were returned to their original organizations, and the battlefront was divided into three national sectors, British, French, and American.

At the beginning of March, the British had about 120,000 men in northern Tunisia, the French about 50,000 in the center, and the Americans about 90,000 in the south. The American II Corps would have three infantry divisions, Allen's 1st, Ryder's 34th, and Major General Manton S. Eddy's 9th, as well as Ward's 1st Armored, all concentrated and held firmly in hand.

Several important questions still awaited resolution. What would be the effect of the beating the Allied troops, particularly the Americans, had absorbed at Kasserine? Would they benefit from their seasoning and experience? Or had they received an inferiority complex that would prevent them from ever attaining status as first-class soldiers? The offensive that opened in March would clearly demonstrate the answers.

35

As THE RAINS came to an end and the smell of spring filled the air, the final phase of the North African campaign opened. While Arnim engaged the British in the north, Patton attacked in the south on March 17. Eight days later the II Corps had regained Gafsa and taken Maknassy.

Montgomery initiated his offensive against the Mareth Line on March 20. On April 6, the two Allied armies in Tunisia made contact and formed a single battlefront. Four days later, they took Sfax, two days afterward Sousse.

On April 15, Patton was promoted to lieutenant general, sent to Algeria to prepare for the invasion of Sicily in July, and put in command of the Seventh U.S. Army. Bradley took his place at the head of the II Corps.

Pushing the Axis forces into the northeastern corner of Tunisia, the Allies launched their final offensive on April 22 and entered Bizerte and Tunis on May 7. The last organized Axis resistance in North Africa came to an end on the 13th.

A total of 200,000 Axis soldiers was taken prisoner during the latter stage of the campaign.

Kesselring, immediately after authorizing Rommel to break off the Battle of Kasserine, had sent a telegram to Hitler telling him that the operation had hurt the Americans and parts of the British and French forces so severely that it would take the Allies four to six weeks to recover enough strength for a large-scale offensive.

They regained their strength far more quickly. Returning almost at once to the ground from which they had been ejected, they found their capabilities hardly impaired. Their casualties had been serious rather than devastating. British losses had been chiefly in tanks, for which replacements had been planned in any event. Less than a month after Rommel drew back, the Allies went over to the offense, and in less than two months swept the Axis armies from the field.

In retrospect, the disaster and tragedy of Kasserine produced a shock that proved beneficial to the Allies. The defeat shook down the command and the logistical establishment.

The American, British, and French forces emerged from Kasserine strengthened by adversity. "Every Yank Outfit Did Great Job," Ernie Pyle reported, reassuring the folks back home that in the final phase of the campaign the Americans had fought like veterans, with good commanders and enough supplies. Everything had, he said, meshed perfectly. "So you at home need never be ashamed of our American fighters. Even though they didn't do too well in the beginning, there was never at any time any question about the American bravery. It is a matter of being hardened and practiced by going through the flames."

The London *Times* also tendered compliments. The Americans had been, the paper reported, "exposed to some of the severest of the fighting, and had suffered heavy casualties; but the event proves that hard buffeting has only hardened their resolution and equipped them with tactical experience that they are quick to turn to account."

After six months of varying fortune, Eisenhower later wrote, Africa was cleared of all Axis forces. There was no longer need to make the long sea voyage around the continent of Africa, and on May 17, four days after the campaign ended, a British convoy passed through the Straits of Gibraltar bound directly for Alexandria, Egypt; on the 24th, an unopposed convoy of ships reached Malta directly from England, the first since 1940.

"I had originally hoped to achieve these results," Eisenhower wrote, "nearly six months earlier than this, by exclud-

THE AFTERMATH 313

ing the Axis entirely from Tunisia and by trapping Rommel in Libya; our initial failure had the unforeseen effect of enhancing the magnitude of our ultimate success, because it tempted the Axis into making what proved to be an excessive investment in the Tunisian Bridgehead."

Hoping to maintain indefinitely a bridgehead in Tunisia, like the Allies at Salonika during World War I, the Axis nations lost more than 320,000 men killed, wounded, or captured, together with all their equipment. The defeat exceeded the disaster at Stalingrad, which had cost the Germans about 200,000 men.

"The turn of the tide at Kasserine," Eisenhower wrote, "proved actually to be the turn of the tide in all of Tunisia."

If Rommel had aimed merely to push the Allied troops back from the coastal plain in the east in order to protect his own lines of communication, he was lured into an operation at Kasserine that was hardly worth the effort. If he envisioned getting to Le Kef to destroy the Allied supply lines, he was tempted into a battle that was beyond his strength. If he intended only to inflict damage on men and equipment, he was misled into an experience that had only temporary effect.

Eisenhower himself took responsibility for the defeat at Kasserine. "I am now convinced," he wrote after the war, "that regardless of consequences, I should have compelled an earlier acceptance by the French of the principle of Allied command on the fighting front, and insisted on their placing their divisions directly under the British commander." By the time Anderson took command of the entire battle line, his headquarters and communications were so established that, for all practical purposes, he was confined to control of the northern part of the front only. The recurring crises prevented him from rearranging the command system and, according to Eisenhower, "unquestionably contributed to the error, in the Sbeitla–Kasserine battle, of committing a United States Armored Division to action in driblets."

But the major factor in the defeat, Eisenhower believed,

was his miscalculation of the ability of the French to hold the central sector. When the French caved in during January, he explained, the British and Americans weakened their own fronts to buttress the French, thus facilitating Rommel's triumph.

The explanation is oversimplified. Without the French army in Tunisia, as Koeltz has justly remarked, the Allies would have been unable to enter Tunisia at all. Without the French, they would certainly have been pushed back twice to Constantine, once in December, 1942, and again in February, 1943.

There is much truth, despite the emotion, in what Koeltz has said of "all the combatants of the [French] army of Africa who took part in the campaign of Tunisia . . . ; who, during six long months, suffered and worked in the djebels, under the rain, in the mud, in the cold, without tents; who had no tanks, no planes, no machine guns, no antitank cannons, no trucks, and who, in spite of everything, resisted the enemy, seized two times from him the passages of the eastern Dorsale and finally pushed him back . . . , pierced his front, fell on his rear, and made him capitulate."

The Battle of Kasserine disclosed an absence of mutual understanding and confidence among the coalition forces on both sides of the front. In the Allied camp, impatience with the different national organizations, tactical methods, and command and staff procedures had created bitterness; personal and petty motivations, resentments, and jealousies had inhibited cooperation. On the Axis side, misunderstanding and lack of confidence between Italians and Germans, plus the personal ambitions of commanders, had prompted distrust, friction, and insubordination; the Italians were riddled with bureaucracy and failed to comprehend the demands and the tempo of modern warfare, while the efficient Germans were arrogant and officious.

At Kasserine, the Axis forces achieved a tactical success,

not a major victory that changed the Allied strategy for the European campaigns. Kasserine lengthened the operations in Tunisia, delayed the invasions of Sicily and the Italian mainland, postponed the invasion of southern France, and retarded the decisive events marking the unfolding strategy. Yet at the same time, the longer duration of the Tunisian campaign resulting from Kasserine intensified the Allied blows against the Axis, gave the Allies more prisoners of war, weakened the Axis military machine, facilitated the invasion of Europe, including the Normandy landings, speeded the subsequent campaigns, and brought closer the ultimate victory.

Kasserine produced the commanders who would gain that victory. Eisenhower, above all, demonstrated his capacity for high responsibility, and he would lead the Allies into Sicily and the Italian mainland, bring about the surrender of the first Axis government, Italy, and engineer the switch of Italy to the Allied side as a cobelligerent. In 1944, at the head of the Allied forces invading northwest Europe, he would direct the march that would end in the capitulation of Germany.

Patton came into prominence after Kasserine, when the American public needed a hero. Catapulted into the spotlight, he captured the imagination of the world and started toward fame. After Tunisia, he would take the Seventh Army into the invasion of Sicily and finally head the Third Army in the campaigns of France and Germany that would forever mark him as one of the great captains.

If Harmon, who displayed many of the same military virtues and characteristics, had accepted command of the II Corps in Tunisia, would he have become the Patton of World War II?

Harmon returned to Tunisia in April, this time to take command of a unit rather than, as before, a battle. He replaced Ward at the head of the 1st Armored Division.

For a cloud had gathered around Ward much like the one about Anderson. How much Ward was to blame for the defeats at Faid, Sidi bou Zid, Sbeitla, and Kasserine was difficult to determine. By ignoring Ward, Fredendall had deprived him of his proper place in the command structure and thereby excused him of fault or blame. But would Harmon, for example, have accepted such treatment? And would Harmon, or anyone else, have permitted McQuillin to fumble at Sidi bou Zid after his display of ineptness at Faid?

Eisenhower had given Patton a task that Eisenhower himself had been unable to perform. "You must not retain for one instant," he warned, "any man in a responsible position where you have become doubtful of his ability to do the job. . . . This matter frequently calls for more courage than any other thing you will have to do, but I expect you to be perfectly cold-blooded about it. . . . I will give you the best available replacement or stand by any arrangement you want to make."

Patton heeded the instruction. Finding Ward somewhat pale for his taste, preferring the colorful exuberance of Harmon, he gave Ward a virtually impossible battle assignment early in April. Ward personally led the assault, was slightly wounded, and failed to capture his objective. Patton relieved him.

Ward returned to the United States. But his relief had been manifestly unfair, and in the following year he received command of another armored division, which he took to Europe early in 1945 and led with distinction during the closing months of the war.

Yet the Battle of Kasserine would haunt him. "I well remember those days," he later wrote, "and feel in retrospect that I could have handled it much better."

Harmon and the 1st Armored Division sat out the Sicilian campaign, then went to southern Italy. The terrain was ill-suited for armor, and the division and Harmon were largely wasted. Toward the end of the war, Harmon received command of a corps, which he directed with his usual vigor and competence.

Clark, who had eschewed Tunisia in favor of commanding the Fifth Army in Morocco, took his army into southern Italy at Salerno, proved his capacity for combat leadership, became army group commander in Italy, and emerged from the war with four stars and distinction.

Truscott, who took command of a division shortly after Kasserine, invaded Sicily, campaigned in southern Italy, and made the landings at Anzio, where he was accorded command of a corps. After invading southern France, he succeeded Clark in command of the Fifth Army in Italy. At the end of the war, he had three stars and recognition as one of America's finest combat leaders.

Bradley, who succeeded Patton in command of the II Corps, participated in the invasion and campaign of Sicily, then took the First U.S. Army ashore in Normandy, assumed command of the 12th Army Group in Europe, and acquired five-star rank and a reputation as one of America's most brilliant soldiers.

Irwin's distinguished performance at Thala gained him command of a division, which he took to Europe, and his continuing competence and success brought him command of a corps. Ryder and Allen were two of the finest division commanders in the European area. Eddy led his division in Sicily, then became a corps commander in Europe. Stack became a brigadier general and an assistant division commander. Drake was repatriated in September, 1944, on a prisoner of war exchange and served for a few months before retiring because of physical disability. Hightower, Hains, and Alger became major generals ten years after the war. Waters returned from internment, handled increasing responsibilities brilliantly, and became a four-star general.

Robinett was wounded during the final few days of the Tunisian campaign, and his promising career was cut short. McNabb and Welvert were killed on the Tunisian battlefield.

Barré, the first French general officer to battle the Germans in Tunisia, had the honor at the end of the campaign of retaking Tunis and marching into the city at the head of his troops. Shortly thereafter, he was excluded from the Regular Army by the Gaullist Committee of National Liberation. Charges were made against him for having collaborated with the Axis, but he was never brought to trial, and he retired from active service after the war.

Derrien, who had commanded the naval base at Bizerte, preferred to be relieved from active duty and returned to France upon the demobilization of French forces in the Tunisian bridgehead. But upon the request of the Vichy Government, he remained at his post. After the Allied conquest of Tunisia, he was remanded for trial. Tried by a special tribunal in March, 1944, he was sentenced to dismissal from the Navy and imprisonment for life. He was released from prison on suspended sentence in May, 1946, and he died twelve days later. He was buried with full military honors.

Giraud retired from public life after the war. Koeltz completed a distinguished career as a soldier. Juin brilliantly led the French Expeditionary Corps in the Italian campaign and became a Marshal of France.

Alexander, who had gained an unfortunate impression of the American soldier at Kasserine, drew American protests for giving British units more favorable assignments during the remainder of the Tunisian campaign and for placing the Americans in a secondary role in Sicily. Patton's stunning triumphs in Sicily dispelled his notion, and, in Eisenhower's words, Alexander became "broad-gauged." He took command of the Mediterranean theater in 1944 and emerged from the war a field marshal and one of Britain's finest soldiers.

Montgomery took his Eighth Army to Sicily and Italy, led the Allied ground forces in the Normandy invasion and the British and Commonwealth troops in the subsequent campaigns of northwest Europe as an army group commander. Known for his excessive caution, he achieved his greatest victory at El Alamein. He too became a field marshal and one of Britain's heroes.

Anderson returned to England after the North African campaign, was later sent to command the British troops in East Africa, and eventually served a tour as Governor and Commander-in-Chief of Gibraltar, a prize reserved for retired generals of good repute. Keightley commanded a division, later a corps in Italy, and rose to full general rank. Dunphie became a major general, served as the War Office Director of Royal Armoured Corps, and retired to become chairman of Vickers, Ltd. Nicholson became a division commander, then the War Office Director of Artillery, and was promoted to four-star rank.

Messe, after the Italian surrender and declaration of war against Germany in the fall of 1943, helped to rehabilitate Italian combat forces for participation, alongside the Allied forces, in the campaign in Italy.

Nehring, after returning to Germany, was sent to the Russian front where he commanded an armored corps and later a panzer army. Hildebrandt returned to Germany and became a liaison officer with an Italian division loyal to Mussolini. Ziegler escaped capture in Tunisia, commanded a division in Italy, then a corps until he was injured by Italian partisans and disabled for further duty.

Arnim, who had been seriously at fault in Tunisia by reason of his self-centered, independent, and arbitrary attitude, had contributed significantly to the Axis failure at Kasserine. Unable to free himself from his fixed ideas and to generate proper feelings of subordination to his superiors, he subverted and sabotaged, by his captious behavior, the foundations of a great opportunity. Together with Broich and Buelowius, he was taken prisoner in Tunisia and spent the rest of the war in prison camp.

Kesselring, one of Germany's most competent soldiers in

World War II, placed the blame for the inability to exploit the near-success at Kasserine on the Italian High Command — for failing to secure the water route to Africa by an unconditional commitment of all available means of combat and transport; and on Hitler — for having a surplus of consideration for his friend, Mussolini. He forgot to take a good part of the fault for himself. His coordination of what he called the "big operation" was defective, and his endeavors to marshal the efforts of Rommel and Arnim toward a single goal were inept. Despite his inadequate performance in Tunisia, he served with distinction as commander-in-chief of the Italian theater until March, 1945, when Hitler placed him in command of the crumbling Western front in the waning days of the war.

Rommel, after a long rest in Germany, took command of an army group in northern Italy in the fall of 1943, then was sent by Hitler to supervise the defenses of the Atlantic Wall, and finally took the brunt of the Allied invasion of Normandy. Disenchanted by Hitler and the war, he became defeatist in attitude and conspiratorial in outlook. Injured by a concussion in July, 1944, when his car was strafed by a plane and forced into a ditch, he was recovering when he was forced to commit suicide in the autumn of 1944.

Despite his brilliance as a commander, it was he who was most responsible for the inconclusive ending at Kasserine. Visionary, instigator, protagonist, and, finally, failure, he ascribed his inability to achieve more at Kasserine to the stubborn Allied defense, to Axis errors, to the lack of Axis command unity, and to Arnim's egotism. But he overlooked his own lack of judgment, his own vacillation, his own unwillingness to recognize the state of his exhaustion. Burned out physically and psychologically, he had victory in his grasp, and he lost his nerve.

The first defeat that Rommel administered to the Americans at Kasserine was his last triumph on the battlefield.

NOTE

THE ALLIED COMMAND

A BRIEF CHRONOLOGY

INDEX

NOTE

KASSERINE is history not fiction. The facts, including the conversations among the participants, can be verified in the following sources.

The basic sources are the official records of the North African campaign — the unit journals, messages, and reports — which are open to scholars and writers. They frequently reveal far more drama and immediacy than one normally expects to find in an archival collection.

Supplementing these documents are manuscripts written shortly after the war by German generals — Kesselring, Nehring, Liebenstein, Gause, and others; interviews of commanders that were transcribed soon after the war — with Harmon, Irwin, Hains, Crosby, and others; and letters and conversations I have had from and with knowledgeable persons.

Of all the accounts I have consulted, the books of Dr. George F. Howe listed below are, by far, the most thoroughly authenticated, reliable, and complete. Rommel's papers, superbly edited by Captain B. H. Liddell Hart, and the memoirs of Generals Truscott, Robinett, and Koeltz furnish professional views and personal recollections.

The principal secondary sources I have used are:

Field Marshal the Viscount Alexander of Tunis, *The African Campaign from El Alamein to Tunis, 10 August 1942 to 13 May 1943.* Supplement to the London *Gazette*, February 3, 1948.

Lieutenant General K. A. N. Anderson, *Operations in Northwest Africa from 8 November 1942 to 13 May 1943.* Supplement to the London *Gazette*, November 8, 1948.

General Georges Barré, *Tunisie, 1942-1943*. Paris, 1950.

Lowell Bennett, *Assignment to Nowhere: The Battle for Tunisia*. New York, 1943.

Omar N. Bradley, *A Soldier's Story*. New York, 1951.

Captain Harry C. Butcher, *My Three Years with Eisenhower*. New York, 1946.

Lieutenant Colonel Bogardus Cairns, "Employment of Armor in the Invasion of Oran," *Military Review*, September, 1948.

Paul Carell, *The Foxes of the Desert*. London, 1960.

Captain Freeland A. Daubin, Jr., "The Battle of Happy Valley," Advanced Officers Class #1, Fort Knox, Kentucky, April, 1948.

Dwight D. Eisenhower, *Crusade in Europe*. New York, 1948.

Colonel Henry E. Gardiner, "We Fought at Kasserine," *Armored Cavalry Journal*, March-April, 1948.

George F. Howe, *The Battle History of the 1st Armored Division*. Washington, 1954.

George F. Howe, *Northwest Africa: Seizing the Initiative in the West*. U.S. ARMY IN WORLD WAR II. Washington, 1957.

Ralph Ingersoll, *The Battle is the Pay-off*. New York, 1946.

H. A. Jacobsen and J. Rohwer, eds., *The Decisive Battles of World War II: The German Side*. New York, 1965.

General Louis Koeltz, *Une Campagne que nous avons Gagnée: Tunisie, 1942-1943*. Paris, 1959.

B. H. Liddell Hart, ed., *The Rommel Papers*. London, 1953.

George S. Patton, Jr., *War as I Knew It*. Boston, 1947.

Colonel Edson D. Raff, *We Jumped to Fight*. New York, 1944.

Brigadier General Paul M. Robinett, *Armor Command*. Washington, 1958.

Service Historique, Etat-Major General, Marine Nationale,

Les Debarquements Alliés en Afrique du Nord (*Novembre 1942*). Paris, 1960.

General Lucian K. Truscott, Jr., *Command Missions.* New York, 1954.

Marcel Vigneras, *Rearming the French.* U.S. ARMY IN WORLD WAR II. Washington, 1957.

War Department Field Manual 5-31, *Land Mines and Booby Traps,* 1 November 1943.

Desmond Young, *Rommel.* London, 1950.

I wish to thank Brigadier General Hal C. Pattison, the Army's Chief of Military History, for his encouragement; Mr. Billy C. Mossman, for his maps and his counsel; Messrs. Joseph R. Friedman, Charles B. MacDonald, and Harry J. Middleton, for their advice and guidance; Mrs. Lois Aldridge, Dr. Hervé Cras, Colonel Thomas D. Drake, Mr. Detmar Finke, Colonel Albert W. Jones, Mr. Richard C. Kugler, Mrs. Lida Mayo, Lieutenant General Sir Frederick Morgan, and General John K. Waters, for their assistance; Mr. Craig Wylie and Mr. David Harris, for their patient and considerable help; and, most of all, my wife, for her support, including her presence during our trip in the summer of 1963 to Kasserine.

All responsibility rests with me. The views and opinions are my own and are not to be construed as an official expression of the Department of Defense or any other government agency.

M. B.

THE ALLIED COMMAND

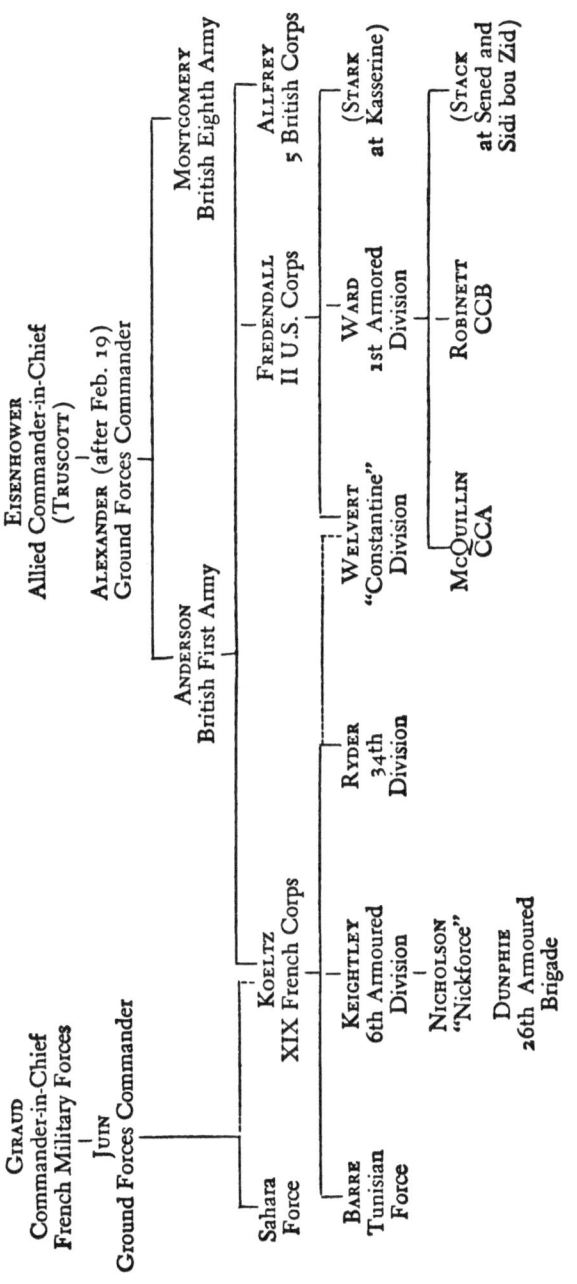

A BRIEF CHRONOLOGY

1942

October

23 — British under Alexander and Montgomery attack at El Alamein, Egypt

November

8 — Anglo-Americans under Eisenhower invade northwest Africa
10 — Allied forces under Anderson start from Algeria toward Tunisia
15 — French in North Africa take up arms against the Axis
17 — Allied and Axis fronts are in contact in Tunisia

December

9 — Arnim takes command of the Axis forces in the Tunisian bridgehead
25 — Arnim takes Pichon Pass

1943

January

3 — Arnim takes Fondouk Pass
26 — Rommel moves his headquarters from Libya across the border into Tunisia
30 — Arnim takes the Faid Pass

February

13 — Eisenhower visits II Corps front
14 — Ziegler, under Arnim, surrounds Djebels Lessouda and

Ksaira and takes Sidi bou Zid (loss of Hightower's battalion)
15 — Ward counterattacks at Sidi bou Zid (loss of Alger's battalion)
— Rommel's Italo-German Panzerarmee enters Mareth Line
— Liebenstein, under Rommel, enters Gafsa, abandoned by Allied forces
16 — Lessouda forces under Moore reach safety
— Ziegler attacks Sbeitla
17 — Ksaira forces under Drake try to break out to safety
— Ward retires from and Ziegler enters Sbeitla
— Liebenstein enters Feriana
18 — Rommel receives authority to attack Le Kef
19 — Rommel attacks at Sbiba and Kasserine
— Alexander takes command of the Allied ground forces in Tunisia
20 — Rommel takes the Kasserine Pass
21 — Robinett and Dunphie stop Rommel
22 — Irwin's artillery pieces defend Thala
— Rommel decides to end his attack
— Anderson gives up Sbiba
23 — Harmon arrives; countermands Anderson's order to give up Thala
— Rommel starts withdrawal; receives appointment as commander, Army Group Afrika
24 — Allied forces reenter Sbiba
25 — Allied forces reenter Kasserine
26 — Arnim attacks British in north Tunisia

March

6 — Messe attacks Montgomery at Mareth Line
9 — Rommel departs Africa
17 — Patton attacks in southern Tunisia
20 — Montgomery attacks Mareth Line

April

22 — Allies launch final offensive

May

7 — Allied troops enter Bizerte and Tunis
13 — Axis resistance in North Africa ends

Index

Afrika Korps. *See* Buelowius; German Forces; Liebenstein; Nehring; Rommel

Air forces: American, 60, 108, 127, 142, 198, 204, 266, 281-82; British, 11, 60, 108; German, 43, 60-62, 86, 108, 110, 141-42, 147, 151, 160-61, 206, 217, 262-63, 266, 281, 284; Royal Canadian, 59

Alamein. *See* El Alamein

Alexander, General Sir Harold R. L., 318; commands Middle East forces, 15-16; selected for North African invasion, 27-28; at Casablanca Conference, 93; takes command in Tunisia, 175, 225-26; role during battle of Kasserine, 305; judges Fredendall, 306; reorganizes front, 310

Alexandria, 13, 22, 312

Alger, Lt. Col. James D., 155, 317; at Sidi bou Zid, 159-63, 180-81, 184

Algeria, 4, 23-24, 78, 219; Allied landings, 20, 27, 32-33; German objective, 41, 48, 50, 80, 130, 183, 215; Allied base, 46, 73, 224, 273, 304

Algiers, 45, 63, 280; invasion of, 27; Eisenhower's headquarters, 31, 82, 90, 93, 120, 124, 175, 224, 288, 297; French headquarters, 38-39, 90

Allen, Maj. Gen. Terry, 96, 102, 115, 240, 247, 310, 317; defense at Kasserine, 248, 260-61, 277, 279, 293-95

Allfrey, Lt. Gen. Sir C. W., 96, 125

Allies. *See* American Forces; British Forces; French Forces

American Forces. ARMY GROUP: 12th, 317. ARMIES: First, 317; Third, 315; Fifth, *see* Clark; Seventh, 311, 315. CORPS: II, *see* Fredendall. DIVISIONS: 1st Infantry, *see* Allen; 9th Infantry, *see* Eddy; 34th Infantry, *see* Ryder; 1st Armored, *see* Ward; 2d Armored, 117, 224, 288, 297. INFANTRY REGIMENTS: 16th, *see* Allen; 18th, *see* Allen; 26th, *see* Stark; 168th, *see* Drake. COMBAT COMMANDS: A, *see* McQuillin; B, *see* Robinett. MISCELLANEOUS: 9th Division Artillery, *see* Irwin; 19th Engineers, *see* Moore, Anderson; 33d Field Artillery Battalion, 277; Rangers, 116, 125, 227, 277; XII Air Support Command, 85

Anderson, Lt. Gen. Sir Kenneth A. N., 319; North African strategy, 27; appointment to command, 28; and French, 30-31, 115; thrusts toward Bizerte and Tunis, 57, 73, 79, 81, 100, 105, 208; command arrangements, 89-92, 95-96, 313; and Maknassy, 102; and Faid, 107, 111; and Pichon, 110; and Sidi bou Zid, 12-26, 117, 122, 128, 155-57, 159; and Sbeitla, 175-76, 181, 183, 185-86, 192-93; and Kasserine, 227, 240-42, 253-54, 258-59, 263, 272, 276, 278, 282; shifts command post, 280-81; orders withdrawal from Thala, 291; role in the battle, 305-6, 315

Anzio, 317

Arabs, 6, 7, 24, 30, 60, 74, 178, 203, 208, 212, 228, 252, 303; intelligence information, 120; use by

Arabs *cont'd*:
  Germans, 142, 164-65, 204; withdrawal from Gafsa, 157; and American casualties, 165, 200; and French, 295, 308
Armored Division. *See* American Forces; British Forces; German Forces; Italian Forces; Panzer Divisions
Army Group Afrika, 99, 132, 285, 294, 300. *See also* Arnim; Comando Supremo; Kesselring; Rommel
Arnim, Generaloberst Juergen von, 54, 319-20; takes command, 52, 55, 76, 79, 81, 98-99; attacks Pichon, 80, 110-11; attacks Fondouk, 91; attacks in northern Tunisia, 93, 95, 299-300; attacks Faid, 104-5, 111; attacks Sidi bou Zid, 130-36, 154; attacks Sbeitla, 177, 179, 186-87, 207; and Kasserine, 216-20, 222, 245, 256-57, 262, 272-73, 281, 283-84, 286-87; under Rommel, 294, 298-99; takes army group command, 311
Atlantic Wall, 320
Atlas Mountains, 76
Austria, 16
Axis. *See* German Forces; Italian Forces; Hitler; Mussolini
Axis Sally, 308

Baldwin, Hanson, 303
Balkans, 5, 15
Barbary States, 23
Barré, General Georges, 78, 318; and Allied invasion of North Africa, 32-44; attacked by Germans, 47, 93
Ben Gardane, 97-98
Benson, Col. C. C., 295
Berbers, 7, 21, 24, 77
Berlin, 46
Bersaglieri. *See* Italian Forces
Bey of Tunis, 24
Bizerte, 28, 31, 32-44, 47-48, 51, 57, 59, 73-74, 81, 96, 98, 115, 131, 311, 318
Bled Foussana. *See* Foussana

Bone, 131-32, 215, 217-18, 220
Bou Chebka, 226-28, 240, 247-48, 261, 264, 276, 278, 293
Bradley, Maj. Gen. Omar N., 307, 311, 317
Britain, battle of, 9
British Forces: Derbyshire Yeomanry, 116, 125, 227, 277; Eighth Army, *see* Montgomery; First Army, *see* Anderson; Hampshires, 274; Lancers, 227, 243, 274-75; Leicesters, 259, 268-69, 271, 274-75; Lothians, 274; Middle East, 8-9, 11, 13, 15-16, 23, 27-28; 6th Armoured Division, *see* Keightley; 26th Armoured Brigade, *see* Dunphie
Broich, Gen. Fritz Freiherr von, 249-50, 319; attacks at Kasserine, 254, 261-64, 268-69, 271, 275-76, 281, 283; withdraws from Kasserine, 286, 294
Buelowius, Gen. Karl, 319; assumes command, 204; enters Feriana and Thelepte, 207; attacks Kasserine Pass, 217, 221, 238-42, 245, 246, 249-50, 254, 261-64, 266, 270-71, 277-78; withdraws from Kasserine, 286
Buerat el Hsur, 52-53
Byzantium, 7, 74, 178

Cairo, 15
Cape of Good Hope, 16
Carthage, 7, 74, 77
Casablanca, 27, 224, 232, 304
Casablanca Conference, 92-93, 119, 175, 304
Casualties. *See* Losses
Caucasus, 13
Centauro Division. *See* Italian Forces
Chambi. *See* Djebel Chambi
Churchill, Winston S., 22, 29, 92, 118-20
Clark, Gen. Mark W., 26-27, 29, 82, 317
Coley, Sgt. Clarence W., 149-53
Comando Supremo, 12, 14, 19, 50-51, 54, 135, 179, 257, 300, 320;

INDEX

Comando Supremo *cont'd:*
   orders attack at Faid, 105, 130-33, 187; authorizes attack on Le Kef, 217-23; authorizes withdrawal from Kasserine, 285-87; names Rommel to army group, 294; authorizes Arnim to attack, 298-99
Combat Command. *See* American Forces; McQuillin; Robinett
Committee of National Liberation. *See* Free French; De Gaulle
Constantine, 33, 38-39, 74, 76-77, 80, 82; Eisenhower's forward command post, 90-91, 93, 108-9, 124, 129, 288-89, 296; German objective, 98, 183, 279-80, 314; and supplies, 119, 304; and reinforcements, 273; *see also* Truscott
Constantine Division. *See* Welvert
Corsica, 29
Crosby, Lt. Col. Ben, 155, 184-85, 190-91

Dakar, 22-23
Darlan, Admiral Jean François, 25, 28-29, 33
Daubin, 2d Lt. Freeland A., Jr., 56-69, 81
De Gaulle, General Charles, 22-23, 25-26, 29, 305, 318
Derbyshire Yeomanry. *See* British Forces
Dernaia, 207, 221, 226-28, 278
Derrien, Admiral Louis, 32-44, 318
Detachment Guinet, 227
Dirtie Gertie from Bizerte, 308
Divisions. *See* American Forces; British Forces; German Forces; Italian Forces
Djebel Chambi, 228, 239, 248
Djebel Hamra, 229, 252, 261-64, 266, 270-71, 277, 279, 282, 293, 295-96
Djebel Ksaira, 121-23, 126-27, 129, 138-39, 143-49, 154, 159-60, 162, 168, 171, 177, 184, 194-96, 201-2, 260, 306
Djebel Lessouda, 108-9, 121-23, 127, 129, 134, 136-43, 145, 148-50,

Djebel Lessouda *cont'd:*
   154-55, 159-61, 163-70, 172, 185, 189, 195, 200, 202
Djebel Semmama, 228, 238-39, 249, 254
Dorsale. *See* Eastern Dorsale; Western Dorsale
Drake, Col. Thomas D., 115-16, 128, 138-39, 143-49, 159, 166, 168, 171, 180, 184, 194-204, 206, 306, 317
Dryden, 1st Lt. Edwin C., 234-37
Duce. *See* Mussolini
Dunkirk, 49
Dunphie, Brig. Charles A. L., 186, 227, 240-41, 253-55, 258-60, 262, 267-69, 271, 274, 276, 292

Eastern Dorsale, 76, 79, 91-93, 98-99, 105, 108-9, 115, 117, 127, 130-31, 133-34, 136, 183, 186, 205, 314
Eddy, Maj. Gen. Manton S., 96, 224, 239, 247, 261, 273, 279, 310, 317
Egypt, 9, 11-13, 15, 19-20, 49, 222
Eighth Army. *See* Montgomery
Eisenhower, Gen. Dwight D., 296, 312, 318; and North Africa landings, 26-28; and French forces, 30-79; thrust toward Bizerte and Tunis, 51, 73, 80; and Rommel's retreat across Libya, 54; and Fredendall, 83-84, 111; command arrangements, 82, 88-89, 91, 95-96, 108, 175-76, 248, 282, 288, 297, 305-7, 315-16; at Casablanca Conference, 93; and intelligence information, 117; and supplies, 117-20, 183, 224-25; visits front, 124-29, 137, 139, 294; and Gafsa, 155-56
El Alamein, 13, 16, 18, 48, 50, 97, 133, 177, 285, 319
El Ma el Abiod, 77, 207, 221, 226-28, 231, 248, 278, 282

Faid, 3, 76-77, 79, 82, 92, 129, 200, 202, 287, 316; attack on, 99-104, 107-11, 116, 121, 125-26, 231,

INDEX

Faid *cont'd*:
278; attack from, 131, 134, 136, 138-41, 143, 149, 155, 165-66, 305
Feriana, 74-75, 192, 215, 226-27, 245; defense of, 115-16, 126, 139, 155-57, 176, 181; attack on, 134, 177, 186-87, 193, 204, 207, 217, 293; Rommel's command post, 221, 239, 284; German withdrawal through, 286, 295
Fifth Panzer Army. *See* Arnim
First Army, American. *See* Bradley
First Army, British. *See* Anderson
First Army, Italian. *See* Messe
Fondouk, 76, 102, 116-17, 125, 159, 177, 185; occupied by French, 79, 92; taken by Germans, 91, 93, 95, 99-100, 134, 137, 154-55, 175, 186, 207, 216
Foussana, 228-30, 238, 242, 247-49, 252, 254, 259, 261-62, 266, 294-95
France, 5, 23, 315, 317; defeat and armistice of 1940, 21, 24-25, 28-29, 36
Franco, Generalissimo Francisco, 27
Frascati, 12
Fredendall, Maj. Gen. Lloyd R., 82-87, 306; North African invasion, 27, 83-85; headquarters, 84, 86-87, 205, 280-82; command, 90-96, 99-101, 258-60, 280-82, 288-97; and Maknassy, 99-104; and Faid, 107-11; and Sidi bou Zid, 115-17, 120-29, 137-39, 144-45, 155-57, 163; supplies, 119; and Sbeitla, 176, 180, 183-84, 188, 191-94, 201, 205; and Kasserine, 224-25, 228, 231-32, 238, 242, 247-50, 253-55, 274, 276, 278-80, 303-4
Free French, 22, 25, 305, 318; *see also* De Gaulle
French Equatorial Africa, 23
French fleet, 22
French Forces: "Constantine Division," *see* Welvert; Detachment Guinet, 227; French Expeditionary Corps, 318; Goums, 277; Light Armored Brigade, *see* Saint-Didier; XIX Corps, *see* Koeltz; Senegal-

French Forces *cont'd*:
ese, 261; Spahis, 277; *see also* Barré; Juin; Koeltz
French Morocco, 20, 23-24, 27, 32, 36, 80, 82, 96, 117, 224, 273, 288, 297, 304, 307, 317
French Resident General, 24, 32, 34, 36-38, 40
Fruehlingswind, 132-36, 177, 207, 215-16, 222
Fuehrer. *See* Hitler

Gabes, 74, 76-79, 131; Axis defense of, 45, 49-50, 52-54, 105, 135; French threaten, 79, 92; and Rommel, 97-98, 284, 286-87, 299; and Fredendall, 100
Gafsa, 74-77, 107, 143, 149, 186-87, 234; Allied occupation, 79, 92; and Fredendall, 100-2; Axis attack, 105, 107-8; Allied withdrawal, 115-17, 124-26, 128, 130-35, 155-57, 177, 293, 204, 206-7, 280; and Rommel, 216-17, 221, 286; Patton takes, 311
Gardiner, Lt. Col. Henry E., 206-12, 264-67, 278, 293, 295
Garet Hadid, 138, 143, 146-47, 149, 159, 165-66, 177, 194-97, 201
Gause, Gen. Alfred, 43-44, 46
Gerhardt Group, 134, 143, 149, 162, 217
German Armed Forces High Command, 16, 33
German Forces: Afrika Korps, 9, 11, 19, 46, 132, 135, 197, 216-17, 220-21, 245, 278, 286, 294, *see also* Buelowius, Liebenstein, Nehring, Rommel; Fifth Panzer Army, *see* Arnim; *see also* Army Group Afrika, Panzer Divisions, Panzerarmee Afrika
Gibraltar, 20, 26, 28, 312, 319
Giraud, Gen. Henri, 26, 29, 78-79, 280, 305, 318; command arrangements, 89-90; reaction to German attacks, 111, 115, 117
Goering, Hermann, 50-51
Gore, Lt. Col. A. C., 243, 248-49, 254

INDEX   337

Gott, Lt. Gen. W. H. D., 15, 28
Goums, 277
Grande Dorsale. *See* Eastern Dorsale
Greece, 11
Group Rommel, 220

Haidra, 77-78, 226, 229, 245, 247, 250, 252-53, 259-60, 263-64, 270-71, 282, 291-92, 294
Hains, Col. Peter C., III, 140, 142, 148, 159, 189-91, 290, 317
Hampshires. *See* British Forces
Hamra. *See* Dejbel Hamra
Harmon, Maj. Gen. Ernest N., 282, 287-97, 305-6, 315-16
Hatab River, 77, 193, 211-12, 228-31, 238, 241, 246, 253-54
Hightower, Lt. Col. Louis V., 138-44, 147, 149-53, 155, 159, 164, 184-85, 190, 290, 317
Hildebrandt, Col. Hans Georg, 243-45, 251, 261, 272, 284, 286, 319
Hitler, Adolf, 8, 21, 136, 177, 218, 311, 320; strategy, 9, 11-12, 14-18, 43, 45, 48, 50-54, 300
Hoffman, 1st Lt. Harry P., 201-3
Homs, 97

Infantry. *See* American Forces; British Forces; German Forces; Italian Forces
Irwin, Brig. Gen. S. LeRoy, 271, 273-75, 281, 287, 291-92, 305, 317
Italian Armed Forces High Command. *See* Comando Supremo
Italian Forces: Bersaglieri, 245, 250, 278; Centauro Division, 135, 216-17, 220-21, 245, 250, 257, 287; First Army, *see* Messe; *see also* Comando Supremo; Panzer Group Afrika; Panzerarmee Afrika
Italo-German Forces. *See* Arnim; German Forces; Italian Forces; Liebenstein; Panzer Group Afrika; Panzerarmee Afrika; Rommel
Italo-German Panzerarmee. *See* German Forces; Italian Forces; Panzerarmee Afrika; Rommel
Italy, 12, 14, 23, 27, 45, 47, 51, 165, 200, 315-19

Juin, Gen. Alphonse, 35-36, 38-39, 42, 78, 90, 93, 95, 101, 107, 279-80, 318
Junker 88 planes. *See* Air forces, German

Kairouan, 178
Kasserine, 3, 39, 74, 76-77, 82, 86, 115, 299, 303, 309, 313, 315-16, 319; movements to, 158, 171, 176, 184, 191, 193-94, 200, 202, 207, 211; defenses, 181, 193, 205-6, 212; operations, 217-19, 221, 225-28, 230-31, 235, 239-40, 242, 244-51, 253, 255, 257-60, 263-65, 267, 270, 272, 274, 283, 285-86, 291, 294-96
Keightley, Maj. Gen. Sir Charles F., 185-86, 225, 227, 244, 254, 258, 272, 274, 281-82, 290, 319
Kern, Lt. Col. William B., 108, 143, 148, 184-85
Kern's Crossroads, 148-49, 153-54, 158-60, 162-63, 171, 177, 180-81, 184, 187-88, 190, 197
Kesselring, Field Marshal Albert, 49-52, 319-20; command, 12, 17-19; and Allied landings, 33, 45-57; and Faid, 105; and Sidi bou Zid, 130-36; and Sbeitla, 177, 179, 187; and Kasserine, 217-18, 221-23, 251, 256-57, 261-62, 283-86; and final Tunisian operations, 298-300, 311
Koeltz, Gen. Louis-Marie, 286, 314, 318; command arrangements, 78-80, 90, 95-96, 99; and Sidi bou Zid, 115, 117, 125-26, 128; defense of Sbiba, 158, 183, 185-86, 192, 205, 226, 240, 244, 247, 263, 272-73, 280-82, 293, 295-96
Koenig, 23
Kouif, 205, 226, 231, 250, 260, 274, 279, 289, 296
Ksaira. *See* Djebel Ksaira

Lancers. *See* British Forces
Le Kef: German objective, 219-23, 226, 256-57, 261, 263, 270, 286, 299, 313; defense of, 259, 272-73, 279-81, 285

Leclerc, 23
Leicesters. See British Forces
Lessouda. See Djebel Lessouda
Libya, 23, 45-46, 313; operations, 5, 9, 13, 15; Rommel's retreat, 19, 27, 48-51, 217-18
Liebenstein, Col. Freiherr Kurt von, 135, 176-77, 186, 204
Light Armored Brigade, 227
Line, Lt. Col. Gerald C., 171, 195, 197-98, 200-1
Logistics, Allied, 118-20, 304
London, 22
London Times, 312
Losses: at El Alamein, 18; at Bizerte, 44; of withdrawal in Libya, 97; at Maknassy, 100-1, 104; at Faid, 116; at Sid bou Zid, 148-49, 153-54, 163, 172; at Sbeitla, 185, 194, 201, 203, 205, 207, 224-25; at Thelepte, 204; at Sbiba, 244, 251, 293; at Kasserine, 247, 252, 255-56, 269-70, 278, 285, 293; final Tunisian operations, 299, 311; cumulative, 303-4, 313
Lothians. See British Forces

Maizila, 92, 103, 116, 133-34, 139, 143-44, 195
Maknassy, 76, 92, 311; raid, 100, 102-4, 111; Sidi bou Zid operations, 134, 138-39, 146, 195
Malta, 12, 312
Mareth Line, 4, 53-54; Rommel occupies, 98-99, 105, 132-34, 176, 187, 216, 219-20, 298, 300; Montgomery threatens, 130, 176-77, 216, 218, 226, 245, 250, 254, 283-84, 311
Marsa el Brega, 48-52
McNabb; Brig. C. V. O'N., 242, 258-59, 267, 317
McQuillin, Brig. Gen. Raymond E., 306, 316; at Faid, 107-9, 111; at Sidi bou Zid, 116, 121, 126-29, 137, 139-47, 149, 151, 154-56; at Sbeitla, 180-81, 184-85, 187, 189-91, 193, 195-97, 205-6; at Kasserine, 227-28, 231, 282, 294
ME 109's. See Air forces, German

Mediterranean, 11, 23, 27
Mers-el-Kebir, 22
Messe, Gen. Giovanni, 98-99, 132, 219-20, 294, 298-300, 319
Metlaoui, 126, 177
Middle East. See British Forces
Middleton, Drew, 4
Montgomery, Lt. Gen. Sir Bernard L., 318; commands Eighth Army, 15, 28; in Egypt, 16; in Libya, 48-49, 54, 93, 97, 130; in Tunisia, 175-77, 193, 216, 226, 245, 250, 283-85, 287, 294, 298, 300, 305, 311
Moore, Col. Anderson T. W., 193, 201, 230-31, 238-39, 241-42, 246, 249, 252
Moore, Maj. Robert R., 137-38, 165-72
Morgenlust, 132, 134-35, 177, 207, 215-16
Morocco. See French Morocco; Spanish Morocco
Munich, 45
Mussolini, Benito, 17, 319-20; strategy, 9, 11, 19, 48, 50-54, 218, 300; command, 12, 14, 98

National Committee of Liberation. See De Gaulle; Free French
Nebelwerfer, 15, 249
Nehring, Gen. der Panzertruppen Walther, 46-47, 50-52, 319
Nicholson, Brig. Cameron G. C., 253-54, 258-60, 274, 276, 278, 282, 291-92, 319
Nickforce. See Nicholson.
Nile River, 9, 13
Nogues, Gen. Auguste, 36, 38
Normandy landings, 315, 317, 318, 320
Numidia, 7, 74, 77-78

Oran, 22, 80; Allied invasion, 27, 56-57, 83, 208; base, 63, 82, 158, 224, 232, 273, 304

Pantelleria, 27
Panzer Divisions: 10TH, 105, 110-11, 130, 132-36, 154-55, 177, 179,

Panzer Divisions *cont'd:*
207, 216-22, 245, 249-50, 256-57, 261-62, 270, 286-87, 298-99; 21ST; 98, 105, 111, 130, 132-35, 143, 177, 179, 207, 216-22, 243, 244, 251, 256, 281, 283-84, 286-87, 299
Panzer Group Afrika, 11, 13; *see also* Rommel
Panzerarmee Afrika, 13, 16-17, 20, 52, 98, 130, 217, 219-20. *See also* Rommel
Paris, 24
Patton, Maj. Gen. George S., Jr., 27, 288, 297, 307-8, 310-11, 315-18
Pétain, Marshal Henri Philippe, 21, 23-24, 28-29, 32-44
Petite Dorsale. *See* Western Dorsale
Pichon, 76; occupied by French, 79; seized by Germans, 80, 91, 93; and Faid, 105, 110-11, 131-34, 137, 154-55; and Sidi bou Zid, 175, 177, 186, 207-8; and Kasserine, 216-17, 222, 256, 287
Poland, 165, 200
President. *See* Roosevelt, Franklin D.
Prime Minister. *See* Churchill, Winston S.
Pyle, Ernie, 137, 312

Rangers. *See* American Forces
Rastenburg, 45, 48, 50; *see also* Hitler
Rebaou, 92, 102, 105, 108, 110
Reimann Group, 134, 143
Resident General. *See* French Resident General
Robinett, Brig. Gen. Paul M., 317; command, 94-95, 101; and Pichon, 110; and Sidi bou Zid, 116, 127-28, 140, 155; and Sbeitla, 176, 181, 184, 187, 191, 193, 205-10; and Kasserine, 227-28, 240, 247, 249-50, 252-54, 258-62, 264, 267-68, 276-79, 292-93, 295
Rohia, 280-81
Romans of antiquity, 6-7, 9, 74-75, 77-78, 178, 303
Rome: and Mussolini, 9, 51; and Comando Supremo, 11, 13-14, 51, 218, 257, 286, 298; and Rommel, 14, 16-17, 50-51; and Kesselring,

Rome *cont'd:*
12, 19, 46, 51, 179, 218, 256-57, 283, 286, 298; and Nehring, 46-47; and Arnim, 298
Rommel, Field Marshal Erwin, 3-4, 8-9, 87, 89, 311-314, 320; retreat across Libya, 5, 18-20, 27, 45-46, 73; withdraws after Kasserine, 5, 283-87, 293-94, 296-97; enters North Africa, 9, 11; first attack on Egypt, 11; first withdrawal from Egypt, 12; second attack on Egypt, 13; leaves North Africa, 14-15; returns to North Africa, 16-17; strategic views, 47-55, 97-99, 105, 215-23, 298-300; enters Tunisia, 76, 79, 81, 93, 97-99, 115-17; and Sidi bou Zid, 130-36, 154; and Sbeitla, 177, 179, 186-87, 204; and Kasserine, 224, 226, 238-39, 243-45, 249-52, 254-57, 261-63, 266, 269-71, 273, 275-76, 305-6
Roosevelt, Franklin D., 29, 92, 306
Russian front, 11, 14, 52-54, 130, 319
Ryder, Maj. Gen. Charles W., 96, 102, 115, 308, 310, 317; North African invasion, 27; defense of Sbiba, 158, 183, 186, 205, 227; and German attacks at Sbiba, 243-44, 263, 272, 281, 293, 295

Saint-Didier, General, 186, 227
Salerno, 317
Salonika, 313
Sardinia, 27
Sbeitla, 3, 77, 79, 82, 137, 169, 171, 202, 212, 226, 228, 230, 240, 278, 286, 296, 313, 316; German threat, 91, 98, 102-3; defense of, 107, 109-10, 116, 121-22, 126-27, 139, 154-58, 197, 264; German attack on, 129-31, 133-34, 142-43, 145, 147-49, 176-94, 204-9; German attack from, 215-17, 219, 221-22, 243, 245, 249
Sbiba, 76, 299, 305; defense of, 157-58, 183, 186, 205-7, 225-27, 242, 254, 258-59, 263, 272-74, 280-81, 293, 295-96; German attacks, 217, 221-22, 239, 243-45, 250-51, 261,

Sbiba cont'd:
283-84, 286
Schutte Group, 134, 143-44
Screaming Meemies. See Nebelwerfer
Secretary of War. See Henry L. Stimson
Semmama. See Djebel Semmama
Sened, 100-2, 111, 115-16, 128, 165
Senegalese, 261
Sfax, 76, 105, 134, 165, 200, 207, 283; Allied threats, 79, 81, 92-93, 100, 104, 285, 311; Axis build-up, 98, 130, 284, 287, 294, 299
Sherman tanks, 16, 17, 225; see also American Forces
Sicily, 12, 27, 31, 47, 311, 315-18
Sidi bou Zid, 92, 200, 231, 234, 278, 296, 306, 316; Maknassy raid, 102-3; and Faid attack, 107-9; defense of, 116, 121, 124, 127-29, 137-41, 153-58; German attack, 132, 134, 141-45, 147, 149-50, 181, 184; American counterattack, 159-61, 163-64, 175-77
Sousse, 76, 165, 200, 284, 311
Spahis, 277
Spain, 23, 48, 80
Spanish Morocco, 23, 27, 80
Stack, Col. Robert I., 317; Maknassy raid, 101-3; and Faid, 108, 116, 125; and Sidi bou Zid, 159-62
Stalingrad, battle of, 53-54, 130-31, 313
Stark, Col. Alexander N., Jr., at Faid, 108-9, 111; at Sidi bou Zid, 115-16; at Feriana, 139, 156, 193; at Kasserine, 231, 238-42, 247-49, 252-56, 258-59, 274
Stenkhoff Group, 134, 143-45, 147, 149, 162
Stimson, Henry L., 4-6
Stukas. See Air forces, German
Suez Canal, 13, 15
Sultan of Morocco, 24
Summerall, Lt. Col. Charles P., Jr., 154, 185
Syria, 23

Tebessa, 39, 74, 82, 109, 201, 203, 208, 212; German objective, 76,

Tebessa cont'd:
81, 98, 105, 131-33, 135, 157, 186, 207; German attack, 215-23, 244-46, 256-57, 263-64, 271, 277-78, 283-84; Allied defense, 78-80, 92, 102, 116-17, 139, 183, 193, 206, 226-29, 238-39, 242, 248-53, 259-61, 280, 289, 294; and airfields, 81, 93, 204; and Fredendall, 86-87, 95, 107, 110, 124, 128; and supplies, 99, 115, 119, 205, 273, 304; commanders' conference, 126-27, 129
Thala, 78, 171, 226, 229, 299; movements to, 193, 207, 227, 263; defenses of, 230-31, 234, 238, 243, 248-55, 266-76, 278-84, 290-93, 306, 317; headquarters in, 240-42, 258-60; German attacks, 245-55, 257, 261, 263-64, 266-76, 278-84; German withdrawal from, 286, 295-96
Thelepte, 75, 217-18, 286; in antiquity, 78; airfields, 81, 99, 108, 116; defense of, 155, 157, 176, 184, 192; abandoned by Americans, 193, 204-5, 207
Thompson, Jack, 137
Tiger tanks, 15; see also German Forces
Tlemcen, 273
Toulon, 25, 29
Tozeur, 126, 131-32, 135, 177
Tripoli, 49, 53-54, 93, 97
Truscott, Maj. Gen. Lucian K., Jr., 90-91, 317; command arrangements, 90-91, 95-96; and Maknassy raid, 108-9; and Faid, 108-9; visits front with Eisenhower, 124-29; and Sbeitla, 180, 183, 188, 192-94, 205; and Kasserine, 248, 288, 294, 296-97
Tunis, 59, 74, 76, 165, 200, 256-57, 283; Allied objective, 28, 51, 57, 73, 81, 96, 115, 311, 318; Axis strategy, 31, 33-34, 46, 48-49, 97, 131
Tunisia, 23-24, 179, 221, 251, 283, 303; Allied withdrawal, 3; Allied invasion, 27, 31-44, 83, 208; Ger-

INDEX

Tunisia *cont'd*:
   man build-up, 45; Axis strategy, 48-49, 51, 97, 215, 217-19, 222, 262; French forces, 78; American build-up, 82, 224, 273, 304; command arrangements, 88-89, 226; Allied strategy, 117, 133, 184, 258-59; supplies, 118-19, 224, 273, 304; Montgomery's approach, 130
Tunisian bridgehead, 45-48, 50-54, 76, 311, 313, 318
Turks, 7

United States. *See* American Forces

Valentine tanks, 225; *see also* British Forces
Van Vliet, Lt. Col. John H., 195-97, 201-2
Vandals, 7
Vichy Government, 23, 26, 29, 32-44, 318; *see also* Pétain
Vienna, 15

Ward, Maj. Gen. Orlando, 56-69, 81-82, 100, 306, 310, 315-16; command arrangements, 93-95; Maknassy raid, 102-3; and Faid, 107, 109; and Sidi bou Zid, 116, 121-25, 127, 137, 139, 142-45, 147-49, 154-55, 158, 162-63, 166, 169-70; and Sbeitla, 176, 180-81, 183-84, 186-88, 191-93, 205, 207-8; and Kasserine, 225, 228, 240, 247-48, 258, 277, 279, 282, 288-92, 295-97
Waters, Lt. Col. John K., 81, 317; in northern Tunisia, 57, 59, 63, 65; on Djebel Lessouda, 137-42, 144, 148, 159, 163-66, 168, 171, 180-81
Wells, Lt. Col. W. W., 242, 248-49, 254
Welvert, Gen. Joseph E., 78-79, 90, 92, 317; Maknassy raid, 100, 103; and Faid, 107-8, 110, 125-26, 128; and Sbeitla, 183; and Kasserine, 227-28, 260, 277-80
Western Dorsale, 76, 79, 115, 117, 132, 175-76, 183, 193, 216, 220-21, 226, 228, 230, 245, 248, 250
Weygand, Gen. Maxime, 21, 25
Williams, Lt. Marvin E., 147, 149

Youks-les-Bains, 79, 81, 204, 232, 264, 280-81

Ziegler, Generalleutnant Heinz, 52, 319; at Sidi bou Zid, 134-36, 154, 162-63; at Sbeitla, 177, 179, 186-87, 192, 194, 206-7

For Product Safety Concerns and Information please contact our EU
representative GPSR@taylorandfrancis.com
Taylor & Francis Verlag GmbH, Kaufingerstraße 24, 80331 München, Germany

www.ingramcontent.com/pod-product-compliance
Lightning Source LLC
Chambersburg PA
CBHW071149300426
44113CB00009B/1140